THE SOCIOLOGY
OF PERSONALITY

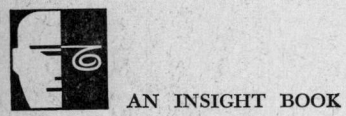 AN INSIGHT BOOK

THE SOCIOLOGY OF PERSONALITY

An Enduring Problem in Psychology

Edited by
STEPHAN P. SPITZER
University of Minnesota

VAN NOSTRAND REINHOLD COMPANY
NEW YORK   CINCINNATI
TORONTO   LONDON   MELBOURNE

Van Nostrand Reinhold Company Regional Offices:
  Cincinnati, New York, Chicago, Millbrae, Dallas

Van Nostrand Reinhold Company Foreign Offices:
  London, Toronto, Melbourne

Copyright © 1969 by LITTON EDUCATIONAL PUBLISHING, INC.

All rights reserved. No part of this work covered by the copyrights hereon may be reproduced or used in any form or by any means—graphic, electronic, or mechanical, including photocopying, recording, taping, or information storage and retrieval systems—without written permission of the publisher. Manufactured in the United States of America.

Published by Van Nostrand Reinhold Company
450 West 33rd Street, New York, N.Y. 10001

Published simultaneously in Canada by
D. Van Nostrand Company (Canada), Ltd.
15 14 13 12 11 10 9 8 7 6 5 4 3 2 1

Preface

The editorial conception guiding the selection of readings for this volume has been to provide a brief coverage of contemporary sociological writings in the area of personality theory. The purpose is to present the major theoretical approaches to this field. Consequently, attention is focused on a number of writings which are believed to be of special importance and which reflect the major directions that personality theory has taken in sociology. In this respect the book is representative.

The book is eclectic in that articles have been selected from various theoretical schools rather than from a singular theoretical position. At the same time the volume is built around a general framework which is intended to help the student see how selections from diverse sources are related to one another.

The organization of the book progresses logically. Part I includes articles which examine, from various perspectives, the relationship between personality and society. Part II brings together a number of papers which concentrate more heavily upon the organization and dynamics of personality and how it arises in the process of interaction. Part III is organized around concepts such as roles and reference groups since these are integral parts of personality theory as developed from various sociological perspectives. Part IV is concerned with the history of personality theory, with its present directions of development, and with some issues and problems now facing the field.

Several criteria were used for selecting the readings. I sought to intersperse "classics" with recent works, to include items not already reprinted elsewhere, and to assure that all selections could be read without undue difficulty by undergraduate college students. With the exception of *The Social Psychology of G. H. Mead*, the selections are the original writings of the personality theorists. The periodical articles appear in their entirety, and the excerpts from books are self-sufficient units of thought.

This book is designed to serve in several capacities. In respect to teaching it can be used as: (1) a supplement for an introductory course in social psychology, (2) a supplement for courses in personality theory, socialization, and developmental processes, or (3) one of a series of brief readings for various interdisciplinary courses which include but are not limited to the field of personality theory. The lay reader may find this book useful for establishing a foundation of knowledge in the area of personality theory; the professional may find it useful for expanding his appreciation of the area. The suggested reading listed at the end of each section should be a helpful guide for further inquiry into the sociology of personality.

Acknowledgments

I am grateful to Professors Norman K. Denzin, Boyd A. Duncan, Helen M. Duncan, Harold A. Mulford, and James L. Price, and students Barbara J. Bank, David B. Graeven, Judy A. Lewis, and James D. Orcutt for discussions concerning what this volume should include. I acknowledge with thanks the review and critical comments concerning the preparatory materials and an earlier version of the summary article from Professors Carl J. Couch, John R. Stratton, and Robert M. Terry. Mrs. Susanne L. Eichler and Mrs. Patricia A. Swanson read the entire manuscript and offered valuable editorial help. Mrs. Eichler also provided necessary secretarial assistance. I am indebted to Mr. Robert M. Swanson who worked on all aspects of this reader. I am especially appreciative of the perceptive suggestions, criticisms, and editorial assistance of my wife, Nancy S. Spitzer.

STEPHAN P. SPITZER

Introduction

> ... sociological analysis—the attempt to understand the structure and functioning of social systems—will often require the use of a general theory of personality and knowledge of the distinctive personality characteristics of participants in the system as a whole or in major subsystems and in particular roles.[1]

Sociologists have become increasingly interested in personality theory and research during the last two decades. While sometimes thought of as part of the realm of psychology and psychiatry, the study of personality has come to hold a position of importance in modern sociology.

The reasons for this interest are severalfold. First, to understand the maintenance and functioning of social systems it is necessary to know not only the role expectation of the system and how that social system transmits and integrates those expectations, but also how the characteristics of the individuals impinge upon the system in order to perpetuate and change it. Second, personality theory is a useful tool to account for the divergences in role performances that cannot be attributed to the demands of the social system. Third, a theory of personality is helpful for explaining the distinctive characteristics of the large and small groups that make up the society. Fourth, personality theory is informative of the distribution of personality characteristics within groups, irrespective of any consequences that personality might have for the social system.

---

[1] Alex Inkeles, "Personality and Social Structure," in Robert K. Merton, Leonard Broom, and Leonard S. Cottrell, Jr. (Eds.), *Sociology Today,* Basic Books, Inc., New York, 1959, p. 272.

Partly as a function of the traditional subject matter of sociology and partly because of present concerns, it is not surprising that the direction taken differs in some respects from the direction taken in other disciplines. Obviously, a sociological approach to personality favors emphasis of social influences. But the issue is deeper than this. The sociologist is prone to view personality as an *open system* that society produces rather than a *closed system*[2] that society merely activates and directs. Rarely is personality seen as an unfolding process of innate determinants of behavior. Instead, personality is viewed as the consequence of social participation, with the form and structure taken the resultant of social experience. Consequently personality from a sociological perspective can be regarded broadly as a system of self-other relationships.

A clearly articulated conception of personality is essential for sociologists and other behavioral scientists in order to differentiate the area of personality from other research which deals with individuals. The study of individuals is not necessarily equivalent to the study of personality. The sociologist must be explicit about his conception of personality in order to alleviate any confusion as to whether personality is actually being studied when it is expressed in a nontraditional way, for example, in terms of interaction or self-presentation. Work in personality theory in sociology has sometimes been a reaction against personality theory in psychology and psychiatry, and an attempt to provide sociological alternatives to such usage. Thus, it should not be expected that the way sociologists regard personality be synonymous with personality as developed in related disciplines. The important consideration is that a conception of personality is both specifically delimited and consonant with ongoing theory and research. Otherwise, personality would not be a very useful or, for that matter, necessary concept for sociological inquiry.

In order to develop a comprehensive sociological theory of

---

[2] The most restricting examples of closed systems embody the notion of instinct. According to Montagu instincts are commonly assumed to be: "(1) *innate* determiners of some kinds which, (2) when affected by particular stimuli, (3) call into function certain neural, glandular, and muscular mechanisms, (4) that underlie particular patterns of behavior or even 'psychological states.'" See M. F. Ashley Montagu, *Man and Aggression,* Oxford University Press, New York, 1968, p. x.

personality, concern needs to be directed toward the units to be utilized and the criteria by which these units may be identified.

From this perspective, then, personality can be conceptualized as a behavioral or cognitive unit of study. The unit of study must show individual differences within a population. Either there should be a nominal distinction among individuals (such as being present or absent) or there should be a range of variation along a continuum. It must also be possible to account for the observed variation by social factors. The factor may be a learned response or cognition, another person, a social grouping, or some aspect of social structure. It must not be possible to account for the observable by innate factors, such as heredity, physiological functions, or neurological processes. But most important, the units of study must comprise a domain. There must be at least an itemization of the components of the domain, and preferably a specification of the interrelationships among the components. For example, personality might be taken to refer to the interrelationships of a number of traits, characteristics, identities, etc., or the enumeration of particular traits, characteristics, or identities, etc. that a person may display. Thus, if an investigator studies how the self-concept arises or perhaps how the self-concept is influenced by some external experience, and conceives of the self as an integrated system of identifications, this would be a personality study. It would remain a personality study even if the investigator did not know exactly how the identifications are interrelated and conceived of the self solely as an inventory of identifications.

A personality study requires that the investigator recognize that personality is made up of a universe of attributes. He need not incorporate all of the attributes, for he may wish to confine his study to one or several components of the domain. But personality must not simply be taken to refer to a singular observable component apart from any consideration of the domain from which it is selected. A study focusing on an isolated trait, characteristic, or identity is not a study of personality. Consequently, a study of submission is not a study of personality. Similarly, a study of submission to bureaucratic authority is not a study of personality. The former is a study of submission and the latter is a study of the relationship between social structure and submission.

Contents

PREFACE	iii
INTRODUCTION	vii

Part I—PERSONALITY AND SOCIAL STRUCTURE

1. SOME TYPES OF CHARACTER AND SOCIETY — 5
   David Riesman
2. THE PERSONAL SYSTEM AND THE SOCIOCULTURAL SYSTEM IN LARGE-SCALE ORGANIZATIONS — 24
   Alex Inkeles and Daniel J. Levinson
3. BASIC PERSONALITY STRUCTURE: MODAL CLUSTERING AND DIVERSITY — 40
   Talcott Parsons

Part II—PERSONALITY AND INTERACTION

4. THE SOCIAL PSYCHOLOGY OF GEORGE HERBERT MEAD — 55
   Bernard N. Meltzer
5. A SOCIO-PSYCHIATRIC APPROACH TO PERSONALITY ORGANIZATION — 72
   Bingham Dai
6. EMERGENT HUMAN NATURE — 83
   Walter Coutu
7. THE PRESENTATION OF SELF IN EVERYDAY LIFE — 94
   Erving Goffman

Part III—UNIFYING CONCEPTS IN PERSONALITY THEORY

8. THE IMPACT ON RESEARCH OF DIFFERENT CONCEPTIONS OF ROLE — 111
   S. Frank Miyamoto
9. REFERENCE GROUPS AS PERSPECTIVES — 124
   Tamotsu Shibutani
10. THE SOCIAL ACT: RE-EXAMINATION OF A CONCEPT — 138
    S. Frank Miyamoto

Part IV—ISSUES AND PROBLEMS

11. THE PROBLEMS OF SOCIAL DIMENSIONS IN PERSONALITY — 153
    Ralph H. Turner

12. RESEARCH IMPLICATIONS OF A FIELD VIEW OF PERSONALITY 168
    J. Milton Yinger
13. SOCIOLOGICAL PERSPECTIVES ON THE PERSON 189
    Stephan P. Spitzer and Robert M. Swanson

THE SOCIOLOGY
OF PERSONALITY

Part I

Personality and Social Structure

The relationship between personality and social structure may be visualized from various perspectives. Personality can be seen as a by-product of social structure, or conversely, social structure can be regarded as a by-product of the personality characteristics of the participants. The former perspective raises questions of how social institutions transmit values and orientations, determines the ways in which personality evolves and becomes structured, and exerts social control in order to minimize deviant behavior. The second perspective raises questions of how personality contributes to the maintenance and functioning of social systems and how personality determines the characteristics of social institutions. A third way to visualize the relationship between personality and social structure is to view both as separate although interdependent levels of analysis.[1] The papers in this section exemplify these various approaches.

The topic of the first article is societal consequences for personality. Various theories of national character have been proposed but none has had the impact of one presented by David Riesman in his book The Lonely Crowd. *Riesman contends that, in general, people can be grouped into one of three types according to their society's phase of demographic growth. Tradition-directed persons, those who are oriented in the traditional ways of their forefathers, predominate in societies with a high growth potential. Inner-directed persons, those who turn to their own inner values and standards for guidance in their behavior, are found predominantly in societies in the phase of transitional growth. Other-directed persons, those who depend upon people around them to give direction to their behavior, are prevalent in societies in the phase of incipient population decline. Both inner- and other-directed types may be found in contemporary American society according to Riesman. However, a profound change*

[1] There also appears to be a fourth approach which uses personality as a variable that determines responses to social settings. This approach has only recently emerged, and has neither any particular guiding conceptual framework nor any one champion. It is more fully discussed in Article 13.

in social character is occurring. Whereas people whose character was inner-directed once dominated American society, the shift is now toward the dominance of the other-directed type, particularly within some segments of American society.

The relevance of personality for the functioning of social systems is a perplexing question. This is partly because there are neither agreed upon categories of personality classification nor agreed upon dimensions of social organization. But most importantly, the problem lies in an undeveloped conceptualization of the links between social structure and personality. For the most part, sociologists have directed their attention toward inferring how personality is influenced or determined by social structural variables, or by interaction patterns (such as child-rearing practices) within a given society. However, the impact of personality on social structure is receiving increased attention.

Inkeles and Levinson outline an analytical schema by which the influence of personality on the functioning of large-scale organizations can be examined. They contend that an approach to the problem of the interrelationship between personality and social organization requires not only a systematic conception of the individual and the organization, but also a conception of the links between the two systems. The model is developed by proposing a number of dimensions along which personality organization and social organization can be viewed. The question of the personality-organization relationship is couched in terms of the influence of modal personality on functioning and the stability or change of the organization. Specifically, the question is: ". . . in what sense does an organization 'require' certain personality characteristics in its members, and what are the consequences for the organization if these characteristics do not obtain?" [2]

The view that personality and society represent "discrete" systems is identified with the work of Talcott Parsons; on one side are the need dispositions of the person, and on the other, the claims and values of the social system. Each of these systems has consequences for the other although neither has primacy nor is superordinate to the other. In the excerpt printed here Parsons reviews the process of childhood socialization, the social context in which personality is laid down,

---

[2] Alex Inkeles and Daniel J. Levinson, "The Personal System and the Sociocultural System in Large-Scale Organizations," *Sociometry*, 26: 219, 1963, reprinted in this volume.

and the mechanisms by which this is accomplished. The main context of the structure of personality is derived from value orientations originating from the social system, although the need dispositions of the organism play an important part. The point of interaction between the two systems are role expectations and personality becomes an independent system once role expectations are learned and internalized.

1

Some Types of Character and Society*

DAVID RIESMAN

This is a book about social character and about the differences in social character between men of different regions, eras, and groups. It considers the ways in which different social character types, once they are formed at the knee of society, are then deployed in the work, play, politics, and child-rearing activities of society. More particularly, it is about the way in which one kind of social character, which dominated America in the nineteenth century, is gradually being replaced by a social character of quite a different sort. Why this happened; how it happened; what are its consequences in some major areas of life: this is the subject of this book.

Just what do we mean when we speak of "social character"? We do not speak of "personality," which in current social psychology is used to denote the total self, with its inherited temperaments and talents, its biological as well as psychological components, its evanescent as well as more or less permanent attributes. Nor even do we speak of "character" as such, which, in one of its contemporary uses, refers to only a part of personality—that part which is formed not by heredity but by experience (not that it is any simple matter to draw a line between the two): Character, in this sense, is the more or less permanent socially and historically conditioned organization of an individual's drives and satisfactions —the kind of "set" with which he approaches the world and people.

"Social character" is that part of "character" which is shared among significant social groups and which, as most contemporary social scientists define it, is the product of the experience of these

---

* Reprinted by permission of Yale University Press from *The Lonely Crowd*, by David Riesman, Nathan Glazer, Reuel Denney. Doubleday & Company abridged edition, pp. 17–38. Copyright © 1950, 1953 by Yale University Press.

groups. The notion of social character permits us to speak, as I do throughout this book, of the character of classes, groups, regions, and nations.

I do not plan to delay over the many ambiguities of the concept of social character—whether it may properly be ascribed to experience rather than to heredity; whether there is any empirical proof that it really exists; whether it deserves to be regarded here as more important than the elements of character and personality that bind all people everywhere in the world together, or those other elements of character and personality that separate each individual from every other, even the closest. The assumption that a social character exists has always been a more or less invisible premise of ordinary parlance and is becoming today a more or less visible premise of the social sciences. It will consequently be familiar under one name or another to any of my readers who are acquainted with the writings of Erich Fromm, Abram Kardiner, Ruth Benedict, Margaret Mead, Geoffrey Gorer, Karen Horney, and many others who have written about social character in general, or the social character of different people and different times.

Most of these writers assume—as I do—that the years of childhood are of great importance in molding character. Most of them agree—as I do—that these early years cannot be seen in isolation from the structure of society, which affects the parents who raise the children, as well as the children directly. My collaborators and I base ourselves on this broad platform of agreement, and do not plan to discuss in what way these writers differ from each other and we from them.

CHARACTER AND SOCIETY

What is the relation between social character and society? How is it that every society seems to get, more or less, the social character it "needs"? Erik H. Erikson writes, in a study of the social character of the Yurok Indians, that ". . . systems of child training . . . represent unconscious attempts at creating out of human raw material that configuration of attitudes which is (or once was) the optimum under the tribe's particular natural conditions and economic-historic necessities."[1]

From "economic-historic necessities" to "systems of child training" is a long jump. Much of the work of students of social character has been devoted to closing the gap and showing how the satisfaction of the largest "needs" of society is prepared, in some half-mysterious way, by its most intimate practices. Erich Fromm succinctly suggests the line along which this connection between society and character training may be sought: "In order that any society may function well, its members must acquire the kind of character which makes them *want* to act in the way they *have* to act as members of the society or of a special class within it. They have to *desire* what objectively is *necessary* for them to do. *Outer force* is replaced by *inner compulsion*, and by the particular kind of human energy which is channeled into character traits."[2]

Thus, the link between character and society—certainly not the only one, but one of the most significant, and the one I choose to emphasize in this discussion—is to be found in the way in which society ensures some degree of conformity from the individuals who make it up. In each society, such a mode of ensuring conformity is built into the child, and then either encouraged or frustrated in later adult experience. (No society, it would appear, is quite prescient enough to ensure that the mode of conformity it has inculcated will satisfy those subject to it in every stage of life.) I shall use the term "mode of conformity" interchangeably with the term "social character"—though certainly conformity is not all of social character: "mode of creativity" is as much a part of it. However, while societies and individuals may live well enough—if rather boringly—without creativity, it is not likely that they can live without some mode of conformity—even be it one of rebellion.

---

[1] "Observations on the Yurok: Childhood and World Image," *University of California Publications in American Archaeology and Ethnology*, XXXV (1943), iv.

[2] "Individual and Social Origins of Neurosis," *American Sociological Review*, IX (1944), 380; reprinted in *Personality in Nature, Society and Culture*, edited by Clyde Kluckhohn and Henry Murray (New York, Alfred A. Knopf, 1948).

My concern in this book is with two revolutions and their relation to the "mode of conformity" or "social character" of Western man since the Middle Ages. The first of these revolutions has in the last four hundred years cut us off pretty decisively from the family- and clan-oriented traditional ways of life in which mankind has existed throughout most of history; this revolution includes the Renaissance, the Reformation, the Counter-Reformation, the Industrial Revolution, and the political revolutions of the seventeenth, eighteenth, and nineteenth centuries. This revolution is, of course, still in process, but in the most advanced countries of the world, and particularly in America, it is giving way to another sort of revolution—a whole range of social developments associated with a shift from an age of production to an age of consumption.

The first revolution we understand moderately well; it is, under various labels, in our texts and our terminology; this book has nothing new to contribute to its description, but perhaps does contribute something to its evaluation. The second revolution, which is just beginning, has interested many contemporary observers, including social scientists, philosophers, and journalists. Both description and evaluation are still highly controversial; indeed, many are still preoccupied with the first set of revolutions and have not invented the categories for discussing the second set. In this book I try to sharpen the contrast between, on the one hand, conditions and character in those social strata that are today most seriously affected by the second revolution, and, on the other hand, conditions and character in analogous strata during the earlier revolution; in this perspective, what is briefly said about the traditional and feudal societies which were overturned by the first revolution is in the nature of backdrop for these later shifts.

One of the categories I make use of is taken from demography, the science that deals with birth rates and death rates, with the absolute and relative numbers of people in a society, and their distribution by age, sex, and other variables, for I tentatively seek to link certain social and characterological developments, as cause and effect, with certain population shifts in Western society since the Middle Ages.

It seems reasonably well established, despite the absence of reliable figures for earlier centuries, that during this period the curve of population growth in the Western countries has shown an

S-shape of a particular type (as other countries are drawn more closely into the net of Western civilization, their populations also show a tendency to develop along the lines of this S-shaped curve). The bottom horizontal line of the S represents a situation where the total population does not increase or does so very slowly, for the number of births equals roughly the number of deaths, and both are very high. In societies of this type, a high proportion of the population is young, life expectancy is low, and the turnover of generations is extremely rapid. Such societies are said to be in the phase of "high growth potential"; for should something happen to decrease the very high death rate (greater production of food, new sanitary measures, new knowledge of the causes of disease, and so on), a "population explosion" would result, and the population would increase very rapidly. This in effect is what happened in the West, starting with the seventeenth century. This spurt in population was most marked in Europe, and the countries settled by Europeans, in the nineteenth century. It is represented by the vertical bar of the S. Demographers call this the stage of "transitional growth," because the birth rate soon begins to follow the death rate in its decline. The rate of growth then slows down, and demographers begin to detect in the growing proportion of middle-aged and aged in the population the signs of a third stage, "incipient population decline." Societies in this stage are represented by the top horizontal bar of the S, again indicating, as in the first stage, that total population growth is small—but this time because births and deaths are low.

The S-curve is not a theory of population growth so much as an empirical description of what has happened in the West and in those parts of the world influenced by the West. After the S runs its course, what then? The developments of recent years in the United States and other Western countries do not seem to be susceptible to so simple and elegant a summing up. "Incipient population decline" has not become "population decline" itself, and the birth rate has shown an uncertain tendency to rise again, which most demographers think is temporary.[3]

It would be very surprising if variations in the basic conditions

[3] The terminology used here is that of Frank W. Notestein. See his "Population—The Long View," in *Food for the World*, edited by Theodore W. Schultz (University of Chicago Press, 1945).

of reproduction, livelihood, and chances for survival, that is, in the supply of and demand for human beings, with all these imply for change in the spacing of people, the size of markets, the role of children, the society's feeling of vitality or senescence, and many other intangibles, failed to influence character. My thesis is, in fact, that each of these three different phases on the population curve appears to be occupied by a society that enforces conformity and molds social character in a definably different way.

The society of high growth potential develops in its typical members a social character whose conformity is insured by their tendency to follow tradition: these I shall term *tradition-directed* people and the society in which they live *a society dependent on tradition-direction*.

The society of transitional population growth develops in its typical members a social character whose conformity is insured by their tendency to acquire early in life an internalized set of goals. These I shall term *inner-directed* people and the society in which they live *a society dependent on inner-direction*.

Finally, the society of incipient population decline develops in its typical members a social character whose conformity is insured by their tendency to be sensitized to the expectations and preferences of others. These I shall term *other-directed* people and the society in which they live one *dependent on other-direction*.

Let me point out, however, before embarking on a description of these three "ideal types" of character and society, that I am not concerned here with making the detailed analysis that would be necessary before one could prove that a link exists between population phase and character type. Rather, the theory of the curve of population provides me with a kind of shorthand for referring to the myriad institutional elements that are also—though usually more heatedly—symbolized by such words as "industrialism," "folk society," "monopoly capitalism," "urbanization," "rationalization," and so on. Hence when I speak here of transitional growth or incipient decline of population in conjunction with shifts in character and conformity, these phrases should not be taken as magical and comprehensive explanations.

My reference is as much to the complex of technological and institutional factors related—as cause or effect—to the development of population as to the demographic facts themselves. It would be almost as satisfactory, for my purposes, to divide societies according to the stage of economic development they have reached. Thus, Colin Clark's distinction between the "primary," "secondary," and "tertiary" spheres of the economy (the first refers to agriculture, hunting and fishing, and mining; the second to manufacturing; the third to trade, communications, and services) corresponds very closely to the division of societies on the basis of demographic characteristics. In those societies which are in the phase of "high growth potential," the "primary" sphere is dominant (for example, India); in those that are in the phase of "transitional" growth, the "secondary" sphere is dominant (for example, Russia); in those that are in the phase of "incipient decline," the "tertiary" sphere is dominant (for example, the United States). And of course, no nation is all of a piece, either in its population characteristics or its economy—different groups and different regions reflect different stages of development, and social character reflects these differences.

High Growth Potential: Tradition-Directed Types

The phase of high growth potential characterizes more than half the world's population: India, Egypt, and China (which have already grown immensely in recent generations), most preliterate peoples in Central Africa, parts of Central and South America, in fact most areas of the world relatively untouched by industrialization. Here death rates are so high that if birth rates were not also high the populations would die out.

Regions where the population is in this stage may be either sparsely populated, as are the areas occupied by many primitive tribes and parts of Central and South America; or they may be densely populated, as are India, China, and Egypt. In either case, the society achieves a Malthusian bargain with the limited food supply by killing off, in one way or another, some of the potential surplus of births over deaths—the enormous trap which, in Malthus' view, nature sets for man and which can be peaceably escaped only by prudent cultivation of the soil and prudent uncultivation of the species through the delay of marriage. Without the prevention of childbirth by means of postponement of marriage or other contraceptive measures, the population must be limited by taking the life of living beings. And so societies have "invented" cannibalism, induced abortion, organized wars, made human sacrifice, and practiced infanticide (especially female) as means of avoiding periodic famine and epidemics.

Though this settling of accounts with the contradictory impulses of hunger and sex is accompanied often enough by upheaval and distress, these societies in the stage of high growth potential tend to be stable at least in the sense that their social practices, including the "crimes" that keep population down, are institutionalized and patterned. Generation after generation, people are born, are weeded out, and die to make room for others. The net rate of natural increase fluctuates within a broad range, though without showing any long-range tendency, as is true also of societies in the stage of incipient decline. But unlike the latter, the average life expectancy in the former is characteristically low: the population is heavily weighted on the side of the young, and generation replaces generation far more rapidly and less "efficiently" than in the societies of incipient population decline.

In viewing such a society we inevitably associate the relative stability of the man-land ratio, whether high or low, with the tenacity of custom and social structure. However, we must not equate stability of social structure over historical time with psychic stability in the life span of an individual: the latter may subjectively experience much violence and disorganization. In the last analysis, however, he learns to deal with life by adaptation, not by innovation. With certain exceptions conformity is largely given in the "self-evident" social situation. Of course nothing in human life is ever really self-evident; where it so appears it is because perceptions have been narrowed by cultural conditioning. As the precarious relation to the food supply is built into the going culture, it helps create a pattern of conventional conformity which is reflected in many, if not in all, societies in the stage of high growth potential. This is what I call tradition-direction.

A definition of tradition-direction. Since the type of social order we have been discussing is relatively unchanging, the conformity of the individual tends to reflect his membership in a particular age-grade, clan, or caste; he learns to understand and appreciate patterns which have endured for centuries, and are modified but slightly as the generations succeed each other. The important relationships of life may be controlled by careful and rigid etiquette, learned by the young during the years of intensive socialization that end with initiation into full adult membership. Moreover, the culture, in addition to its economic tasks, or as part of them, provides ritual, routine, and religion to occupy and to orient everyone. Little energy is directed toward finding new solutions of the age-old problems, let us say, of agricultural technique or medicine, the problems to which people are acculturated.

It is not to be thought, however, that in these societies, where the activity of the individual member is determined by characterologically grounded obedience to traditions, the individual may not be highly prized and, in many instances, encouraged to develop his capabilities, his initiative, and even, within very narrow time limits, his aspirations. Indeed, the individual in some primitive societies is far more appreciated and respected than in some sectors of modern society. For the individual in a society dependent on tradition-direction has a well-defined functional relationship to other members of the group. If he is not killed off, he "belongs" —he is not "surplus," as the modern unemployed are surplus, nor is he expendable as the unskilled are expendable in modern society. But by very virtue of his "belonging," life goals that are *his* in terms of conscious choice appear to shape his destiny only to a very limited extent, just as only to a limited extent is there any concept of progress for the group.

In societies in which tradition-direction is the dominant mode of insuring conformity, relative stability is preserved in part by the infrequent but highly important process of fitting into institutionalized roles such deviants as there are. In such societies a person who might have become at a later historical stage an innovator or rebel, whose belonging, as such, is marginal and problematic, is drawn instead into roles like those of the shaman or sorcerer. That is, he is drawn into roles that make a socially acceptable contribution, while at the same time they provide the individual with a more or less approved niche. The medieval monastic orders may have served in a similar way to absorb many characterological "mutations."

In some of these societies certain individuals are encouraged toward a degree of individuality from childhood, especially if they belong to families of high status. But, since the range of choice, even for high-status people, is minimal, the apparent social need for an individuated type of character is also minimal. It is probably accurate to say that character structure in these societies is very largely "adjusted," in the sense that for most people it appears to be in tune with social institutions. Even the few misfits "fit" to a degree; and only very rarely is one driven out of his social world.

This does not mean, of course, that the people are happy; the society to whose traditions they are adjusted may be a miserable one, ridden with anxiety, sadism, and disease. The point is rather that change, while never completely absent in human affairs, is slowed down as the movement of molecules is slowed down at low temperature; and the social character comes as close as it ever does to looking like the matrix of the social forms themselves.

In western history the Middle Ages can be considered a period in which the majority were tradition-directed. But the term tradition-directed refers to a common element, not only among the people of precapitalist Europe but also among such enormously different types of people as Hindus and Hopi Indians, Zulus and Chinese, North African Arabs and Balinese. There is comfort in relying on the many writers who have found a similar unity amid diversity, a unity they express in such terms as "folk society" (as against "civilization"), "status society" (as against "contract society"), "*Gemeinschaft*" (as against "*Gesellschaft*"), and so on. Different as the societies envisaged by these terms are, the folk, status, and *Gemeinschaft* societies resemble each other in their relative slowness of change, their dependence on family and kin organization, and—in comparison with later epochs—their tight web of values. And, as is now well recognized by students, the high birth rate of these societies in the stage of high growth potential is not merely the result of a lack of contraceptive knowledge or techniques. A whole way of life—an outlook on chance, on children, on the place of women, on sexuality, on the very meaning of existence—is the basis of distinction between the societies in which human fertility is allowed to take its course and toll and those which prefer to pay other kinds of toll to cut down on fertility by calculation, and, conceivably, as Freud and other observers have suggested, by a decline in sexual energy itself.

Transitional Growth: Inner-Directed Types

Except for the West, we know very little about the cumulation of small changes that can eventuate in a breakup of the tradition-directed type of society, leading it to realize its potential for high population growth. As for the West, however, much has been learned about the slow decay of feudalism and the subsequent rise of a type of society in which inner-direction is the dominant mode of insuring conformity.

Critical historians, pushing the Renaissance ever back into the Middle Ages, seem sometimes to deny that any decisive change occurred at all. On the whole, however, it seems that the greatest social and characterological shift of recent centuries did indeed come when men were driven out of the primary ties that bound them to the western medieval version of tradition-directed society. All later shifts, including the shift from inner-direction to other-direction, seem unimportant by comparison, although of course this latter shift is still under way and we cannot tell what it will look like when—if ever—it is complete.

A change in the relatively stable ratio of births to deaths, which characterizes the period of high growth potential, is both the cause and consequence of other profound social changes. In most of the cases known to us a decline takes place in mortality prior to a decline in fertility; hence there is some period in which the population expands rapidly. The drop in death rate occurs as the result of many interacting factors, among them sanitation, improved communications (which permit government to operate over a wider area and also permit easier transport of food to areas of shortage from areas of surplus), the decline, forced or otherwise, of infanticide, cannibalism, and other inbred kinds of violence. Because of improved methods of agriculture the land is able to support more people, and these in turn produce still more people.

Notestein's phrase, "transitional growth," is a mild way of putting it. The "transition" is likely to be violent, disrupting the stabilized paths of existence in societies in which tradition-direction has been the principal mode of insuring conformity. The imbalance of births and deaths puts pressure on the society's customary ways. A new slate of character structures is called for or finds its opportunity in coping with the rapid changes—and the need for still more changes—in the social organization.

A definition of inner-direction. In western history the society that emerged with the Renaissance and Reformation and that is only now vanishing serves to illustrate the type of society in which inner-direction is the principal mode of securing conformity. Such a society is characterized by increased personal mobility, by a rapid accumulation of capital (teamed with devastating technological shifts), and by an almost constant *expansion*: intensive expansion in the production of goods and people, and extensive expansion in exploration, colonization, and imperialism. The greater choices this society gives—and the greater initiatives it demands in order to cope with its novel problems—are handled by character types who can manage to live socially without strict and self-evident tradition-direction. These are the inner-directed types.

The concept of inner-direction is intended to cover a very wide range of types. Thus, while it is essential for the study of certain problems to differentiate between Protestant and Catholic countries and their character types, between the effects of the Reformation and the effects of the Renaissance, between the puritan ethic of the European north and west and the somewhat more hedonistic ethic of the European east and south, while all these are valid and, for certain purposes, important distinctions, the concentration of this study on the development of modes of conformity permits their neglect. It allows the grouping together of these otherwise distinct developments because they have one thing in common: *the source of direction for the individual is "inner" in the sense that it is implanted early in life by the elders and directed toward generalized but nonetheless inescapably destined goals.*

We can see what this means when we realize that, in societies in which tradition-direction is the dominant mode of insuring conformity, attention is focused on securing strict conformity in generally observable words and actions, that is to say, behavior. While behavior is minutely prescribed, individuality of character need not be highly developed to meet prescriptions that are objectified in ritual and etiquette—though to be sure, a social character *capable* of such behavioral attention and obedience is requisite. By contrast, societies in which inner-direction becomes important, though they also are concerned with behavioral conformity, cannot be satisfied with behavioral conformity alone. Too many novel situations are presented, situations which a code cannot encompass in advance. Consequently the problem of personal choice, solved in the earlier period of high growth potential by channeling choice through rigid social organization, in the period of transitional growth is solved by channeling choice through a rigid though highly individualized character.

This rigidity is a complex matter. While any society dependent on inner-direction seems to present people with a wide choice of aims—such as money, possessions, power, knowledge, fame, goodness—these aims are ideologically interrelated, and the selection made by any one individual remains relatively unalterable throughout his life. Moreover, the means to those ends, though not fitted into as tight a frame of social reference as in the society dependent on tradition-direction, are nevertheless limited by the new voluntary associations—for instance, the Quakers, the Masons, the Mechanics' Associations—to which people tie themselves. Indeed, the term "tradition-direction" could be misleading if the reader were to conclude that the force of tradition has no weight for the inner-directed character. On the contrary, he is very considerably bound by traditions: they limit his ends and inhibit his choice of means. The point is rather that a splintering of tradition takes place, connected in part with the increasing division of labor and stratification of society. Even if the individual's choice of tradition is largely determined for him by his family, as it is in most cases, he cannot help becoming aware of the existence of competing traditions—hence of tradition as such. As a result he possesses a somewhat greater degree of flexibility in adapting himself to ever changing requirements and in return requires more from his environment.

As the control of the primary group is loosened—the group that both socializes the young and controls the adult in the earlier era—a new psychological mechanism appropriate to the more open society is "invented": it is what I like to describe as a psychological gyroscope.[4] This instrument, once it is set by the parents and other authorities, keeps the inner-directed person, as we shall see, "on course" even when tradition, as responded to by his character, no longer dictates his moves. The inner-directed person becomes capable of maintaining a delicate balance between the demands upon him of his life goal and the buffetings of his external environment.

This metaphor of the gyroscope, like any other, must not be taken literally. It would be a mistake to see the inner-directed man

[4] Since writing the above I have discovered Gardner Murphy's use of the same metaphor in his volume *Personality* (New York, Harper, 1947).

as incapable of learning from experience or as insensitive to public opinion in matters of external conformity. He can receive and utilize certain signals from outside, provided that they can be reconciled with the limited maneuverability that his gyroscope permits him. His pilot is not quite automatic.

Huizinga's *The Waning of the Middle Ages* gives a picture of the anguish and turmoil, the conflict of values, out of which the new forms slowly emerged. Already by the late Middle Ages people were forced to live under new conditions of awareness. As their self-consciousness and their individuality developed, they had to make themselves at home in the world in novel ways. They still have to.

Incipient Decline of Population: Other-Directed Types

The problem facing the societies in the stage of transitional growth is that of reaching a point at which resources become plentiful enough or are utilized effectively enough to permit a rapid accumulation of capital. This rapid accumulation has to be achieved even while the social product is being drawn on at an accelerated rate to maintain the rising population and satisfy the consumer demands that go with the way of life that has already been adopted. For most countries, unless capital and techniques can be imported from other countries in still later phases of the population curve, every effort to increase national resources at a rapid rate must actually be at the expense of current standards of living. We have seen this occur in the U.S.S.R., now in the stage of transitional growth. For western Europe this transition was long-drawn-out and painful. For America, Canada, and Australia—at once beneficiaries of European techniques and native resources—the transition was rapid and relatively easy.

The tradition-directed person, as has been said, hardly thinks of himself as an individual. Still less does it occur to him that he might shape his own destiny in terms of personal, lifelong goals or that the destiny of his children might be separate from that of the family group. He is not sufficiently separated psychologically from himself (or, therefore, sufficiently close to himself), his family, or group to think in these terms. In the phase of transitional growth, however, people of inner-directed character do gain a feeling of control over their own lives and see their children also as individuals with careers to make. At the same time, with the shift out of agriculture and, later, with the end of child labor, children no longer become an unequivocal economic asset. And with the growth of habits of scientific thought, religious and magical views of human fertility—views that in an earlier phase of the population curve made sense for the culture if it was to reproduce itself—give way to "rational," individualistic attitudes. Indeed, just as the rapid accumulation of productive capital requires that people be imbued with the "Protestant ethic" (as Max Weber characterized one manifestation of what is here termed inner-direction), so also the decreased number of progeny requires a profound change in values—a change so deep that, in all probability, it has to be rooted in character structure.

As the birth rate begins to follow the death rate downward, societies move toward the epoch of incipient decline of population. Fewer and fewer people work on the land or in the extractive industries or even in manufacturing. Hours are short. People may have material abundance and leisure besides. They pay for these changes however—here, as always, the solution of old problems gives rise to new ones—by finding themselves in a centralized and bureaucratized society and a world shrunken and agitated by the contact—accelerated by industrialization—of races, nations, and cultures.

The hard enduringness and enterprise of the inner-directed types are somewhat less necessary under these new conditions. Increasingly, *other people* are the problem, not the material environment. And as people mix more widely and become more sensitive to each other, the surviving traditions from the stage of high growth potential—much disrupted, in any case, during the violent spurt of industrialization—become still further attenuated. Gyroscopic control is no longer sufficiently flexible, and a new psychological mechanism is called for.

Furthermore, the "scarcity psychology" of many inner-directed people, which was socially adaptive during the period of heavy capital accumulation that accompanied transitional growth of population, needs to give way to an "abundance psychology" capable of "wasteful" luxury consumption of leisure and of the surplus product. Unless people want to destroy the surplus product in war, which still does require heavy capital equipment, they must learn to enjoy and engage in those services that are expensive in terms of man power but not of capital—poetry and philosophy, for instance.[5] Indeed, in the period of incipient decline, nonproductive consumers, both the increasing number of old people and the diminishing number of as yet untrained young, form a high proportion of the population, and these need both the economic opportunity to be prodigal and the character structure that allows it.

Has this need for still another slate of character types actually been acknowledged to any degree? My observations lead me to believe that in America it has.

A definition of other-direction. The type of character I shall describe as other-directed seems to be emerging in very recent years in the upper middle class of our larger cities: more prominently in New York than in Boston, in Los Angeles than in Spokane, in Cincinnati than in Chillicothe. Yet in some respects this type is strikingly similar to the American, whom Tocqueville and other curious and astonished visitors from Europe, even before the Revolution, thought to be a new kind of man. Indeed, travelers' reports on America impress us with their unanimity. The American is said to be shallower, freer with his money, friendlier, more uncertain of himself and his values, more demanding of approval than the European. It all adds up to a pattern which, without stretching matters too far, resembles the kind of character that a number of social scientists have seen as developing in contemporary, highly industrialized, and bureaucratic America: Fromm's "marketer," Mills's "fixer," Arnold Green's "middle class male child." [6]

It is my impression that the middle-class American of today is decisively different from those Americans of Tocqueville's writings who nevertheless strike us as so contemporary, and much of this book will be devoted to discussing these differences. It is also my impression that the conditions I believe to be responsible for other-direction are affecting increasing numbers of people in the

[5] These examples are given by Allan G. B. Fisher, *The Clash of Progress and Security* (London, Macmillan, 1935).

[6] See Erich Fromm, *Man for Himself;* C. Wright Mills, "The Competitive Personality," *Partisan Review*, XIII (1946), 433; Arnold Green, "The Middle Class Male Child and Neurosis," *American Sociological Review*, XI (1946), 31. See also the work of Jurgen Ruesch, Martin B. Loeb, and co-workers on the "infantile personality."

metropolitan centers of the advanced industrial countries. My analysis of the other-directed character is thus at once an analysis of the American and of contemporary man. Much of the time I find it hard or impossible to say where one ends and the other begins. Tentatively, I am inclined to think that the other-directed type does find itself most at home in America, due to certain unique elements in American society, such as its recruitment from Europe and its lack of any feudal past. As against this, I am also inclined to put more weight on capitalism, industrialism, and urbanization—these being international tendencies—than on any character-forming peculiarities of the American scene.

Bearing these qualifications in mind, it seems appropriate to treat contemporary metropolitian America as our illustration of a society—so far, perhaps, the only illustration—in which other-direction is the dominant mode of insuring conformity. It would be premature, however, to say that it is already the dominant mode in America as a whole. But since the other-directed types are to be found among the young, in the larger cities, and among the upper income groups, we may assume that, unless present trends are reversed, the hegemony of other-direction lies not far off.

If we wanted to cast our social character types into social class molds, we could say that inner-direction is the typical character of the "old" middle class—the banker, the tradesman, the small entrepreneur, the technically oriented engineer, etc.—while other-direction is becoming the typical character of the "new" middle class—the bureaucrat, the salaried employee in business, etc. Many of the economic factors associated with the recent growth of the "new" middle class are well known. They have been discussed by James Burnham, Colin Clark, Peter Drucker, and others. There is a decline in the numbers and in the proportion of the working population engaged in production and extraction—agriculture, heavy industry, heavy transport—and an increase in the numbers and the proportion engaged in white-collar work and the service trades. People who are literate, educated, and provided with the necessities of life by an ever more efficient machine industry and agriculture, turn increasingly to the "tertiary" economic realm. The service industries prosper among the people as a whole and no longer only in court circles.

Education, leisure, services, these go together with an increased consumption of words and images from the new mass media of communications. While societies in the phase of transitional growth step up the process of distributing words from urban centers, the flow becomes a torrent in the societies of incipient population decline. This process, while modulated by profound national and class differences, connected with differences in literacy and loquacity, takes place everywhere in the industrialized lands. Increasingly, relations with the outer world and with oneself are mediated by the flow of mass communication. For the other-directed types political events are likewise experienced through a screen of words by which the events are habitually atomized and personalized—or pseudo-personalized. For the inner-directed person who remains still extant in this period the tendency is rather to systematize and moralize this flow of words.

These developments lead, for large numbers of people, to changes in paths to success and to the requirement of more "socialized" behavior both for success and for marital and personal adaptation. Connected with such changes are changes in the family and in child-rearing practices. In the smaller families of urban life, and with the spread of "permissive" child care to ever wider strata of the population, there is a relaxation of older patterns of discipline. Under these newer patterns the peer-group (the group of one's associates of the same age and class) becomes much more important to the child, while the parents make him feel guilty not so much about violation of inner standards as about failure to be popular or otherwise to manage his relations with these other children. Moreover, the pressures of the school and the peer-group are reinforced and continued—in a manner whose inner paradoxes I shall discuss later—by the mass media: movies, radio, comics, and popular culture media generally. Under these conditions types of character emerge that we shall here term other-directed. To them much of the discussion in the ensuing chapters is devoted. *What is common to all the other-directed people is that their contemporaries are the source of direction for the individual–either those known to him or those with whom he is indirectly acquainted, through friends and through the mass media. This source is of course "internalized" in the sense that dependence on it for guidance in life is implanted early. The goals toward which the other-directed person strives shift with that guidance: it is only the process of striving itself and the process of paying close attention to the signals from others that remain unaltered throughout life.* This mode of keeping in touch with others permits a close behavioral conformity, not through drill in behavior itself, as in the tradition-directed character, but rather through an exceptional sensitivity to the actions and wishes of others.

Of course, it matters very much who these "others" are: whether they are the individual's immediate circle or a "higher" circle or the anonymous voices of the mass media; whether the individual fears the hostility of chance acquaintances or only of those who "count." But his need for approval and direction from others—and contemporary others rather than ancestors—goes beyond the reasons that lead most people in any era to care very much what others think of them. While all people want and need to be liked by some of the people some of the time, it is only the modern other-directed types who make this their chief source of direction and chief area of sensitivity.[7]

[7] This picture of the other-directed person has been stimulated by, and developed from, Erich Fromm's discussion of the "marketing orientation" in *Man for Himself*, pp. 67–82. I have also drawn on my portrait of "The Cash Customer," *Common Sense*, XI (1942), 183.

ns of personality than those which are now
2

The Personal System and the Sociocultural System in Large-scale Organizations*

ALEX INKELES AND DANIEL J. LEVINSON

There is general agreement, we would suppose, that an individual's personality may exert some influence upon his role-performance. It has been more difficult to get social scientists to entertain the hypothesis that personality factors enter *systematically* as significant influences in the performance of whole sets of roles such as those of the occupational realm, the kinship system, or the political order. After the extensive, and often intense, post-war discussion of the relevant issues, however, many are now prepared to accept that idea, at least in principle, as a basis for further exploration. Those of us who hold strongly to this position have the responsibility to specify more precisely what we assume to be the relation of personality patterns to the functioning of social systems.

There is still a good deal of uncertainty as to which aspects of personality are most relevant for, and how they enter into, the functioning of institutions. This requires that we develop different, and broader, conceptions of personality than those which are now commonly used in organizational analysis. We will not pursue the interrelations of personality and social structure for long, however, before realizing that we must also adjust our thinking about social systems. We must treat these not only in the usual sociological terms of norms, statuses and roles, but also as characteristic milieus which confront individuals with demands, cross-pressures, dilemmas,

---

* By permission, from Alex Inkeles and Daniel J. Levinson, "The Personal System and the Sociocultural System in Large-scale Organizations," *Sociometry*, 26: 217–229, 1963.

Revised version of paper read at the Special Meeting of The Section on Social Psychology, American Sociological Association, St. Louis, August, 1961.

stresses, opportunities, and supports which cannot be understood without reference to their psychological as well as their social meanings.

We shall deal here with the interrelations of personality and sociocultural system in the case of the large-scale organization (industrial firm, government agency, college, hospital, and the like).[1] Our chief purpose is to present the outlines of a systematic theoretical framework. We make no special claims for originality. Virtually all of the single components of this framework may be found at one place or another in the existing literature of organizational theory or of personality theory. However, very few attempts have previously been made to bring these diverse notions together into a reasonably comprehensive, integrated scheme.

The question guiding our inquiry may be stated as follows: if we wish to develop a genuine social psychology of organizational life, an understanding of the reciprocal impact of personality and organization, what theoretical domains must be taken into account? Three broad domains immediately suggest themselves, and they form the major rubrics of our scheme.

(a) A sociopsychological conception of the individual. Contemporary theories in psychology and sociology differ considerably in their emphasis upon, and their conceptualization of, different aspects of personality. Some focus primarily upon more central or underlying features such as unconscious fantasies and modes of ego defense, whereas others deal almost exclusively with more conscious values, attitudes, and self-concepts. Clearly, many aspects and levels of personality may influence, and be influenced by, the individual's participation in organizational life. A comprehensive sociopsychological analysis must therefore have room, theoretically and empirically, for diverse personal characteristics. We shall indicate below what seem to us the major analytic areas in this domain.

(b) A sociopsychological conception of the organization. Once again, different theoretical approaches in the social sciences empha-

[1] With appropriate modifications, the same general approach may be used in the analysis of smaller collective units, such as primary groups, and of larger structures and societies. For an earlier treatment of over-all societal analysis, and the problem of "national character," see Alex Inkeles and Daniel J. Levinson, "National character: The study of Modal Personality and Sociocultural Systems," in Gardner Lindzey, ed., *Handbook of Social Psychology*, Cambridge, Mass.: Addison-Wesley, 1954.

size different aspects of the organization as a collective enterprise. Technology, stratification, leadership, division of labor, informal structure—these and other aspects have claimed the attention of research workers. Most often, however, there is a focus on one or two and a neglect of the others. Our concern here is to designate the major analytic areas that merit inclusion in any attempt to characterize systematically an organization. In addition, from a sociopsychological point of view we wish to consider the organizational properties not merely in impersonal terms but rather in terms of their potential impact upon, and their influence by, the personalities of the individual members.

(c) A conception of the links and interrelation between person and organization. The forms of linkage are clearly numerous and complex. For illustrative purposes we have chosen one: the influence of modal personality on the functioning and the stability or change of the organization. Our question here is: in what sense does an organization "require" certain personality characteristics in its members, and what are the consequences for the organization if these characteristics do not obtain?

The approach taken here is, so to say, "anti-sectarian." We are trying to lay out, in a systematic fashion, the conceptual domains that must ultimately be utilized in a general theory of person-organization interrelations, and in the conduct of organizational research. We shall not take a sectarian stand—although we have our own preferences—regarding the relative merits of alternative theoretical conceptions within a domain, or regarding the causal importance of the various domains. It is not that we eschew theoretical controversy. Rather, we would suggest that controversy can be carried forward most fruitfully when it is placed within a broader intellectual framework.

Finally, we believe that current organizational research suffers greatly from the lack of an inclusive analytic scheme. Although there have been a number of excellent studies, the empirical work in this field has been generally haphazard and uncumulative. More systematic and comparative organizational research must be guided by a more broadly conceived analytic scheme. The following proposals concerning the study of the individual, the organization, and their interrelations, are offered as a first step toward that end.

THE PERSONAL SYSTEM

At the present time, there is no generally agreed upon set of categories for describing the personal properties of any individual. Two conceptions of the individual, commonly held by psychologists and sociologists, have led investigators to omit from systematic consideration aspects of the person which figure prominently in his organizational role. These have been characterized by Levinson as the "mirage" and the "sponge" theories.[2] The former, particularly characteristic of the psychoanalytic literature, regards unconscious motives and defenses as the essential features of personality; values, ideologies and behavior are treated explicitly or implicitly as mere epiphenomena or by-products. The "sponge" theory, more common among sociologists, treats the individual's ideas, values, goals and behavior as mere reflections of social structure, and by default leaves as the distinctly personal only those modes of reaction which are assumed to be unique or idiosyncratic. Both approaches fail to treat the person's values, ideas, role-conceptions, and role-behaviors as important phenomena in their own right, which cannot be understood merely by deduction from social norms nor by induction from unconscious fantasies and impulses.

This state of affairs is unfortunate. Clearly, very different conceptions of personality are involved here. When the psychoanalytically oriented psychologist uses the concept of personality almost exclusively to represent certain features of individual psychodynamics, the sociologist finds it too limited and lacking in social relevance. Similarly, when the sociologist conceives of personality solely in terms of the individual's orientations and values in regard to political and social issues the psychologist finds it too superficial and narrow.

We propose the adoption of a much broader and more neutral term, "the personal system," to represent the totality of the relatively enduring attributes which characterize an individual. For purposes of defining the personal system we do not care whether

[2] Daniel J. Levinson, "Idea Systems in the Individual and in Society," in George Zollschan and Walter Hirsch, ed., *Explorations in Social Change*, Boston: Houghton Mifflin, 1963.

these attributes are widely shared with others or are distinctive for the given individual. It is of course important to know whether a given view is held by one man alone, by most men of his class, or by all men in his society. However, the meaning of such facts in any specific case cannot be determined without reference to a large number of other facts. Moreover, we include characteristics from all "levels" of personality: those which are, psychodynamically speaking, more peripheral, and those conceived to be more central or underlying. Those who wish may apply the term "personality" to any part of the personal system, and assign that part whatever role their theoretical orientation prescribes. Our concern here is with comprehensiveness. We wish to avoid prejudging questions of relevance, importance and the like. We leave for empirical exploration the relative "significance," however defined, of any particular element of the personal system.

The personal system may be encompassed analytically in four major areas. These areas are essentially heuristic; they are not yet adequately conceptualized and the boundaries between them are unclear at many points. Nonetheless, they have some utility in pointing up the wide variety of personal characteristics that must ultimately be taken into account.

1. *Psychophysical and Psychosocial Attributes*

This is an especially amorphous area. It contains a number of attributes that have been used frequently in empirical research by sociologists and psychologists; but their theoretical status remains vague. We would include here such attributes as age, sex, body-type; general intelligence and specific skills (manual, artistic, mathematical, etc.); and temperamental qualities such as energy level, excitability, and the like.

We shall perhaps generate some controversy by including under this rubric various psychosocial attributes of the person, such as his income, occupation, political membership and reference groups, class of origin, and so on. A class and a political party are, of course, collective units and components of a broader social structure. However, membership in a class of party is an attribute of an individual, an element of his "personal system." A study of the relation between class level and child-rearing attitudes is concerned with two properties of the individual. It becomes a study of class as such only when it inquires into the sociocultural system encompassing all members of a given class and providing an environment within which certain kinds of child-rearing attitudes tend to evolve.

It is important to distinguish between the group membership or other "external" attributes and the more intrinsically psychological properties of the person (noted below). For example, "years of education" is a commonly used and empirically significant variable. While continuing to use it, we must go further and study independently such personal attributes as intellectual sophistication, values, and modes of cognitive functioning, which are imperfectly related to educational level. It is a persistent defect of sociological research that investigators assume too simple and direct a correlation between group-membership attributes of the person and other attributes falling in the areas noted below. The degree of relationship, and the causal context of the relationship, must be determined empirically and not taken for granted.

2. *The Idea System*

We are concerned here with the context and patterning of ideas in the individual. This area includes level and kind of factual information, technical knowledge, and empirical knowledge as culturally defined and validated. It includes, also, more general beliefs, attitudes, and values, and the patterning of these into broad conceptions of the cosmos, nature, society, and man. Within the organizational setting, it includes the person's ideology regarding the nature and the purposes of the organization and his conception of the various roles within it. A value, ideology or specific attitude is a part of the personal idea-system to the extent that it is held with some conviction and durability by the individual. Ideas do not qualify as part of the personal system merely because they are "widespread" in a given group or important in its culture. Ideologies, role-conceptions, values, and the like have their existence independently of any given individual, and have usually been studied by sociologists as properties of the sociocultural system. From a sociopsychological point of view, we are interested in them equally as components of the sociocultural system and as components of the personal system—and, ultimately, in the interrelations between the two.

3. Personality Structure: The Patterning of Psychodynamic Dispositions

The focus here is on the personal attributes most commonly emphasized in dynamic personality theories: character traits; core values and moral standards; unconscious motives, fantasies, conflicts and anxieties; modes of ego defense; ego ideal and life goals; and the like. To be included here, an attribute must be relatively enduring and difficult to change (though by no means unchangeable); it must play an important part in the internal functioning of personality and find manifold expression in a variety of life situations. A person will, we would suppose, find one organizational system more congenial than another to the extent that it more adequately meets his inner structural requirements—sustains his defenses, gratifies his wishes, permits fulfillment of his values, treads lightly on his vulnerabilities. When the organization makes demands that are initially stressful or otherwise incompatible with major dispositions of the person, this may lead in time to intrapsychic change, to efforts on his part toward inducing organizational change, to some form of accommodation or deviance, or to his leaving the organization. At any rate, the relevance of central personality dispositions for the person's functioning in the organization can be studied only if we conceptualize and measure these dispositions within the over-all framework of organizational analysis.

4. Modes of Adaptation and Behavioral Striving

We refer here to the personality in action, as it were, to the ways in which the individual comes to grips with the demands and opportunities of the external world. These aspects of the personal system are more "peripheral" than those in (3) above, in the sense that they represent the ego's contact with the external world. They are accordingly subject to influence both from external sources and from "central" motives, defenses, and the like. To conceive of them as peripheral is not, however, to suggest that they are unimportant. Indeed, their position at the "outer face" of personality gives them a crucial significance for social psychology; they provide an essential link between depth psychology and sociology.

We include here the person's everyday modes of cognitive, affective, and conative functioning. What kinds of relationships does he tend to establish with other persons generally, and differentially with authorities, peers, subordinates, strangers, deviants? What kinds of feelings does he communicate to others; and what feelings does he evoke in others? What are the qualities of his cognitive functioning: diffuse, precisely analytic, hyper-intellectual, imaginative? What are his preferred modes of behavioral striving (conation)? Does he prefer a steady, even pace, or does he rather engage in bursts of furious activity which punctuate longer periods of relative quiescence or apathy? Is he firmly determined or capricious in his efforts; is he fiercely competitive, cooperative, solitary? These qualities are often regarded purely as matters of personal "style" having little social relevance. We would suggest, however, that they may have substantial consequences for the "fit" between individual and organization, and for organizational stability or change.

THE SOCIOCULTURAL SYSTEM OF THE ORGANIZATION

Since large-scale organizations have been the focus of concerted research efforts in the past 10–15 years, it might be assumed that the task of structural analysis has been largely solved. Can one not go to any of the strandard sources and find there a generally accepted scheme for the sociological analysis of the organization? Apparently not. The various studies use widely different schemes even at the descriptive level. The variations are due only in part to differences in general theory. They reflect even more, perhaps, the lack of a truly systematic comparative approach in empirical work: each investigator focuses on specific aspects of the organization studied, and his delineation of the organization's over-all system is largely idiosyncratic. In short, we have a number of organizational case studies but no generally applicable scheme that would provide a framework for comparative analysis.[3]

In formulating our own suggestions for a standard analytic scheme, we have been more concerned with inclusiveness than with taking one side or the other in current theoretical disputes. Our first goal is to develop the outlines of a truly comprehensive scheme embracing the major properties of any large-scale organization. A scheme of this kind would be useful as well in the analysis of other durable collectivities. We posit four sets of properties as comprising the "sociocultural system" of an organization. We shall briefly describe each of these in turn, giving a few illustrative examples.

[3] See, for example, the following organization studies: Alvin W. Gouldner, *Patterns of Industrial Bureaucracy*, Glencoe, Ill.: Free Press, 1954; Peter M. Blau, *The Dynamics of Bureaucracy: A Study of Interpersonal Relations in Two Government Agencies*, Chicago: University of Chicago Press, 1955; Philip Selznick, *TVA and the Grass Roots: A Study in the Sociology of Formal Organization*, Berkeley: University of California Press, 1949; Seymour M. Lipset, Martin Trow, and James Coleman, *Union Democracy: The Inside Politics of the International Typographical Union*, Glencoe, Ill.: Free Press, 1956; Alfred H. Stanton and Morris S. Schwartz, *The Mental Hospital: A Study of Institutional Participation in Psychiatric Illness and Treatment*, New York: Basic Books, Inc., 1954; William A. Caudill, *The Psychiatric Hospital as a Small Society*, Cambridge; Harvard University Press, 1958; Chris Argyris, *Personality and Organization: The Conflict Between System and the Individual*, New York: Harper Bros., 1957; Robert N. Rapoport (in collaboration with Rhona Rapoport and Irving Rosow), *Community as Doctor: New Perspectives on a Therapeutic Community*, London: Tavistock Publications, 1960; Temple Burling, Edith M. Lentz, and Robert N. Wilson, *The Give and Take in Hospitals: A Study of Human Organization in Hospitals*, New York: Putnam, 1956; Morris Janowitz, *The Professional Soldier: A Social and Political Portrait*, Glencoe, Ill.: Free Press, 1960.

For recent proposals in the direction of a more inclusive framework, see: Talcott Parsons, "The Mental Hospital as a Type of Organization," in Milton Greenblatt, Daniel J. Levinson, and Richard H. Williams, eds., *The Patient and the Mental Hospital*, Glencoe, Ill.: Free Press, 1957; Alvin W. Gouldner, "Organizational Analysis," in Robert K. Merton, et al., *Sociology Today: Problems and Prospects*, New York: Basic Books, 1959; Philip Selznick, *Leadership in Administration: A Sociological Interpretation*, Evanston, Ill.: Row, Peterson, 1959. However there is still a serious gap between general theory and empirical work in this field.

1. Ecological Properties

These include, broadly speaking, the physical properties, technology, and resources of the organization. Technological change is coming increasingly to be recognized as a crucial aspect of organizational life, one that significantly influences and is influenced by other aspects. Additional ecological properties include architecture, size, density, or dispersion of population, life-span (duration), nature of the facilities and resources available for its work, and general degree of affluence or scarcity of rewards and conditions of work. Also relevant are the properties of the organization's external environment, and its relationships with various sectors of that environment. Is it competitive or monopolistic, revered or despised or taken for granted, free-acting or subject to scrutiny and control by outside agencies?

2. Cultural Properties

These include the guiding traditions, values, and "philosophy" as well as the major long-range goals and purposes of the organization. In the minds of its members, what is the organizational image, myth, or mystique? Is it conceived of as an extended family, controlled by an all-powerful, capriciously indulgent leader? Is it regarded primarily as a competitive, impersonal, profit-seeking machine, without moral obligation to anyone, or as a noble enterprise devoted selflessly to public service? Is it trying merely to survive from year to year, or to expand and conquer, or to achieve and maintain an elite status, widely respected for the excellence of its work? The more explicitly stated goals are virtually always multiple and have to do with such things as production, profit, fostering of human health-education-welfare, social control, and the like. The organizational goals and myths may be consensually agreed upon. When they are defined differently by different groups (or by the same group at different times), the differences may become a source of internal strain.

3. Structural Properties

The study of social structure has, of course, been a major concern in sociology; indeed, at times the structural properties of organizations have been emphasized to the relative exclusion of all others. The organizational structure has at least the following components: a series of interrelated positions (offices, niches) providing for a division of labor; an ordering of positions into some form of status hierarchy providing for a distribution of authority and power, together with rules governing super ordinate-subordinate relations; a system for the recruitment of new members; a system by which new members learn about the nature of the organization and the requirements and opportunities of their particular positions; a system of sanctions providing myriad forms of reward and punishment, presumably on the basis of the degree to which members fulfill or violate organizational values and norms; a system of communication providing for the transmission of ideas, information, and orders throughout various status-levels and sectors of the organization.

Systematic organizational analysis must take account of the above subsystems within the over-all structure. How shall they be described? We sorely need a list of theoretically relevant dimensions or properties that can be used in the delineation of social structure in various types of organization.

4. Social Process Characteristics

The social structure provides a framework—a set of normative requirements, a form of patterning, and various devices for integrating and coordinating the members' activities. It is important, in addition, to describe the actual workings of the organization, which we refer to here as its "social process" characteristics. These are influenced in part, but only in part, by the structural arrangements. For the moment, the causal relations between these and other properties of the organization are not our primary concern. They can be interrelated only after they have been systematically distinguished and described.

Examples of social process characteristics are: rhythms of work (slow or fast, steady or pulsating); the degree of formality or informality in personal relationships; the formation of cliques and alliances (which in varying degrees foster or hinder organizational objectives); the emotional climate and types of emotional interchange (mutual support, subtle intimidation, periodic explosiveness, apathetic conformity, enthusiastic effort, ingratiation); qualities of mind such as bland or critical, inquiring or non-reflective, concrete or abstract.

It will be noted that the four areas used in the analysis of the sociocultural system closely parallel those of the personal system. There are conceptual similarities between the ecological properties of the organization and the psychophysical and psychosocial attributes of the individual; between the culture and the personal idea system; between the structural properties of the organization and of the individual; between the social process characteristics and the modes of individual adaptation. Although we are not committed to the maintenance of a complete isomorphism, we have found it useful thus far to proceed with this possibility in mind.

PERSONAL SYSTEM AND ORGANIZATIONAL FUNCTIONING

We turn now to our final question: What is the relevance of the personal system for the functioning and the stability or change of the organizational system? To illustrate our proposed mode of analysis, let us take "rhythm of work" as a property of the organization.

Organizations differ markedly in the rhythms which the nature of the work permits or unrelentingly imposes. Factories with moving production lines experience a steady, unremitting pressure which demands evenness and continuity even though there can be substantial variation in the speed with which the line moves. Newspapers and magazines are also tied to a domineering schedule, but here time asserts itself in terms of a series of emergencies—the periodic and immutable deadlines. The content of certain kinds of magazines can, of course, be planned well ahead, but newspapers and news magazines cannot. Retail establishments reveal less regular rhythmic patterns. Saturdays are intensely busy, but shopping bursts are otherwise scattered throughout the year in connection with holidays and seasonal events. By contrast, many organizations work on an extremely smooth, regular or repetitive schedule which is traditionally established and involves few crises of any kind. This is true of schools (except perhaps at examination time) and to some extent libraries, many business offices such as insurance companies, some printing establishments, many small manufactories and large units producing standard items but not tied to a moving production line. Scheduling problems are again altogether different in organizations in which work involves a low level of standardization—for example shops fabricating special machines or parts, repair organizations, and the like.

Let us consider organizations characterized by a markedly uneven pattern in the rhythm of work. The functioning of these organizations will, we suggest, be significantly influenced by the conative patterns which are typical or modal among its personnel. In particular we would make the following hypotheses.

1. Recruitment will be more difficult for such organizations than for others lacking this characteristic.

2. Personnel in such organizations will display greater homogeneity in conative patterns than in other organizations, that is, there will be fewer modal categories and perhaps one really dominating mode.

3. Individuals having characteristics congruent with the required rhythms of work will, as a group, be relatively more "stable" members; they will have a lower rate of turnover than members having non-congruent characteristics.

4. Individuals whose conative style is incongruent with the required rhythms of work will show high rates of turnover; and those who remain longer with the firm will have shifted to positions largely free of the time pressures characteristic of the organization as a whole.

5. Comparing organizations in the same line of work, those having a higher proportion of members whose personal pattern of conative functioning is congruent with the rhythms of the organization will be more effective and efficient[4] in production.

We know of no standard test of conative patterns in the personality. If one exists, we doubt that it has been applied systematically

---

[4] By effectiveness we mean the extent to which the organization is able to meet the goals set for it or by it. We ask, is it a high or low producer, are its products outstanding or mediocre? Efficiency expresses the relation between output and the costs necessary to attain it. These costs include not only inputs expressed in terms of quality and quantity of resources consumed, but also a special category of outputs such as morale, rates of turnover and frequency of work stoppages or strikes which are obvious "costs" to the organization.

to the personnel of any organization in a research design which would provide evidence to the hypotheses stated above. Our illustration thus remains for the moment little more than an academic exercise. Unfortunately, the situation is not greatly different even in the case of those features of the personal system, such as values, which have loomed larger in the attention of social scientists. A useful beginning has been made in a few studies which give some attention to the relevant dimensions. We cite two of them in order to suggest in broad outline the pattern which we hope will be set in future research.

In a study of unusually high quality Arthur Kornhauser and his associates explored the interrelations of personality and political participation as they affect a trade union organization, specifically the United Auto Workers' Union.[5] Their personal system measures included tests of authoritarianism, life satisfaction, social alienation and sense of futility in politics. These were related to measures of political interest, participation in Union affairs, pattern of voting, and the like. The research does not present truly independent measures of organizational functioning as influenced by personal system factors, but the authors make a number of interesting observations on this theme and point out the direction in which we should go.

Those high on authoritarianism tended to take extremist positions, either pro-union or anti-union, denying basic rights to those with whom they disagreed. For example, those who were extremely pro-union felt it was right for labor to support Stevenson, but would have denied business the right to support Eisenhower. Clearly such people could be a threat to democratic processes within their own organization. The authors comment: "Altogether our results show that these people (extremists, whether left or right) present a special challenge to political leadership both in the union and in the general society. . . . Their faith in powerful leaders, absolute obedience, and violence against deviates points to the danger of their being potential adherents of anti-democratic movements . . ." [6] (p. 176). And again: "The problem of democracy in a large-scale society like ours, and more concretely in large-scale organizations like the union,

[5] Arthur Kornhauser, Harold I. Sheppard and Albert J. Mayer, *When Labor Votes*, New York: University Books, 1956.
[6] *Ibid.*, p. 176.

is partly the problem of maintaining an adequate proportion of members who are capable of engaging in the market place of proposals and counter-proposals, immune from the feeling that 'the leader knows best' and from the temptation to condone, or to resort to, desperate measures of social and political crises" [7] (pp. 249–250). The feared organizational outcome, the breakdown of union democracy, has not come about in this union. We can only speculate as to whether in those unions in which the breakdown of democracy is well advanced, the relative incidence of high authoritarianism and extremism is not greater than in the Auto Union. To suggest this possibility is, of course, not to minimize the role which the quality of leadership, the organizational structure, and the objective situation of any union may play in determining the outcome of the political process within it.

We may cite one other outstanding study relating elements of the personal system to organizational functioning, in this case a college. Stern, Stein, and Bloom[8] developed a broad synthetic characterization of two antipolar personality types. One type, the stereopaths, were more authoritarian and rigid, tending to depersonalize relations, to be exocathective and extraceptive. They were students in a college that stressed "abstract analysis, relativity of values and judgment rather than fixed standards, and an intraceptive rather than an impersonal orientation." In other words, the students having a stereopathic personality, sixteen percent of the total, constituted a modal group whose personality characteristics were markedly incongruent with the predominant values and mode of action of the college. Those at the opposite pole, the nonstereopaths, manifested qualities which were highly congruent with the values of the college and its typical class and study room procedures.

The stereopaths, although matched in intelligence to the nonstereopaths, performed less well on tests distinctive of this college, and were evaluated and graded lower by their instructors. Of those who withdrew at the end of the first year, 38 percent were stereopaths, 61 percent came from the middle range, and only 1 percent were non-stereopaths. In other words stereopaths contributed to

[7] *Ibid.*, pp. 249–250.
[8] George Stern, Morris I. Stein, and Benjamin S. Bloom, *Methods in Personality Assessment: Human Behavior in Complex Social Situations*, Glencoe, Ill.: The Free Press, 1956.

withdrawals at twice the rate warranted by their weight in the student body, and non-stereopaths contributed only 1/16 of what they should have if all groups had contributed in proportion to their weight in the student body as a whole.

Clearly if the college wished to reduce the number withdrawing, it would be well advised to select its students from the non-stereopathic side of the distribution. If it did so, of course, other consequences perhaps not intended would follow. The student body would be more homogeneous in personality, and the challenge and stimulus of contrast and even conflict previously made possible by greater diversity would be lost.

In relating the person to the organization, both studies deal with members of only one position, namely, union member in the U.A.W. and student in the college. However, it cannot be assumed that the qualities, pressures, and needs of the organizations are exerted equally on all of its component parts; the general characteristics of an organizational setting may impinge quite differently on groups occupying different positions within the organization. Thus, the deadlines which dominate the occupational life of the reporter and editorial worker on a newspaper cannot be assumed to be terribly important pressures for the accountants and bookkeepers in the personnel or treasurer's office of the same organization. Also, members of these groups are deeply involved in other memberships which "cross-cut" that which is nominally their prime organizational involvement. Factory workers have their union, hospital doctors their medical association, and so on. The pressures created by these different organizational memberships are not necessarily wholly consistent or congruent. Thus, a further complication is introduced.

We cannot afford to neglect the ways in which the properties of the organization as a whole impinge upon its multiple component groups. At the same time, in studying the interaction of the personal system and the organizational system, we must consider the mediation of occupational and other subgroups within the organization. This will, of course, require that we develop a separate set of analytic categories adequate to the description of occupations. The task ultimately is to merge "occupational" and "organizational" perspectives in the analysis of "positions-in-organizations."

3

Basic Personality Structure: Modal Clustering and Diversity*

TALCOTT PARSONS

We have seen that each one of the pattern variables is intimately involved in that aspect of the socialization process which concerns the acquisition of value-orientation patterns. It has been possible, in a rough way, to show that each of them may present crucial alternatives at different stages of the socialization process, and that it is within the possibility of variation of the role taken by alter to swing the balance one way or the other. Of course what has been presented above is in this respect a very crude sketch. These alternatives in fact appear not once but many times, and there are very complex combinations of influences emanating from the role-expectations of the various socializing agents. But this sketch has been sufficient to show the relevance of the pattern-variable scheme to the analysis of socialization, and the kind of theoretical approach which would be indicated to carry the analysis farther with genuine empirical rigor.

It follows, then, from the above analysis that in principle any one of the major pattern variable combinations can become internalized as a result of socialization processes and presumably, though this question has not been explored here, without a primary part being played by recourse to the operation of mechanisms other than the learning mechanisms, that is, without "neurotic" complications. At least the indications are very strong indeed that there is *no one* humanly "normal" pattern of internalized value-orientation so that all others could be considered to be "neurotic" deviations from it; for example some pattern of the "mature personality" *in general*.

It seems to be without serious qualification the opinion of com-

* Reprinted with permission of The Macmillan Company from *The Social System* by Talcott Parsons. Copyright 1951 by Talcott Parsons.

petent personality psychologists that, though personalities differ greatly in their degrees of rigidity, certain broad fundamental patterns of "character" are laid down in childhood (so far as they are not genetically inherited) and are not radically changed by adult experience. The exact degree to which this is the case or the exact age levels at which plasticity becomes greatly diminished, are not at issue here. The important thing is the fact of childhood character formation and its relative stability after that.

Secondly, if the above account of the process of value-acquisition is correct only in its broadest lines, it follows that the combination of value-orientation patterns which is acquired *must in a very important degree be a function of the fundamental role structure and dominant values of the social system.*

This statement needs to be qualified in two ways. First, as we shall show presently, it cannot be a function *only* of this fundamental role structure. Secondly, the roles in which socialization takes place are predominantly kinship roles, and we have seen that these are in certain structural respects among the less variable as between primacies in the values of the pattern variables.

We are then justified in concluding that the weight of evidence is strongly in favor of the existence and importance of an element of "basic personality" as Kardiner has called it, which is a function of socialization in a particular type of system of role relationships with particular values. Patterns of value-orientation play a peculiarly strategic part *both* in the definition of role-expectation patterns and in personality structure. Hence it may be concluded that it is the internalization of the value-orientation patterns embodied in the role-expectations for ego of the significant socializing agents, which *constitutes the strategic element of this basic personality structure.* And it is because these patterns can only be acquired through the mechanism of identification, and because the basic identification patterns are developed in childhood, that the childhood structure of personality in this respect is so stable and unchangeable.

The value-orientation patterns are so crucial in this regard because they are in fact the principal common denominator between personality as a system and the role-structure of the social system. If the whole analysis of action systems presented up to this point is correct this *must* be the strategic set of features of personalities which is most directly shaped by socialization processes. The same analysis of action, however, enables us to introduce certain very important qualifications and limitations relative to the concept of basic personality structure.

The most important is that such a concept must be interpreted to refer to a *component* of the normal personality structure in a society, not to that personality structure as a concrete entity. Secondly, such a personality structure cannot be uniform for a whole society, but it must be regarded as differentiated with regard to those status-differentiations in which kinship groups function as units within the same society, and also by sex within the same classes of kinship units.

We assume that all normal early socialization of children occurs within the context of kinship, though often, of course, supplemented by other agencies such as schools and peer groups. The fundamental lines of differentiation in socialization patterns will then be by sex within any given status group, and relative to the more general role-structure in which the parents are involved. The fact that it is the status differentiations which involve kinship units as units which are significant means that class, community and ethnic differences would be the most important within the same society. We must speak, then, of broad differentiations of basic personality structure between major types of societies, and of narrower differentiations by these status categories within the same society.

But even so the basic personality structure will be *only one aspect* not only of the total concrete structure of the personality, but of its concrete value-orientation aspect. This is because of a variety of factors. In the first place no two human organisms are alike by genetic constitution. Therefore the same influences operating on different genetic material will not necessarily bring about the same result. It is a case analogous to that of the same beam of light refracted through different prisms; the spectra will not be identical.

But, secondly, it is the concrete constellation of reciprocal role relationships which constitutes the socializing influence, and within the same broad status groupings of the society these are different in a variety of ways. One of the most obvious is the age, sex, birth-order composition of kinship units. Even though there is a broad similarity of pattern, in detail the relationship of a first child and a second child to the mother is never identical, first, because the mother is older when the second child is born, second, because of the presence of the first child. The relation of a second child to the mother is never quite the same if the first is a brother as it is if it is a sister, and so on. These variations may be almost random within certain status-groups, and their consequences thus "iron out," but they nevertheless produce differences of result for people who are, broadly, being socialized for the same adult roles. There is also, thirdly, the fact that the individual idiosyncrasies of the socializing agents enter in. It is the concrete reciprocal role relationship to the particular person in the particular situation which influences the learning process, and this may be more or less "typical"; no two cases are absolutely identical.

It must be kept in mind that a personality is a distinctive action system with its own focus of organization in the living organism and its own functional imperatives. Given the initial diversity of genetic constitution, plus the diversity of situational influences, *including* the combination or role-interactions, it would be strictly impossible for socialization, even in a relatively uniform milieu, in terms of major differentiations of social structure, to produce a strictly uniform product. The diversity of personality structures of those occupying the same status in the social structure, which is one of the best attested facts of clinical observation, is thus not fortuitous but is fundamentally grounded in the nature of the relations between personality and the social system. The two systems of action are inextricably bound together, but they *not only are not, they cannot be identical* in structure or in the process of functioning.

This diversity of personality structures relative to the role structure of the social system implies that we cannot rely on the building up of basic personality structures alone to explain the fundamental motivational processes of social systems. There are, it would seem, three further places we must seek. The first of these is to the capacity of the individual to make rational adaptations to the exigencies of his situation. This capacity is clearly along with genetic endowment a product of the processes of socialization in which identifications and value-acquisition will have played a prominent part. Once *given* the value-orientation patterns of the personality as internalized these processes of rational adaptation are not theoretically problematical to the sociologist and will not be further treated here.

Second we must look for additional mechanisms of socialization than the acquisition of basic value-orientations as sketched above, and third, where motivation to deviance exists, for mechanisms of social control. The latter will be deferred to the following chapter, but before approaching the former a few further remarks may be made about types of basic personality structure and their relations to the distribution of variations from them.

The facts concerning the nature of the acquisition of value-orientations, which we have reviewed, make it quite clear that the empirically observed diversity of concrete personality types cannot, relative to the dominant value-pattern system of the society or subsystem of it, vary at random. The point of reference for analyzing the distribution will, of course, have to be the relevant institutionalized pattern-type. This, it is to be remembered, will always be differentiated by sex role. The "modal personality type" for a social system or sub-system then will be that which predisposes to conformity with the major role-expectations of the sex role patterns in that part of the society, will be that is, the type which, in personality terms, is most congruous with these expectations.

The variability from this modal type may be, in principle, analyzed with respect to any one or any combination of the pattern variables. Where the modal type is achievement-oriented some individuals may incline to passivity; where it is also universalistically oriented some may, while retaining the achievement-orientation, incline to particularism and so on. . . . The strength of the socialization mechanisms is, however, sufficiently great so that it would seem very improbable that the completely antithetical types would be as common as those which varied from the modal type with respect to one, or possibly two, of the variables.

In addition to this general consideration, however, something can be said about specific factors which would tend to influence the distribution of more or less variant[1] types. Of these, three may be mentioned. First, the source of the deviation from the modal type may have been an identification with a model alternative to that which might be regarded as normal. Of course in these terms there are many different shadings possible because of the diversity of concrete adult personalities in any child's situation. But some of

[1] The term *variant* in a meaning similar to this has been used by Florence Kluckhohn. Cf. "Dominant and Substitute Profiles of Cultural Orientation," *Social Forces*, May, 1950.

BASIC PERSONALITY STRUCTURE

these alternatives may be relatively definitely structured. Perhaps the most obvious of these possibilities is the identification with a model of the wrong sex, so far as sex-role orientations are concerned, since both sexes are so readily available and so crucially important. This is apt to be a highly complicated matter, with, for instance, connections with the problem of homosexuality. But apart from such considerations, the value-pattern elements in the character for example of the parent of opposite sex may be taken over instead of those of the parent of the same sex. Thus in a given population one would expect to find that a certain proportion of the men leaned toward the value-patterns appropriate to the feminine role in that society or sub-system and vice versa. For example, in a sector of our own society, where universalistic-specific values are particularly prevalent, a minority of men might lean more in the particularistic-diffuse direction, hence be more inclined to assume roles primarily emphasizing informal organization.

Cross-sex identification is, of course, by no means the only possibility of finding an alternative role model. There may well be other, slightly variant persons of the same sex.[2] Here perhaps particularly uncles, aunts and substantially older siblings may be highly important if they are substantially different from the parent of the same sex. Also in a complex and heterogeneous society like our own, an identification process started in such a direction may well take on association with various sub-cultures within the society, including perhaps the ethnic. Such a society offers a rich fund of alternative value-patterns, often without being defined as radically deviant.

The second direction in which the distribution of variant personality types may be organized is that of the "hierarchy of regression possibilities" discussed above. The important process here would not be regression itself, but the failure in the course of socialization to make some of the last steps successfully. This would seem to apply particularly to universalistic orientation trends and the affectively neutral-specific combination. Regression to particularistic orientations is one of the most important possibilities in a universalistically oriented role-system, and further "overemotional" types in situations which call for affective neutrality are familiar.

[2] Which may, of course, relative to the modal type, include the parent of the same sex.

A failure on these levels may, of course, be a result of failure in the early years to achieve a diffuse affective attachment to the mother, but it might be manifested in these other types of orientation context. It should be kept in mind that the relevant structure of the regression hierarchy will vary according to the value-orientation pattern in question; it is not constant for all types, not even for the sex roles within a social sub-system—thus the manifestation of affectivity by crying in certain types of situations is "childish" for a man, but not for a woman. It must, of course, also be kept in mind that we are here speaking of regression in relation to the order and conditions of acquisition of value-orientation patterns, not of object-attachments as such. Though the two are, of course, closely related, the fact that psychoanalysts particularly so often have the latter in mind when speaking of regression should not be a source of confusion. Indeed the failure to distinguish these two things is characteristic of much psychoanalytic thinking. The capacity, through generalization, to abstract a value-orientation pattern from the original object through identification with which it was first acquired, is obviously one of the most important results of successful socialization.

It is highly probable that no process of socialization occurs without an important part being played by the special mechanisms of defense and adjustment. But this exposition has deliberately attempted to abstract from such considerations in order to throw the operation of the mechanisms of socialization into full relief. It seems obvious, however, that in seeking role-models alternative to the parent of the same sex and in failing to attain what is for the role system in question the normal order of steps of value-acquisition, that it is extremely likely that such mechanisms will be involved in the total process in important ways. Here attention will, however, be called to only one important aspect of their operation. We have seen that conformity-alienation is inherently a primary dimension of all interaction systems. The assumption of a role by the socializee means ipso facto that he comes to be faced with a conformity problem, and therefore the development of an alienative predisposition toward alter's expectations is always an immediate possibility. Those elements of such alienation which are built into the personality in the course of the elementary socialization process we may call the *primary* alienative (and conversely conformative) need-dispositions. Both the mechanisms of defense and those of adjustment, where such a need-disposition exists, may be various. These will be analyzed more fully when the problems of deviance and social control are taken up. But here it may merely be noted that alienation is always a possible product of something going wrong in the process of value-acquisition through identification.

It may be presumed that in the genesis of alienative need-dispositions the negative affect is in the first instance directed against the object of attachment as a person. But the phenomenon of interest here is the more generalized alienation from the value-patterns involved in the role-expectation. This, then, would motivate the actor to avoid conformity with these patterns, whenever encountered, either by withdrawal or by actively seeking a counter-orientation. This can be a source of motivation to seek alternative identifications and may also reinforce regressive tendencies. In any case the possibilities of primary alienation are among the most important factors giving *direction* to the distribution of variability from the modal personality type.

What will be called *secondary* alienation is not built into the primary value-orientation patterns of the personality, but is a consequence of the fact that a personality with a given value-orientation pattern in his character structure is faced, *in a specific role*, with role-expectations which are uncongenial to his need-dispositions and that, therefore, he is motivated to try to avoid conformity with them, though of course this component of his motivation may be outweighed by others such as a fear of the consequences of sanctions.

Even without primary alienative need-dispositions the diversity of personality types within a given role-system is such that further mechanisms would be necessary in order to secure the level of uniformity of behavior which is required by most roles in a social structure. There are three sets of facts, however, which cut down considerably the need for further mechanisms on the socialization level. These may be briefly mentioned before taking up the latter.

First, there are the mechanisms of social control, which operate to secure conformity with role-expectations in spite of need-dispositions to avoid that conformity. The simplest and most obvious of these are the reward-punishment mechanisms which may give sufficient rewards for conformity and punishments for deviance to tip the balance in favor of conformity. This aspect of reward and punishment will, however, have to be taken up later.

Secondly, to a widely varying degree for different roles and in different social systems, there is institutionalized a range of toleration, so that conformity does not need to mean absolute uniformity of behavior. Put a little differently, along with prescriptions and prohibitions, there are also permissions. Very often, however, there is a certain relativity in the permissiveness in that there may be, as some anthropologists say, "preferred patterns," that is, a hierarchy among the permitted ones. Perhaps the most important case of this is that where there are differentiated levels of achievement within a role, as is true for example of most modern occupational roles. Then there will be differential rewards correlated with the differential achievements, so that the actor whose grade of achievement is low, while he may not be deviant, is still "paying a price," in that he fails to get the higher rewards, both, for example, in money earnings and in approval. Finding his place on such an achievement ladder may, however, constitute a tolerable adjustment for a variant personality, and this is an important kind of flexibility in the relation between the social system and the individual. Of course this is still more sure where the place occupied within the permitted range is a "matter of taste" without clear hierarchical distinctions.

Finally, the third element of flexibility is the very important one, which again varies from society to society, of the existence of a system of *alternative role-opportunities* so that there is no one set of role-expectations which every individual who starts at a given status-point must conform with or pay the cost of deviance in sanctions. There seems to be little doubt that in a complex and mobile society like our own, one of the major sorting-out factors between alternative role-opportunities is to be found in differences of the value-orientation patterns of different personalities. When the major family status factors have been taken into account, and such obvious performance-capacity factors as I.Q., there is still a substantial residual variance with respect to occupational career orientation.[3] It seems highly probable that one of the major factors in this residual variance is the variability of basic personality structure within the

[3] This has been clearly demonstrated in an unpublished study of the social mobility of high school students in the Boston area by S. A. Stouffer, Florence Kluckhohn, and the present author.

population concerned, which is not a function of the modal role-expectation patterns of their initial status.

SUGGESTED READINGS

DAVID I. ABERLE and KASPAR D. NAEGELE. Raising Middle-class Sons, *American Journal of Orthopsychiatry*, *22*: 366–378, 1952.

REINHARD BENDIX. Compliant Behavior and Individual Personality, *American Journal of Sociology*, *58*: 292–303, 1952.

URIE BRONFENBRENNER. The Changing American Child—A Speculative Analysis, *Journal of Social Issues*, *17*: 6–18, 1961.

BERT KAPLAN. Personality and Social Structure, in J. B. Gittler (Ed.), *Review of Sociology: Analysis of a Decade*, John Wiley and Sons, Inc., New York, 1957, pp. 87–123.

TALCOTT PARSONS. *Social Structure and Personality*, Free Press, New York, 1964.

WILLIAM H. SEWELL. Social Class and Childhood Personality, *Sociometry*, *24*: 340–356, 1961.

NEIL J. SMELSER and WILLIAM T. SMELSER (Eds.). *Personality and Social Systems*, John Wiley and Sons, Inc., New York, 1963.

MAURICE STEIN, ARTHUR J. VIDICH, and DAVID M. WHITE (Eds.). *Identity and Anxiety*, Free Press, New York, 1960.

BARTLETT H. STOODLEY (Ed.). *Society and Self*, Free Press, New York, 1962.

Part II

Personality and Interaction

The papers in this section have a somewhat different orientation than those found in Part I. Greater emphasis is placed upon the organization and dynamics of personality and how personality arises from interaction. The self is often the central organizing concept.

Symbolic interactionist theory, which guides much of sociological inquiry in personality and interaction, originated in the writings of George H. Mead, Charles H. Cooley, John Dewey, W. I. Thomas and several other theorists at the turn of the century. Symbolic interactionist theory has undergone considerable modification and extension during the last two decades, but it is still based upon the assumptions and philosophical viewpoint presented by Mead in Mind, Self, and Society.[1] *The first article in this section is a summary of Mead's position.*

According to Mead, the self is a set of attitudes or beliefs that an individual comes to hold toward himself. The self or personality is socially formed; it is not there at birth.[2] *There is no self because the person has no information about himself. As other people react to him as an object, the individual learns to think of himself as a social object, begins to develop self-attitudes, and comes to respond to himself as others respond to him. Mead suggests that a number of selves may develop, each of which represents a more or less separate set of responses acquired from different social groups in which the individual holds membership.*

Language is essential for the development of the self, for the self can arise only in those settings where there is social communication. Human beings, according to Mead, respond to one another on the basis of the interpretations given to each other's actions. At first, the individual responds to others in terms of gestures. Later, language is substituted for the gestures and the person responds to language

[1] George H. Mead, *Mind, Self, and Society*, University of Chicago Press, Chicago, Ill., 1934.

[2] It is often the case that sociologists equate the term "self" with "personality," and if not, the self is regarded as one aspect of personality.

symbols. *It is through language that the person acquires the meanings and definitions (significant symbols) around him. Mead is also largely responsible for introducing several terms which are a common part of sociological terminology. By* role taking *Mead means the ability of a person to put himself into the position of another. The* generalized other *refers to a person seeing himself as others see him.*

The content of the paper by Bingham Dai, in many respects, represents a fusion between the symbolic interactionist and psychoanalytic orientation toward personality organization. While the title might convey the impression that Dai is concerned with the abnormal personality, his focus is actually upon the normal personality, especially that aspect which can be called the self.

Dai raises a series of hypotheses about personality organization, among which are several that incorporate Cooley's recognition of the importance of primary groups in personality development and Mead's contention of multiple selves. According to Dai, the self can be divided into a primary and secondary self. The primary self is, in many respects, the core of personality and arises from experiences acquired in primary groups, i.e., groups characterized by warm, intimate, and informal relationships and in which early social learning takes place. The secondary self arises in secondary group environments. Here the environment is less intimate, and interpersonal relationships are more formal and constrained. The primary self may be either favorable or unfavorable, but regardless of evaluation it has a very close affinity with the secondary self. Dai hypothesizes that the degree of integration between the two selves appears to depend largely upon the degree of continuity and congruity between a person's early socio-cultural environments. The concept of the primary and secondary self is explored in relationship to behavior and various other personality theories.

A set of excerpts taken from Coutu's Emergent Human Nature: A Symbolic Field Interpretation *make up the next selection. As might be expected from the title, Coutu has integrated aspects of Lewinian field theory with aspects of symbolic interactionist theory. Coutu suggests that the reciprocity of inner (personality) and outer (field or situation) determinants of behavior can best be kept in view if we have words which express that relationship. He has coined the term "tinsit" (abbreviation for tendency-in-situation) to express the relationship between personality and the field. The properties of the "tinsit" are discussed and Coutu demonstrates that accuracy of predicting behavior is enhanced if both person and situation are incorporated into a theory of behavior, rather than being handled as independent events.*

The influence of the drama is not new to personality theory. The term persona *was used by Jung to describe the public personality of the individual—that portion which he displayed to the world. The term role is derived from the Latin* rotula *and originally referred to the "rolls" on which the scripts of ancient Grecian and Roman actors were written.*

Perhaps the most elaborately developed dramaturgical analysis of human behavior is found in the work of Erving Goffman. Goffman uses the terms and concepts of the stage as a maneuver to describe the behavior of participants in interaction. In so doing he develops ". . . a perspective on the world, and the self within it, that renders life a kind of 'theatre' in which a 'show' is 'staged'." [3] *Goffman's dramaturgical theory revolves around a performer whose activities function to create an impression on an audience. In order to prepare for the action that is to occur, the performer engages in various strategies. He puts up a front, manipulating scenery and stage props (furniture, décor, and other background items) and those more personal items identified with the performer himself (posture, voice, clothing, and additional expressive equipment). The performer may act alone, or may act in concert, but whether acting individually or as a team it is necessary to protect against events that could discredit the performance. As a consequence the actors employ defensive practices to safeguard a performance as well as various other techniques to salvage a performance in the face of disruptions and intrusions that inevitably occur.*

As Goffman develops an actor-audience paradigm which has as its core the ways in which impressions are created and sustained, his view of self as a dramatic effect is quite distinct from that found in other theories. In Goffman's words:

> *. . . A correctly staged and performed scene leads the audience to impute a self to a performed character, but this imputation—this self—is a* product *of a scene that comes off, and is not a* cause *of it.*[4]

[3] Sheldon L. Messinger, "Life as Theater: Some Notes on the Dramaturgic Approach to Social Reality," *Sociometry,* 25: 98, 1962.

[4] Erving Goffman, *The Presentation of Self in Everyday Life,* Doubleday and Company, Garden City, New York, 1959, p. 252.

4

The Social Psychology of George Herbert Mead*

BERNARD N. MELTZER

CONTENT OF MEAD'S SOCIAL PSYCHOLOGY

1. Society

According to Mead, all group life is essentially a matter of cooperative behavior. Mead makes a distinction, however, between infrahuman society and human society. Insects—whose society most closely approximates the complexity of human social life—act together in certain ways because of their biological make-up. Thus, their cooperative behavior is physiologically determined. This is shown by many facts, among which is the fact of the fixity, the stability, of the relationships of insect-society members to one another: Insects, according to the evidence, go on for countless generations without any difference in their patterns of association. This picture of infrahuman society remains essentially valid as one ascends the scale of animal life, until we arrive at the human level.

In the case of human association, the situation is fundamentally different. Human cooperation is not brought about by mere physiological factors. The very diversity of the patterns of human group life makes it quite clear that human cooperative life cannot be explained in the same terms as the cooperative life of insects and the lower animals. The fact that human patterns are not stabilized and cannot be explained in biological terms led Mead to seek another basis of explanation of human association. Such cooperation can

---

* By permission, from Bernard N. Meltzer, *The Social Psychology of George Herbert Mead*, Center for Sociological Research, Western Michigan University, Kalamazoo, Mich., 1964, pp. 11–26 (excerpt).

only be brought about by some process wherein: (a) each acting individual ascertains the *intention* of the acts of others, and then (b) makes his own response on the basis of that intention. What this means is that, in order for human beings to cooperate, there must be present some sort of mechanism whereby each acting individual: (a) can come to understand the lines of action of others, and (b) can guide his own behavior to fit in with those lines of action. Human behavior is not a matter of responding directly to the activities of others. Rather, it involves responding to the *intentions* of others, i.e., to the future, intended behavior of others—not merely to their present actions.

We can better understand the character of this distinctively human mode of interaction between individuals by contrasting it with the infrahuman "conversation of gestures." For example, when a mother hen clucks, her chicks will respond by running to her. This does not imply however, that the hen clucks *in order* to guide the chicks, i.e., with the *intention* of guiding them. Clucking is a natural sign or signal—rather than a significant (meaningful) symbol—as it is not meaningful to the hen. That is, the hen (according to Mead) does not take the role, or viewpoint, of the chicks toward its own gesture and respond to it, in imagination, as they do. The hen does not envision the response of the chicks to her clucking. Thus, hen and chicks do not share the same experience.

Let us take another illustration by Mead: Two hostile dogs, in the pre-fight stage, may go through an elaborate conversation of gestures (snarling, growling, baring fangs, walking stiff-leggedly around one another, etc.). The dogs are adjusting themselves to one another by responding to one another's gestures. (A gesture is that portion of an act which represents the entire act; it is the initial, overt phase of the act, which epitomizes it, *e.g.*, shaking one's fist at someone.) Now, in the case of the dogs the response to a gesture is dictated by preestablished tendencies to respond in certain ways. Each gesture leads to a direct, immediate, automatic, and unreflecting response by the recipient of the gesture (the other dog). Neither dog responds to the *intention* of the gestures. Further, each dog does not make his gestures with the intent of eliciting certain responses in the other dog. Thus, animal interaction is devoid of conscious, deliberate meaning.

To summarize: Gestures, at the non-human, or non-linguistic level, do not carry the connotation of conscious meaning or intent, but serve merely as cues for the appropriate responses of others. Gestural communication takes place immediately, without any interruption of the act, without the mediation of a definition or meaning. Each organism adjusts "instinctively" to the other; it does not stop and figure out which response it will give. Its behavior is, largely, a series of direct, automatic responses to stimuli.

Human beings, on the other hand, respond to one another on the basis of the intentions or meanings of gestures. This renders the gestures *symbolic*, *i.e.*, the gesture becomes a symbol to be interpreted; it becomes something which, in the imaginations of the participants, stands for the entire act.

Thus, individual A begins to act, *i.e.*, makes a gesture: for example, he draws back an arm. Individual B (who perceives the gesture) completes, or fills in, the act in his imagination; *i.e.*, B imaginatively projects the gesture into the future: "He will strike me." In other words, B perceives what the gesture stands for, thus getting its meaning. In contrast to the direct responses of the chicks and the dogs, the human being inserts an interpretation between the gesture of another and his response to it. Human behavior involves responses to *interpreted* stimuli.[1]

We see, then, that people respond to one another on the basis of imaginative activity. In order to engage in concerted behavior, however, each participating individual must be able to attach the same meaning to the same gesture. Unless interacting individuals interpret gestures similarly, unless they fill out the imagined portion in the same way, there can be no cooperative action. This is another way

---

[1] The foregoing distinctions can also be expressed in terms of the differences between "signs," or "signals," and symbols. A sign stands for something else because of the fact that it is present at approximately the same time and place with that "something else." A symbol, on the other hand, stands for something else because its users have agreed to let it stand for that "something else." Thus, signs are directly and intrinsically linked with present or proximate situations; while symbols, having arbitrary and conventional, rather than intrinsic, meanings, transcend the immediate situation. (We shall return to this important point in our discussion of "mind.") Only symbols, of course, involve interpretation, self-stimulation and shared meaning.

of saying what has by now become a truism in sociology and social psychology: Human society rests upon a basis of *consensus*, *i.e.*, the sharing of meanings in the form of common understandings and expectations.

In the case of the human being, each person has the ability to respond to his own gestures; and, thus, it is possible to have the same meaning for the gestures as other persons. (For example: As I say "chair," I present to myself the same image as to my hearer; moreover, the same image as when someone else says "chair.") This ability to stimulate oneself as one stimulates another, and to respond to oneself as another does, Mead ascribes largely to man's vocal-auditory mechanism. (The ability to hear oneself implies at least the potentiality for responding to oneself.) When a gesture has a shared, common meaning, when it is—in other words—a *linguistic* element, we can designate it as a "significant symbol." (Take the words, "Open the window": The pattern of action symbolized by these words must be in the mind of the speaker as well as the listener. Each must respond, in imagination, to the words in the same way. The speaker must have an image of the listener responding to his words by opening the window, and the listener must have an image of his opening the window.)

The imaginative completion of an act—which Mead calls "meaning" and which represents mental activity—necessarily takes place through *role-taking*. To complete imaginatively the total act which a gesture stands for, the individual must put himself in the position of the other person, must identify with him. The earliest beginnings of role-taking occur when an already established act of another individual is stopped short of completion, thereby requiring the observing individual to fill in, or complete, the activity imaginatively. (For example, a crying infant may have an image of its mother coming to stop its crying.)

As Mead points out, then, the relation of human beings to one another arises from the developed ability of the human being to respond to his own gestures. This ability enables different human beings to respond in the same way to the same gesture, thereby sharing one another's experience.

This latter point is of great importance. Behavior is viewed as "social" not simply when it is a response to others, but rather when it has incorporated in it the behavior of others. The human being

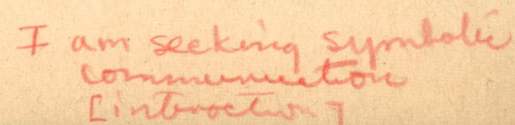

I am seeking symbolic communication [introduction]

responds to himself as other persons respond to him, and in so doing he imaginatively shares the conduct of others. That is, in imagining their response he shares that response.[2]

2. Self

To state that the human being can respond to his own gestures necessarily implies that he possesses a *self*. In referring to the human being as having a self, Mead simply means that such an individual may act socially toward himself, just as toward others. He may praise, blame, or encourage himself; he may become disgusted with himself, may seek to punish himself, and so forth. Thus, the human being may become the object of his own actions. The self is formed in the same way as other objects—through the "definitions" made by others.

The mechanism whereby the individual becomes able to view himself as an object is that of role-taking, involving the process of communication, especially by vocal gestures or speech. (Such communication necessarily involves role-taking.) It is only by taking the role of others that the individual can come to see himself as an object. The standpoint of others provides a platform for getting outside oneself and thus viewing oneself. The development of the self is concurrent with the development of the ability to take roles.

The crucial importance of language in this process must be underscored. It is through language (significant symbols) that the child acquires the meanings and definitions of those around him. By learning the symbols of his groups, he comes to internalize their definitions of events or things, including their definitions of his own conduct.

It is quite evident that, rather than assuming the existence of selves and explaining society thereby, Mead starts out from the prior existence of society as the context within which selves arise. This view contrasts with the nominalistic position of the Social Contract theorists and of various individualistic psychologies.

---

[2] To anyone who has taken even one course in Sociology it is probably superfluous to stress the importance of symbols, particularly language, in the acquisition of all other elements of culture. The process of socialization is essentially a process of symbolic interaction.

GENESIS OF THE SELF

The relationship between role-playing and various stages in the development of the self is described below:

(1) Preparatory Stage (not explicitly named by Mead, but inferable from various fragmentary essays). This stage is one of meaningless imitation by the infant (for example, "reading" the newspaper). The child does certain things that others near it do without any understanding of what he is doing. Such imitation, however, implies that the child is incipiently taking the roles of those around it, *i.e.*, is on the verge of putting itself in the position of others and acting like them.

(2) Play Stage. In this stage the actual playing of roles occurs. The child plays mother, teacher, storekeeper, postman, streetcar conductor, Mr. Jones, etc. What is of central importance in such play-acting is that it places the child in the position where it is able to act back toward itself in such roles as "mother" or "teacher." In this stage, then, the child first begins to form a self, that is, to direct activity toward itself—and it does so by taking the roles of others. This is clearly indicated by use of the third person in referring to oneself instead of the first person: "John wants . . .", "John is a bad boy."

However, in this stage the young child's configuration of roles is unstable; the child passes from one role to another in unorganized, inconsistent fashion. He has, as yet, no unitary standpoint from which to view himself, and hence, he has no unified conception of himself. In other words, the child forms a number of separate and discrete objects of itself, depending on the roles in which it acts toward itself.

(3) Game Stage. This is the "completing" stage of the self. In time, the child finds himself in situations wherein he must take a number of roles simultaneously. That is, he must respond to the expectations of several people at the same time. This sort of situation is exemplified by the game of baseball—to use Mead's own illustration: Each player must visualize the intentions and expectations of several other players. In such situations the child must take the roles of groups of individuals as over against particular roles. The child becomes enabled to do this by abstracting a "composite" role out of the concrete roles of particular persons. In the course of his associa-

tion with others, then, he builds up a *generalized other*, a generalized role or standpoint from which he views himself and his behavior. This generalized other represents, then, the set of standpoints which are common to the group.

Having achieved this generalized standpoint, the individual can conduct himself in an organized, consistent manner. He can view himself from a consistent standpoint. This means, then, that the individual can transcend the local and present expectations and definitions with which he comes in contact. An illustration of this point would be the Englishman who "dresses for dinner" in the wilds of Africa. Thus, through having a generalized other, the individual becomes emancipated from the pressures of the peculiarities of the immediate situation. He can act with a certain amount of consistency in a variety of situations because he acts in accordance with a generalized set of expectations and definitions that he has internalized.

THE "I" AND THE "ME"

The self is essentially a social process within the individual involving two analytically distinguishable phases: The "I" and the "Me."

The "I" is the impulsive tendency of the individual. It is the initial, spontaneous, unorganized aspect of human experience. Thus, it represents the undirected tendencies of the individual.

The "Me" represents the incorporated other within the individual. Thus, it comprises the organized set of attitudes and definitions, understandings and expectations—or simply meanings—common to the group. In any given situation, the "Me" comprises the generalized other and, often, some particular other.

Every act begins in the form of an "I" and usually ends in the form of the "Me." For the "I" represents the initiation of the act prior to its coming under control of the definitions or expectations of others (the "Me"). The "I" thus gives *propulsion* while the "Me" gives *direction* to the act. Human behavior, then, can be viewed as a perpetual series of initiations of acts by the "I" and of acting-back-upon the act (that is, guidance of the act) by the "Me." The act is a resultant of this interplay.

The "I," being spontaneous and propulsive, offers the potentiality for new, creative activity. The "Me," being regulatory, disposes the individual to both goal-directed activity and conformity. In the operation of these aspects of the self, we have the basis for, on the one hand, social control and, on the other, novelty and innovation. We are thus provided with a basis for understanding the mutuality of the relationship between the individual and society.[3]

IMPLICATIONS OF SELFHOOD

Some of the major implications of selfhood in human behavior are as follows:

(1) The possession of a self makes of the individual a society in miniature. That is, he may engage in interaction with himself just as two or more different individuals might. In the course of this interaction, he can come to view himself in a new way, thereby bringing about changes in himself.

(2) The ability to act toward oneself makes possible an inner experience which need not reach overt expression. That is, the individual, by virtue of having a self, is thereby endowed with the possibility of having a mental life: He can make indications to himself—which constitutes *mind*.

(3) The individual with a self is thereby enabled to direct and control his behavior. Instead of being subject to all impulses and

---

[3] At first glance, Mead's "I" and "Me" may appear to bear a close affinity with Freud's concepts of Id, Ego, and Superego. The resemblance is, for the most part, more apparent than real. While the Superego is held to be harshly frustrating and repressive of the instinctual, libidinous, and aggressive Id, the "Me" is held to provide necessary direction—often of a *gratifying* nature—to the otherwise undirected impulses constituting the "I." Putting the matter in figurative terms: Freud views the Id and the Superego as locked in combat upon the battleground of the Ego; Mead sees the "I" and "Me" engaged in close collaboration. This difference in perspective may derive from different preoccupations: Freud was primarily concerned with tension, anxiety, and "abnormal" behavior; Mead was primarily concerned with behavior generically.

It is true, on the other hand, that the Id, Ego, and Superego—particularly as modified by such neo-Freudians as Karen Horney, Erich Fromm, and H. S. Sullivan—converge at a few points with the "I" and "Me." This is especially evident in the emphasis of both the Superego and "Me" concepts upon the internalization of the norms of significant others through the process of identification, or role-taking.

Incidentally, it should be noted that both sets of concepts refer to processes of behavior, *not* to concrete entities or structures. See also, the discussion of "mind" which follows.

stimuli directly playing upon him, the individual can check, guide, and organize his behavior. He is, then, *not* a mere passive agent.

All three of these implications of selfhood may be summarized by the statement that the self and the mind (mental activity) are twin emergents in the social process.

3. Mind

DEVELOPMENT OF MIND

As in the instance of his consideration of the self, Mead rejects individualistic psychologies, in which the social process (society, social interaction) is viewed as presupposing and being a product of, mind. In direct contrast is his view that mind presupposes, and is a product of, the social process. Mind is seen by Mead as developing correlatively with the self, constituting (in a very important sense) the self in action.

Mead's hypothesis regarding mind (as regarding the self) is that the mental emerges out of the organic life of man through communication. The mind is present only at certain points in human behavior, *viz.*, when significant symbols are being used by the individual. This view dispenses with the substantive notion of mind as existing as a box-like container in the head, or as some kind of fixed, ever-present entity. Mind is seen as a *process*, which manifests itself whenever the individual is interacting with himself by using significant symbols.

Mead begins his discussion of the mind with a consideration of the relation of the organism to its environment. He points out that the central principle in all organic behavior is that of continuous adjustment, or adaptation, to an environing field. We cannot regard the environment as having a fixed character for all organisms, as being the same for all organisms. All behavior involves selective attention and perception. The organism accepts certain events in its field, or vicinity, as stimuli and rejects or overlooks certain others as irrelevant to its needs. (For example, an animal battling for life ignores food.) Bombarded constantly by stimuli, the organism selects those stimuli or aspects of its field which pertain to, are functional to, the acts in which the organism is engaged. Thus, the organism has a hand in determining the nature of its environment. What this means, then, is that Mead, along with Dewey, regards all life as ongoing activity, and views stimuli—not as initiators of

[margin top: Sullivan got selective attention from Mead]

activity—but as elements selected by the organism in the furtherance of that activity.

Perception is thus an activity that involves selective attention to certain aspects of a situation, rather than a mere matter of something coming into the individual's nervous system and leaving an impression. Visual perception, *e.g.*, is more than a matter of just opening one's eyes and responding to what falls on the retina.

The determination of the environment by the biologic individual (infrahumans and the unsocialized infant) is not a cognitive relationship. It is selective, but does not involve consciousness, in the sense of reflective intelligence. At the distinctively human level, on the other hand, there is a hesitancy, an inhibition of overt conduct, which is *not* involved in the selective attention of animal behavior. In this period of inhibition, mind is present.

For, human behavior involves inhibiting an act and trying out the varying approaches in imagination. In contrast, as we have seen, the acts of the biologic individual are relatively immediate, direct, and made up of innate or habitual ways of reacting. In other words, the unsocialized organism lacks consciousness of meaning. This being the case, the organism has no means for the abstract analysis of its field when new situations are met, and hence no means for the reorganization of action-tendencies in the light of that analysis.[4]

Minded behavior (in Mead's sense) arises around problems. It represents, to repeat an important point, a temporary inhibition of action wherein the individual is attempting to prevision the future. It consists of presenting to oneself, tentatively and in advance of overt behavior, the different possibilities or alternatives of future action with reference to a given situation. The future is thus present in terms of images of prospective lines of action from which the individual can make a selection. The mental process is, then, one of delaying, organizing, and selecting a response to the stimuli of the environment. This implies that the individual *constructs* his act,

---

[4] The reader should recognize here, in a new guise, our earlier distinction between signs and symbols. Signs have "intrinsic" meanings which induce direct reactions; symbols have arbitrary meanings which require interpretations by the actor prior to his response or action. The former, it will be recalled, are "tied to" the immediate situation, while the latter "transcend" the immediate situation. Thus, symbols may refer to past or future events, to hypothetical situations, to nonexistent or imaginary objects, and so forth.

*[margin bottom: * latency period not accounted for by those of alone & beyond nervous impulse the reflex arc time]*

rather than responding in predetermined ways. Mind makes it possible for the individual purposively to control and organize his responses. Needless to say, this view contradicts the stimulus-response conception of human behavior.

When the act of an animal is checked, it may engage in overt trial and error or random activity. In the case of blocked human acts, the trial and error may be carried on covertly, implicitly. Consequences can be imaginatively "tried out" in advance. This is what is primarily meant by "mind," "reflective thinking," or "abstract thinking."

What this involves is the ability to indicate elements of the field or situation, abstract them from the situation, and recombine them so that procedures can be considered in advance of their execution. Thus, to quote a well-known example, the intelligence of the detective as over against the intelligence of the bloodhound lies in the capacity of the former to isolate and indicate (to himself and to others) what the particular characters are which will call out the response of apprehending the fugitive criminal.

The mind is social in both origin and function. It arises in the social process of communication. Through association with the members of his groups, the individual comes to internalize the definitions transmitted to him through linguistic symbols, learns to assume the perspectives of others, and thereby acquires the ability to think. When the mind has risen in this process, it operates to maintain and adjust the individual in his society; and it enables the society to persist. The persistence of a human society depends, as we have seen, upon consensus; and consensus necessarily entails minded behavior.

The mind is social in function in the sense that the individual continually indicates to himself in the role of others and controls his activity with reference to the definitions provided by others. In order to carry on though, he must have some standpoint from which to converse with himself. He gets this standpoint by importing into himself the role of others.

By "taking the role of the other,"—as I earlier pointed out—we can see ourselves as others see us, and arouse in ourselves the responses that we call out in others. It is this conversation with ourselves, between the representation of the other (in the form of the "Me") and our impulses (in the form of the "I") that constitutes the mind. Thus, what the individual actually does in minded behavior is to carry on an internal conversation. By addressing himself from the standpoint of the generalized other, the individual has a universe of discourse, a system of common symbols and meanings, with which to address himself. These are presupposed as the context for minded behavior.

Mead holds, then, that mental activity is a peculiar type of activity that goes on in the experience of the person. The activity is that of the person responding to himself, of indicating things to himself.

To repeat, mind originates in the social process, in association with others. There is little doubt that human beings lived together in groups before mind ever evolved. But, there emerged, because of certain biological developments, the point where human beings were able to respond to their own acts and gestures. It was at this point that mind, or minded behavior, emerged. Similarly, mind comes into existence for the individual at the point where the individual is capable of responding to his own behavior, *i.e.*, where he can designate things to himself.

Summarizing this brief treatment of mind, mental activity, or reflective thinking, we may say that it is a matter of making indications of meanings to oneself as to others. This is another way of saying that mind is the process of using significant symbols. For, thinking goes on when an individual uses a symbol to call out in himself the responses which others would make. Mind, then, is symbolic behavior.[5] As such, mind is an emergent from non-symbolic behavior and is fundamentally irreducible to the stimulus-response mechanisms which characterize the latter form of behavior.

It should be evident that Mead avoids both the behavioristic fallacy of reduction and the individualistic fallacy of taking for granted the phenomenon that is to be explained.

---

[5] A growing number of linguists, semanticists, and students of speech disorders are becoming aware of the central role of symbols in the *content*, as well as the process, of thought. Edward Sapir and Benjamin Whorf have formulated "the principle of linguistic relativity," which holds that the structure of a language influences the manner in which the users of the language will perceive, comprehend, and act toward reality. Wendell Johnson, in the field of semantics, and Kurt Goldstein, in the study of aphasia, are representative investigators who have recognized the way in which symbols structure perception and thought. Mead's theory clearly foreshadows these developments.

OBJECTS

Returning to Mead's discussion of the organism-in-environment, we can now give more explicit attention to his treatment of *objects*. As we have seen, we cannot regard the environment as having a fixed character for all organisms. The environment is a function of the animal's own character, being greatly determined by the make-up of the animal. Each animal largely selects its own environment. It selects out the stimuli toward which it acts, its make-up and on-going activity determining the kinds of stimuli it will select. Further, the qualities which are possessed by the objects toward which the animal acts arise from the kind of experiences that the animal has with the objects. (To illustrate, grass is not the same phenomenon for a cat and for a cow.) The environment and its qualities, then, are always functional to the structure of the animal.

As one passes on to the human level, the relation of the individual to the world becomes markedly more complicated. This is so because the human being is capable of forming objects. Animals, lacking symbols, see stimuli, such as patches of color—not objects. An object has to be detached, pointed out, "imaged" to oneself. The human being's environment is constituted largely by objects.

Now, let us look at the relation of the individual to objects. An object represents a plan of action. That is, an object doesn't exist for the individual in some pre-established form. Perception of any object has telescoped in it a series of experiences which one would have if he carried out the plan of action toward that object. The object has no qualities for the individual, aside from those which would result from his carrying out of a plan of action. In this respect, the object is constituted by one's activities with reference to it. (For example, chalk is the sum of qualities which are perceived as a result of one's actions: a hard, smooth, white, writing implement.)

The objects which constitute the "effective environment," the individual's experienced environment, are established by the individual's activities. To the extent that his activity varies, his environment varies. In other words, objects change as activities toward them change. (Chalk, for instance, may become a missile.)

Objects, which are constituted by the activities of the human individual, are largely *shared* objects. They stand for common patterns of activity of individuals. This is true, Mead points out, by virtue of the fact that objects arise, and are present in experience, only in the process of being indicated to oneself (and, hence, explicitly or implicitly, to others). In other words, the perspective from which one indicates an object implicates definitions by others. Needless to say, these definitions involve language, or significant symbols. The individual acquires a commonality of perspective with others by learning the symbols by which they designate aspects of the world.[6]

4. The Act

All human activity other than reflex and habitual action is built up in the process of its execution; *i.e.*, behavior is constructed as it goes along, for decisions must be made at several points. The significance of this fact is that people act—rather than merely reacting.

For Mead, the unit of study is "the act," which comprises both overt and covert aspects of human action. Within the act, all the separated categories of the traditional, orthodox psychologies find a place. Attention, perception, imagination, reasoning, emotion, and so forth, are seen as parts of the act—rather than as more or less extrinsic influences upon it. Human behavior presents itself in the form of acts, rather than of concatenations of minute responses.

The act, then, encompasses the total process involved in human activity. It is viewed as a complete span of action: its initial point is an impulse and its terminal point some objective which gives release to the impulse. In between, the individual is in the process of constructing, organizing his behavior. It is during this period that the act undergoes its most significant phase of development. In the case of human behavior, this period is marked by the play of images of

[6] The contrast between this view of learning and the neo-behavioristic "learning theory" of Clark Hull and other psychologists should be clearly evident. Basically, learning theorists attempt to reduce human learning to the mechanisms found in infrahuman learning. This is reflected in their tendency to ignore the role of linguistic symbols in human behavior, their conceptualization of human activity in terms of stimulus-response couplets, and their view of learning as equivalent with conditioning. (For an excellent critique of learning theory from the symbolic interactionist standpoint, see: Manford H. Kuhn, "Kinsey's View of Human Behavior," *Social Problems*, 1 (April 1954), pp. 119–125.)

possible goals or lines of action upon the impulse, thus directing the activity to its consummation.

In pointing out that the act begins with an impulse, Mead means that organisms experience disturbances of equilibrium. In the case of the lower animals, their biological make-up channelizes the impulse toward appropriate goals. In the case of the human being, the mere presence of an impulse leads to nothing but mere random, unorganized activity. This is most clearly—but definitely not exclusively—seen in the instance of the behavior of infants. Until the defining actions of others set up goals for it, the human infant's behavior is unchannelized. It is the function of images to direct, organize and construct this activity. The presence in behavior of images implies, of course, a process of indicating to oneself, or mind.

The act may have a short span (*e.g.*, attending a particular class meeting, or starting a new page of notes) or may involve the major portion of a person's life (*e.g.*, trying to achieve a successful career). Moreover, acts are parts of an interlacing of previous acts, and are built up, one upon another. This is in contradistinction to the view that behavior is a series of discrete stimulus-response bonds. Conceiving human behavior in terms of acts, we become aware of the necessity for viewing any particular act within its psychosocial context.[7]

Using the concept of the act, Mead sets up classes of acts—the

---

[7] The reader may have noted that this discussion makes no explicit reference to the problem of motivation. Mead had little to say regarding motives. Adherents to his general orientation have tended either to regard motives as implicit in the concept of *object* ("a plan of action") or to consider them "mere" verbal labels offered in supposed explanation of the actions of oneself or of others.

In my judgment, a conception of motivation can be formulated that is both useful and consistent with Mead's theories. Motivation can refer to "a process of defining (symbolically, of course) the goal of an act." Thus, while both human and infrahuman behavior may be viewed as goal-directed, only human behavior would be considered "motivated." Just as "motive" would be restricted to the human level, "drive" might serve a comparable function on the infrahuman level.

This would not imply that motives lie back of, or "cause," human acts. Rather, human acts are in constant process of construction, and the goal-definitions by individuals undergo constant reformulation. I mean to designate by "motive," however, the definition the individual makes, *at any given time*, of the objectives of his own specific acts. Such definitions, obviously, would be socially derived.

automatic act, the blocked act, the incomplete act, and the retrospective act—and analyzes them in terms of his frame of reference. Space does not permit presentation of these intriguing analyses.

SUMMARY

At several points in this report the reader must have been aware of the extremely closely interwoven character of Mead's various concepts. In the discussions of society, of self, and of mind, certain ideas seemed to require frequent (and, perhaps, repetitious) statement. A brief summary of Mead's position may help to reveal more meaningfully the way in which his key concepts interlock and logically imply one another.

The human individual is born into a society characterized by *symbolic interaction*. The use of *significant symbols* by those around him enables him to pass from the conversation of gestures—which involves direct, unmeaningful response to the overt acts of others—to the occasional *taking of the roles* of others. This role-taking enables him to *share* the perspectives of others. Concurrent with role-taking, the *self* develops, *i.e.*, the capacity to act toward oneself. Action toward oneself comes to take the form of viewing oneself from the standpoint, or perspective, of the *generalized other* (the composite representative of others, of society, within the individual), which implies defining one's behavior in terms of the expectations of others. In the process of such viewing of oneself, the individual must carry on symbolic interaction with himself, involving an internal conversation between his impulsive aspect (the "I") and the incorporated perspectives of others (The "Me"). The *mind*, or mental activity, is present in behavior whenever such symbolic interaction goes on—whether the individual is merely "thinking" (in the everyday sense of the word) or is also interacting with another individual. (In both cases the individual must indicate things to himself.) Mental activity necessarily involves *meanings*, which usually attach to, and define, *objects*. The meaning of an object or event is simply an image of the pattern of action which defines the object or event. That is, the completion in one's imagination of an act, or the mental picture of the actions and experiences symbolized by an object, defines the act or the object. In the unit of study that Mead calls "the *act*," all of the foregoing processes are usually entailed. The concluding point to be made in this summary is the same as the point with which I began: Mead's concepts intertwine and mutually imply one another. To drive home this important point, I must emphasize that human society (characterized by symbolic interaction) both precedes the rise of individual selves and minds and is maintained by the rise of individual selves and minds. This means, then, that symbolic interaction is both the medium for the development of human beings and the process by which human beings associate as human beings.

Finally, it should be clearly evident by now that any distinctively human act necessarily involves: symbolic interaction, role-taking, meaning, mind, and self. Where one of these concepts is involved, the others are, also, necessarily involved. Here we see, unmistakably, the organic unity of Mead's position.

5

A Socio-Psychiatric Approach to Personality Organization*

BINGHAM DAI

There are many approaches to personality. They have varied from the elementaristic to the holistic, from the peripheralistic to the centralistic, or from the psychoanalytic, personalistic to the topological.[1] This paper, however, is an outgrowth not so much from a logical need to reconcile those opposing theories of personality as from a practical necessity to account for the behavioral phenomena that the writer has encountered from day to day as a lay-analyst and a sociologist for a number of years and in different cultural settings.[2] It is hoped, though, that what is presented in the following may be of some use to those better qualified to discuss strictly theoretical problems.

The approaches employed and found most useful in the writer's work, to use the words of Edward Sapir, may be simply called the sociological and the psychiatric.[3] The sociological approach looks

---

* By permission, from Bingham Dai, A Socio-Psychiatric Approach to Personality Organization, *American Sociological Review*, 17: 44–49, 1952.

Paper read at the annual meeting of the American Sociological Society held in Chicago, September 5–7, 1951.

[1] Angyal, A., *Foundations of a Science of Personality*, 1941; Maslow, A. H., "Dynamics of Personality Organization," *Psychological Review*, 50 (1943): 514–539; Rosenzweig, S., "Converging Approaches to Personality," *Psychological Review*, 51 (1944): 248–275.

[2] The writer started his work as a lay analyst and sociologist at the Peiping Union Medical College in China in 1935 and worked among American Negroes at Fisk University from 1939 to 1942. Since 1943 he has been associated with the Department of Psychiatry, and since 1947 also with the Department of Psychology, Duke University.

[3] Sapir, E., "Personality," *Encyclopedia of the Social Sciences*, 12 (1934), 85–88.

upon the human individual not only as a biological organism but always as a member of society and a carrier of culture and his behavior at any given point of time as a function of the interaction between him and the on-going socio-cultural situation as he defines it.[4] The psychiatric approach, on the other hand, tends to emphasize the unique and the relatively enduring systems of reactivity on the part of the individual, especially those integrative and adjustive processes that are characterized by low degrees of personal awareness. A combination of these views, or what is here called the socio-psychiatric approach, therefore, will incline one to think of man not only as a psychophysical organization, but one that "embodies countless cultural patterns in a unique configuration:[5] one that is characterized by "relatively enduring life processes,"[6] accompanied by different degrees of awareness and functioning almost always in a socio-cultural context, actual or imaginary; and one that responds to any given situation always in terms of its meaning to itself. This approach is increasingly recognized by practically all serious students of personality, although it has been known by different names in different disciplines.[7]

SOME EMPIRICAL CLINICAL OBSERVATIONS

A clinician using the socio-psychiatric approach and working intensively with patients for a long period of time can hardly escape the following empirical observations: (1) Each patient seeking treatment seems to be perennially preoccupied with what kind of person he is, that is, the self as an object. It also seems that each patient has a preferred self-picture that he has had difficulty in realizing,

---

[4] Thomas, W. I., *The Polish Peasant in Europe and America* (1927), pp. 1847–1849.

[5] Sapir, *op. cit.*

[6] Sullivan, H. S., "Multidiscipline Coordination of Interpersonal Data," *Culture and Personality* edited by S. S. Sargent and M. W. Smith (1949), pp. 175–194.

[7] This approach is called the interpersonal theory by Harry S. Sullivan in *Conceptions of Modern Psychiatry*, the field theory by Gardner Murphy in *Personality: A Bio-Social Interpretation*, and the personal frame of reference by Snygg and Combs in *Individual Behavior*.

and because of this he is now beset by anxiety, guilt or aggression, or by half-hearted or unsuccessful attempts to live up to such a self-picture that have resulted in psychiatric symptoms.[8] (2) What has prevented the patient from realizing his preferred self-picture seems to consist of impulses that are accompanied by different degrees of personal awareness; some of these impulses are readily accessible to consciousness while others are not accessible. These conflicting impulses seem to function at the same time in situations emotionally significant to the individual. (3) Not only those life processes of which the individual is fully aware but also those characterized by low degrees of awareness tend to cluster. Such clusters have been variably represented as complexes, traits, trends, themes, or just attitudes.[9] In fact, such clusters of behavior patterns seem to be organized around unitary, though often conflicting, roles or self-concepts that the individual has attempted to play or realize in the socio-cultural situations confronting him. (4) All roles or self-concepts seem to have definite socio-cultural referent situations, or consist of what Sullivan called the "me-you patterns." [10] This is as true of the roles or self-concepts acquired in an individual's primary group environment as it is of those acquired later through membership in the secondary groups. (5) The conflicts of neurotic patients seem to be fundamentally conflicts of roles or self-concepts, having their origins in the conflicting socio-cultural environments with which the individual has been identified in the course of his development. (6) In spite of these conflicts, however, the human individual, it seems, never ceases to strive for a consistent self-picture, one that he considers as appropriate to his present-day socio-cultural environment. In fact, the so-called neurotic symptoms can be shown, in many instances, to be just such conscious or unconscious attempts at self-consistency.[11] (7) A change in behavior is often found to

[8] Cf. Murphy, *Personality*, p. 561.

[9] These clusters of impulses have been called complexes by Freud (*General Introduction to Psychoanalysis*), traits by Allport (*Personality: A Psychological Interpretation*), thema by Murray (*Explorations in Personality*), trends by Horney (*The Neurotic Personality of Our Time*) and attitudes by many sociologists and psychologists.

[10] Sullivan, H. S., "Psychiatry: An Introduction to the Study of Interpersonal Relations," *A Study of Interpersonal Relations*, edited by P. Mullahy (1949), pp. 98–121.

[11] Cf. Lecky, P., *Self Consistency: A Theory of Personality*, 1945.

follow a change in self-concept;[12] in fact, it seldom occurs otherwise. Very frequently when a patient's self-esteem increases, his previous complaints imperceptibly lose their importance. And (8) changes in self-concepts most frequently result from changes in self-other relations, the "other" being either the therapist in the therapeutic situation or the patient's associates in real life situations. This fact has been emphasized in different ways by practically all schools of psychotherapy.[13]

On the basis of such observable facts as mentioned above, certain hypotheses regarding personality organization have appeared to the writer as worthy of consideration. They will be presented first in a summary fashion. Then a discussion will follow.

SOME HYPOTHESES REGARDING PERSONALITY ORGANIZATION

1. Human personality, on its higher levels of integration, may be thought of as an organization of selves or self-concepts.[14]

2. Each of the selves in a personality organization has a definite socio-cultural referent situation, or has resulted from the interaction between the individual and a specific socio-cultural environment.

3. The organization of these selves appears to be hierarchical. The self that is acquired in the first or family group environment seems to be the most basic, while others acquired later in the secondary group environments vary in importance to the individual's self-picture of the moment, depending on the situation he is confronted by.[15]

4. The self that is acquired in the primary group environment may be called the primary self, while the selves acquired in the secondary group environments are the secondary selves. The primary

---

[12] Rogers, C. R., "The Significance of the Self Regarding Attitudes and Perceptions," *Feelings and Emotions*, edited by M. L. Reymert (1950), pp. 374–382.

[13] Alexander, F., French, T. M., *et al.*, *Psychoanalytic Therapy*, 1946; Fromm-Reichmann, F., *The Principles of Intensive Psychotherapy*, 1950; Rogers, C. R., *Client-Centered Therapy*, 1951.

[14] Cf. Allport, *op. cit.*, pp. 139–141.

[15] Cf. Angyal, *op. cit.*, on the vertical dimension of personality organization, pp. 264ff.

self tends to create life goals and set in motion certain basic self-defending and self-enhancing mechanisms or patterns that may persist in some form throughout the individual's life and condition his adaptation to later socio-cultural situations.

5. The primary self is either favorable or unfavorable, acceptable or unacceptable, to the person. The former tends to facilitate personality growth and adaptation to changing situations, while the latter tends to do the opposite.[16] Both kinds of processes may operate with or without the individual's awareness.

6. The relationship between the primary self and the secondary selves seems to be a very intimate one. The primary self almost invariably serves as a selector in the individual's later dealings with the secondary group situations and tends to incorporate or utilize the latter for the solution of its unresolved problems, with or without awareness on the part of the individual. On the other hand, the secondary self at any given point of time, especially if it is very much consciously preferred, tends to assert an inhibiting or integrative influence over the selves acquired earlier in the individual's development.

7. The degree of integration of the primary self and the secondary selves, or the degree of organization in a personality, seems to depend, to a very large extent, on the degree of continuity or congruity between an individual's primary or earlier socio-cultural environments and his secondary or later socio-cultural environments.[17]

8. There seems to be a natural tendency on the part of the human organism toward consistency or integration or to act as a whole. This tendency often necessitates the exclusion or dissociation of those impulses and behavior patterns from personal awareness that are not consistent with the individual's preferred self-picture in a given socio-cultural situation, thus resulting, in certain cases, in the kind of anxiety and defense mechanisms that eventually lead to neurotic symptoms.[18]

9. The behavior of a human individual in any given socio-cultural situation and at any given point of time may be thought of as a

[16] Cf. Allen, F., *Psychotherapy with Children* (1942), pp. 24–29.
[17] Cf. Benedict, R., "Continuities and Discontinuities in Cultural Conditioning," *Personality in Nature, Society and Culture*, edited by C. Kluckhohn and H. A. Murray (1948), pp. 414ff.
[18] May, R., *The Meaning of Anxiety* (1950), pp. 343ff.

function of the interaction between his personality organization as conceptualized above and the situation as it appears to him.[19]

10. The organism is at all times the core of a personality organization. An individual's efforts to integrate his various self-concepts together with their respective behavior patterns may be thought of as manifestations of the organisms' basic homeostatic processes at the self-other and self-culture levels. In other words, the human individual seems to act at all times as a bio-social whole.[20]

DISCUSSION

The idea that the behavior of a human individual is usually organized around his conception of himself and that a human personality consists of a hierarchy of self-concepts, of course, is not new.[21] Ever since the fad of radical behaviorism has subsided, the concept of self has been utilized by an increasing number of academic psychologists as well as clinicians.[22] While some of them, like Allport, tend to stress personality as an intrapsychic organization, others, like Murphy, place great emphasis on the relationship between the selves and the environment. With respect to the latter point of view, of course, the contributions of the sociologists have been the most outstanding and the most consistent, though little recognized in current psychological and psychiatric literature. According to Sorokin, for example, "the structure of the individual's egos may be considered as a microcosm corresponding to the social macrocosm of the groups to which the individual belongs." His thesis, very similar to the writer's, is that "the individual has not one empirical soul, or self, or ego, but several: first, biological; and second, social egos. The individual has as many different social egos as there are different social groups and strata with which he is connected."[23]

To most of these writers, however, the concept of self or ego seems

---

[19] Cf. Lewin, K., *Field Theory in Social Sciences*, edited by S. D. Cartwright (1951).

[20] Cf. Goldstein, K., *The Organism* (1939), pp. 291–340 and Frank, L. K., *Nature and Human Nature* (1951).

[21] James, W., *Psychology* (1948), pp. 176–216.

[22] Among those whose writings have been cited are Allport, Murphy, Rogers, Snygg, Combs, French, Horney and Sullivan.

[23] Sorokin, P. A., *Society, Culture and Personality* (1947), p. 345.

to refer primarily to the conscious system of attitudes and values with which an individual identifies in a given situation. What has been known in psychoanalytic literature as the Id or the Unconscious, that is, impulses and behavior patterns characterized by low degrees of awareness has not been adequately accounted for. One may ask here: Are those impulses and behavior patterns that the clinicians deal with really as primitive and as instinctive as the word Id would signify and do they come directly into conflict with the individual's self-picture of the moment or with Freud's Superego formed in the early genital period of his psychosexual development; or are they rather what Dewey called "habits" organized around roles or self-concepts that the individual has acquired early in life? [24] These questions are not adequately answered by such designations as "neurotic trends" (Horney), or "dissociated tendencies" (Sullivan), or autonomous motives (Allport), or plain unacceptable impulses. If the concept of self or ego is used to refer to the organization of those experiences that an individual had in his primary group environment but that now are repressed or dissociated, we are not told what becomes of those selves acquired early in an individual's life and how they are related to his self-concept of the moment and incorporated into his personality as a whole. The answer to these questions, it seems to the writer, may lie in the concept of primary self as it is used in the foregoing propositions regarding personality organization.

Some of the clinical observations in support of the concept of the primary self have already been mentioned. Further evidences justifying the use of the concept may be found in the so-called transference phenomenon and in the self perceptions often dramatized in the dreams. The former, as all users of intensive psychotherapy can testify, is essentially a relationship in which a patient, knowingly or unknowingly, identifies the treatment situation with his primary group environment and the therapist with the most significant persons in that environment. In other words, in his relations with the therapist at the present time the patient is actually playing a role, or acting according to a self-concept, that he has acquired in his primary group environment, although at the same time he may feel that he ought to act differently or more according to a self-concept appropriate to the real situation. In fact, learning to differentiate be-

[24] Dewey, J., *Human Nature and Conduct* (1922), p. 89.

tween the two constitutes the very essence of the therapeutic process. Such distorted definitions of present-day situations are often dramatized with the most uncanny accuracy in the patient's dreams and they usually take the form of perceiving an on-going interpersonal situation in terms of self-other relations in his primary group environment.[25]

A pertinent question may be asked here. Since there are more than one person in the primary group and since the concept of self implies a self-other relationship, can we say then that there are as many primary selves in an individual's personality as there are persons in his primary group? Logically, the answer seems to be in the affirmative. But empirically and clinically, what we do very often find is that there are always certain key persons in an individual's primary group and certain key experiences that are especially related to the kind of primary self he has acquired. In fact, we may follow Mead and say that what we refer to here is a generalized self that has resulted from the child's taking the role of the primary group "community" as a whole.[26] It is a self-picture that reflects the child's role in the total context of his first socio-cultural environment.[27]

Another related question may be asked. Does this concept of the primary self that has been derived principally from clinical observations apply to the normals, that is individuals who do not appear to have psychiatric symptoms and who do not seek treatment? That it does is strongly suggested by such intensive studies as that of a successful business man, named Orvil, by William Healy[28] and those of over 30 graduate students in psychiatry, clinical psychology, and medicine, made by the writer strictly for purposes of training.[29] In

[25] Freud, S., *The Interpretation of Dreams;* Lowy, S., *Psychological and Biological Foundations of Dream Interpretation*, 1946.

[26] Mead, G., *Mind, Self and Society* (1934), pp. 142, 167. It is to be noted that Mead makes a distinction between the self in its cognitive aspects and the self in its affective aspects (p. 173). This paper admittedly emphasizes the latter.

[27] For a clinical application of this approach, see B. Dai, "Divided Loyalty in War: A Study of Cooperation with the Enemy," *Psychiatry*, 7 (1944), pp. 327–340.

[28] Healy, W., *Personality in Formation and Action* (1938), pp. 53–69.

[29] Each of these trainees was given a 3-month intensive personality study, consisting of 36 didactic interviews, as a part of a program of training in psychotherapy conducted by the writer in the Departments of Psychiatry and Psychology, Duke University.

fact, a certain amount of such distorted definitions of present-day situations in terms of primary group relations seems to be the rule instead of an exception with the normals, and the exponents of the interpersonal theory have insisted that this phenomenon they call parataxia deserves more of the attention of the social scientists than it has been given.[30]

There are other interesting theoretical problems connected with the concept of primary self that we cannot go into here for lack of time. Perhaps the process of self formation and some of its practical implications may be worth a special mention. In the first stage of the development of the primary self, the interaction between the individual and the representatives of his primary group environment probably takes the form of the interplay of what Plant called "psychomotor tensions" [31] and the process involved is probably what Sullivan called "empathy." [32] As the child's language ability develops, the process may be more properly called "symbolic interaction," [33] or in Mead's own terms, "the conversation of significant gestures." [34] In terms of the sequence of events that can be readily reconstructed in the life history of any patient, the steps involved in the formation of the primary self seem to be as follows: first, the significant persons in his primary group environment have felt, thought and acted toward him in a certain way; then he as a child has learned to feel, think and act toward himself in a similar way; and finally, since no important corrective experiences have intervened, he has acquired the type of primary self that we spend a lot of time in discovering and helping to modify in the clinic.[35]

If problems of behavior disorders can be best understood in terms of man's continuous and persistent efforts to be human since infancy, that is to achieve a self-picture acceptable to himself as well as to other humans, therapeutic implications of the approach are obvious. Instead of centering one's attention on the vicissitudes of an instinct from infancy on or any other causal factor required by the various schools of psychopathology, the therapist's principal job will be to

[30] Beaglehole, E., "Interpersonal Theory and Social Psychology," *A Study of Interpersonal Relations*, edited by P. Mullahy (1949), pp. 50–79.
[31] Plant, J., *Personality and the Cultural Pattern* (1937), p. 21.
[32] Sullivan, H. S., *Conceptions of Modern Psychiatry* (1946), p. 8.
[33] Coutu, W., *Emergent Human Nature* (1949), pp. 281–300.
[34] Mead, *op. cit.*, pp. 138–139, 167, 191, 364–370.
[35] Cf. Rogers, *Client-Centered Therapy*, pp. 481ff.

find out what type of a primary self the individual has acquired in the course of his relations with his primary group environment and how this primary self together with the behavior patterns it has produced are now interfering with the individual's attempt at realizing the self-picture he considers as more appropriate to his present-day socio-cultural environment. The types of primary self one may find differ with the individual and with his specific primary personal and cultural environment, and may, in fact, require different therapeutic procedures. Problems related to the handling of biologic impulses will not be ignored, but they will be approached always in the context of the individual's personality organization as a whole and especially in that of his efforts to be human, that is to achieve the kind of self-picture that he can be proud of in relation with other humans. From this point of view, therapeutic relations will be no mere occasions for the recapitulation of the various stages of libidinal development, but primarily experiences through which an inadequate primary self-concept is modified or a new self-picture is developed. Nor does the therapeutic process seem to be simply a matter of internal perceptual reorganization on the part of the individual as Rogers described it,[36] for we can be reasonably sure that no such perceptual reorganization can take place in a social vacuum. In fact, it appears to be literally a process in which a new self appears through a new kind of symbolic interaction, which the individual now experiences for the first time in his life. The steps involved seem to be the same through which the primary self first emerges. First, the therapist feels about and responds to him and his problems in a certain way; then, the patient learns to do the same to himself and his problems; and finally, if the therapist succeeds in performing his professional role and the patient's assets permit, a new and more acceptable self may emerge. A remarkable study of the steps involved in the recovery of a schizophrenic patient made by a Swiss lay-analyst, Mrs. Sechehaye, seems to indicate that the therapeutic process described here is true not only of cases with behavior disorders of the neurotic variety, with which the writer has a fair amount of familiarity, but of the more severe cases as well.[37]

The socio-psychiatric approach to personality organization as out-

[36] Rogers, C. R., "Personality Organization," *Psychological Theory*, edited by M. H. Marx (1951), pp. 517–521.

[37] Sechehaye, M. A., *Symbolic Realization* (1951), pp. 136–137.

lined here may also have some rather far-reaching implications for mental hygiene. According to this view, the most important job in bringing up children is not so much to see that isolated biologic needs are gratified or that specific habits are established as that, through all these need-gratifications and habit-formations, an adequate and favorable primary self-picture is developed. This may mean that we will have to learn to treat the infant as a human being with self-concepts in the process of becoming and not merely as a bundle of reflexes to be severally conditioned or as a concentration of libidinal energy to be zonally discharged. If our description of the process of self-formation is correct, it follows that in order to give the child the proper role to take and thereby to enable him to develop the proper kind of self-concept and eventually become a self-respecting and self-trusting human being among other humans, it may not be quite sufficient for parents just to learn to master the methods of administering rewards and punishments, as some authors seem to think,[38] or even to indoctrinate the child in the best religious teachings of the world.[39] Child rearing methods and ethical principles by themselves may be of little avail unless parents themselves and those having direct dealings with the child have achieved self-concepts of such a kind that they will not, wittingly or unwittingly, utilize their relations with the child mainly for the gratification of their own private needs. Only in this manner can they genuinely and consistently love and respect the child as an individual, and only in this manner can the child, in turn, learn to love and respect himself as a human being and eventually acquire the kind of adequate and growth-facilitating primary self that seems to be the only true foundation of mental health.[40]

[38] Hohman, L. B., *As the Twig Is Bent*, 1940.
[39] Moore, D. T. V., *Personal Mental Hygiene*, 1944.
[40] Dai, B., "Freedom, Discipline and Personal Security," *Progressive Education*, January, 1949.

6

Emergent Human Nature*

WALTER COUTU

THE NATURE OF A CONCEPT

"Personality" is a word; it points to a concept; and a concept symbolizes certain "ways" of acting toward "something." The "ways" are intellectual types of behavior; and the "something" is "human behavior." "Personality," then, refers to a conceptual interpretation of the phenomena of human behavior. Since we can look at these phenomena in many ways, no one can say without qualification that there is a "correct" way and an "incorrect" way. Consequently we define "personality" (state the concept we refer to) to suit our convenience, in accordance with historical usage. The usefulness or truth of the concept will be determined by its adequacy in describing what we wish to portray.

While the concept personality is not given in nature, action *is* given, since we are born as organizations of living protoplasm. If the word "personality" survives, it will be because it refers to a concept which is adequate for a purpose; but our guess is that the term eventually will be abandoned in technical usage, for reasonable doubt exists about its ever coming to refer to a standardized concept. We shall define the term for our purpose, that is, state our concept, so that the reader will know what we are talking about, but we do not mean to imply that this is what personality "really is," for we do not believe in that kind of truth. A concept *is* what it *does;* and a man is what he *does*. In this book the word "truth" is synonymous with "adequacy for a purpose." For one writer to say that another writer's definition, or concept, "misses the point" and does not get

---

* By permission, from Walter Coutu, *Emergent Human Nature: A Symbolic Field Interpretation*, Alfred A. Knopf, New York, 1949, pp. 76–78, 11–17, 18–19, 20–22 (excerpts).

at what personality "really is," exemplifies confusion of a symbol with what it symbolizes.

As our earlier discussion of system suggests, we postulate a variety of unit processes called probable behaviors under stated conditions; we postulate their occurring as if woven together into an interrelated, relatively integrated, relatively stable whole. Thus we are enabled and directed to observe in interaction the emergence of a system of probable behaviors which we arbitrarily call personality. One cannot find or see or observe anything closely corresponding to this phenomenon in any of the individual tinsits, but at some point in the process of integration of many tinsits a whole emerges which could not have been predicted *precisely* from a list of hypothetical separate tinsits. A concept *is* what it *does*.

We can see that a concept is not something given in nature, but an arbitrarily invented mental construct applied *to* nature to mark off stretches or segments of a continuous process for study. In this sense the whole, here called personality, becomes a unit of a larger situational or social process. Such mental constructs are used by man to aid in the ordering and understanding of the natural phenomena of social interaction. They are constructs used as tools for unifying perceptions of phenomena and for discovering new relationships between such phenomena. If we can manipulate phenomena so as to demonstrate that they are to a satisfactory degree representative examples of this concept, we shall consider our operations reasonably successful.

* * *

TENDENCY-IN-SITUATION AS A UNIT PROCESS

The Meaning of Tendency

As the title of this chapter indicates, all behavior of every kind is assumed to represent tendency in some form and to some degree. Tendency-in-situation is the general generic concept of this book, and the term is used to include all other behavioral units on all levels. Although the term is presented as the hyphenated expression "tendency-in-situation," later it will be reduced to another form. We will gain some advantage if, for the moment, we discuss the term part by part.

The Definition of Tendency. "Tendency" is defined as "a probable behavior," and so defined, it must be treated as a continuous variable. Tendency is an inference based on observation of type-acts, a statistical concept based on the frequency of the behavior which specifies the tendency. Even in popular speech people customarily say, when they observe that a person frequently acts in a certain way: "He has a tendency to act that way." Tendency, then, is an inferential unit for action based on the assumption that the behavior of the individual can be described statistically. The concept is justified by the well-authenticated knowledge that treating the behavior of self and others statistically is precisely what people do "informally" in their day to day adjustments to one another throughout their lives. By "informally" is meant "without formal statistical procedures." Probably every person has many times in his life said of a friend or an enemy "he has a tendency to look out for himself," or a tendency to do something else. That people have observed tendencies is the commonest human experience; it is verifiable knowledge without which there could be no friendship, no enmity, no society, no human life at all. The purpose of this book is to state a theory of human behavior in terms of this knowledge.

Examples of Tendency. In defining a tendency as a probable behavior we assume that the act which specifies the tendency is a socially conditioned process of a measurable degree of probability or stability under stated conditions. A person is conditioned to act in a given way in a given situation. Such an act may be a habit, bent, mental set, neuromuscular set, attitude, propensity, inclination, or impulse—all of which specify tendencies in given situations. A tendency thus represents acts which are of sufficient similarity in direction and magnitude to be recognized as of a given type; and such acts occur in situations sufficiently similar to be recognized as type-situations.

In much the same manner in which physicists use the concept energy, we may think of tendency as stress or pressure of a given direction and magnitude under stated conditions. When one hears a statement of another person and says "I am inclined to agree with that," one is announcing a tendency. The term thus covers all forms of readiness. If a person acts in a given way in a given situation, probably he will act in a similar way if that or an equivalent situation presents itself again; and if he acts in much the same way again, the probability of his acting that way in the future in such situations is greater than the probability of his acting in some other way. Any act will, to some degree, predispose a person's future acts in similar situations.

This way of thinking leads to the application of the mathematical theory of probability to human behavior and likewise explains why *tendency* is here defined as a probable behavior. In mathematics "the theory of probability" is a highly conventional and rather rigorous form of behavior. Suppose we ask a person to perform some task one hundred times under prescribed conditions, and we observe that under these conditions he does it one way seventy times and another way thirty times. On this basis we feel reasonably justified in saying that if he were to perform this task again under the same conditions, the *probability* is that he would do it the first way about seventy times out of a hundred, or about 70% of the time. Continued observation of the behavior under the stated conditions will increase the predictability of the behavior in terms of probability.

The Meaning of Situation

When we say that a person has an attitude, we have not made a complete statement because an attitude, like all tendencies, has direction; it always occurs in relation to something. Likewise, one does not merely have an attitude toward something, but an attitude toward something in some *context of behavior*, in some situation. Since the process could not possibly occur except in some situation, tendency is herein always treated as a function of the situation, meaning that the tendency varies with the situation. The situation, then, is an integral part of the tendency. It is not something necessary to, but separate from, tendency. There are not two things here, but one, tendency-in-situation.

A mode of thought is becoming evident which . . . tries to determine the predisposition, not by excluding so far as possible the influence of the environment, *but by accepting in the concept of disposition* its necessary reference to a group of concretely defined situations.[1]

[1] K. Lewin: *A Dynamic Theory of Personality*. New York: McGraw-Hill Book Company; 1935, Chapter I, pp. 40–1. (Italics mine).

Words and phrases like "field," "context," and "social setting" are equivalent to the concept ("situation,") but the present work will consistently use the words "conditions under which" interchangeably with the word "situation." [2]

The Definition of Situation. At this early stage of our discussion we shall have to be content with a tentative definition: a situation is the total configuration of relevant behaviors and stimuli involved in an adjustment problem. For any one person the situation is *for him* those components of the configuration to which he is at the moment sensitive. Situation is difficult to define because, like the term "act," it is a segment of an ongoing process, and discussion depends on how big a segment one is talking about.

Every event that ever occurs in the universe, whether it be the action of men or some other aspect of nature, occurs under certain conditions, and science as we know it today could not have developed if the *conditions under which* phenomena occur had not been given a central position in scientific conceptual systems. Yet, there are well-known students of human behavior who sometimes imply, and sometimes assert, that certain tendencies "exist" or occur "regardless of the situation." But natural phenomena do not just occur whether they are the behavior of electrons or of human beings; they always occur in a configuration of conditions, and this configuration of conditions is here called "the situation." This concept is central to the thought and method of the more exact sciences and of this book.

Examples of Situation. Again we shall have to be content with something vague until we have developed, in the following chapters, concepts in terms of which intelligible examples can be given. We shall at present have to be content with "use-meanings" instead of definitions. For example, everyone continually *uses* the term in such expressions as "the international situation," "the political situation," "the strike situation," and "the financial situation." In a recent broadcast a speaker discussing labor-management relations said: "Now, let's go over all the facts and see just what the situation is." In preparing for a recent camping trip a member of the group said: "O.K., we've got the equipment laid out; now, what's the food situation?" Recently the writer was asked to speak in a small com-

[2] See Lewin: *A Dynamic Theory of Personality*, p. 29, where he discusses the concept "situation" in relation to Aristotelian and Galilean dynamics.

munity on a controversial subject. The person inviting him to speak remarked: "Before you say yes or no, let me tell you what the situation is in this town." A child with emotional problems was taken to a counselor who said to the parent: "Tell me the child's situation as you see it."

Practically everyone *uses* "situation" in this vague manner, but part of the purpose of this book is to provide a way of thinking that will enable us to delimit the concept, and give more precise definition and example.

Tendency-in-Situation. If one were to see a chemical in a laboratory and were to say to a chemist: "What will that chemical do?," the chemist would have to name certain conditions in order to answer the question. He would have to say that under such and such conditions the chemical will probably do thus and thus. The important implication of this is that the *conditions under which* the chemical behaves are an integral part of the behavior as well as of the statement of the behavior. For human beings, likewise, the configuration of conditions, or situations, is not only an integral part of the statement of behavior, but of the behavior itself.

To indicate that this is a practical and not an academic point in the understanding of behavior, we may use some homely illustrations. We all know that iron filings have a tendency to move in relation to a magnet. That a person should say that filings have this tendency when no magnet is present would be incredible. One knows that one of the *conditions under which* this tendency appears is the presence of a magnet. What could be the meaning of such a statement as "iron filings have a tendency to move in relation to a magnet regardless of whether a magnet is present"? The statement is not meaningless, for, says Lewin, this was the position of Aristotelian physics, according to which "the vectors which determine an object's movements are completely determined by the object. . . . The tendency of light bodies to go up *resided* in the bodies themselves. . . ." [3] Modern physics holds a different point of view.

In terms of human behavior, the Aristotelian concept is the equivalent of the now discredited social-instinct theory of man's behavior, a theory which assumed that tendencies exist as entities in people, and which saw everything in the man. The situation was

[3] Lewin: *A Dynamic Theory of Personality*, pp. 28–9. (Italics mine).

irrelevant. Today this is a popular theory in accounting for the behavior of minority groups, Negroes and "Mexicans" (U.S. citizens) for example. Everything is in the people—the situation and the *conditions under which* they live are assumed to have nothing to do with their *behavior*.

As another illustration, few people would immediately challenge the statement that a ball has a tendency to roll. That this is false may be demonstrated by placing a ball on a flat table and watching it. A ball has a tendency to roll only under certain conditions, the conditions being the position of the ball in relation to an inclined, unobstructed plane. The tendency *in* the filings and *in* the ball are analogous to the "trait" *in* the personality as propounded in conventional thinking.

Let us now consider a common human tendency, the tendency to imitate. No one imitates every one he sees, nor every behavior he sees; and a person who, as we have heard, "always imitates" a certain other person, does not do any such thing. There are certain *conditions under which* he imitates.[4] One of these conditions is that he *know how* to imitate the act in question; another condition is that he receive the stimulus to imitate; and another, that the situation in general be appropriate. Furthermore, he does not imitate everything the other person does, *but only those acts which his own tendencies-in-situation select*, and which all other conditions of the situation permit. A boy may like to spit like a famous baseball player, but he does not and probably will not do so in bed, or when reciting before his class at school, or while passing cakes at his mother's tea. *The situation is the immediate determinant of all behavior*. Chapter after chapter will insist that the function of the science of human behavior is to investigate the *conditions under which* behavior takes place, to standardize these conditions conceptually, to make generalizations on this basis, and to determine the *probability* of a given behavior under these conditions.

At this point we should cite another of the several reasons for not using Mead's "act" as our central unit.

An act is an impulse that maintains the life process by the selection of certain sorts of stimuli it needs. The stimulus is the occasion for the

[4] See J. F. Brown: *Psychology and the Social Order*. New York: McGraw-Hill Book Company; 1936, pp. 91-3.

expression of the impulse. Stimuli are the means, tendency is the real thing.[5]

While I am in complete agreement with Mead's idea of selection, the statement that "tendency is the real thing" seems to say that tendency is a kind of entity *residing* in the organism, and that the occasion or situation as stimulus merely releases something that already resides in the organism. In the unit *tendency-in-situation*, however, tendency is no more the "real thing" than is situation, for tendency does not exist except in situation. One can discover no tendency in iron filings, balls, or people except in situation. It would be difficult, in any case, to think of occurrences as "existing," and even more difficult to think of occurrences, that is, behavior, as appearing apart from some situation. This will become increasingly important and central as the discussion develops.

* * *

THE TINSIT AS A UNIT PROCESS OF ACTION

We must now engage in an operation which, to many social scientists, is frequently a source of embarrassment, and which is sometimes thought of as foolish or even flippant. I refer to the coining of new terms to represent units and other concepts, a practice which is almost a daily occurrence in the more exact sciences. Both in speech and in writing the term tendency-in-situation is a long and clumsy name for a unit. In my own writing I have observed an increasingly strong tendency to abbreviate the expression with the symbols T-in-Sit. Since, as indicated earlier, units of measure are inventions, arbitrary symbols for standardizing people's responses to certain phenomena, for purposes of economy I abandoned the hyphens in the above symbols, thus shortening the expression to TINSIT, while continuing to include reference to all the important elements.

Tendency-in-situation will hereafter appear in the form of *tinsit*. Grammatically, tinsit is used in the same manner as tendency, as,

---

[5] G. H. Mead: *Mind, Self and Society* (E. W. Morris, ed.). Chicago: University of Chicago Press; 1939, p. 6.

for example in "John has a tinsit to get angry when teased about girls." *To name a tinsit one must name the situation of which it is a function; one thus avoids the fallacy of conceptually separating the tendency from the situation in which it occurs and of which it is a function. The significance of this will appear in almost every section of the book.*

<u>Every type of act or mechanism earlier referred to as a tendency will hereafter be referred to as a tinsit,</u> whether it be habit, mental <u>act, attitude, disposition, idea, impulse, trait, or any other behavior.</u> Tinsit is defined as a *probable behavior in a given situation*, or a behavior of a given probability under stated conditions. The tinsit is an inference based on frequency of a given behavior in a given situation, or on frequency of type-response in a type-situation, or on frequency of related responses in type-situations. It thus involves the application of statistical operations to the study of individual, as well as group, behavior.[6]

* * *

The Properties of the Tinsit

The tinsit has many properties, two of which are those of a vector quantity: directions and magnitude. The *direction* of a tinsit specifies that-in-relation-to-which it moves, that-in-relation-to-which the person behaves. Direction thus defines the act, as in "attitude-toward-democracy" and "love-of-beauty." *Magnitude* is a continuous variable which measures the intensity or strength of a tinsit as observed in a given situation. A third property of the tinsit is *stability*, a continuous variable measuring the frequency with which the tinsit appears in a given or type-situation. Stability is not to be confused with magnitude. This caution is prompted by the custom in popular speech of such statements as "John has a strong tendency to argue." What is usually referred to in such a statement is not intensity but the frequency (dependability) with

---

[6] There appears to be significant support for this point of view in F. H. Allport: "Teleonomic Description in the Study of Personality," *Character and Personality* (1937), vol. 5, pp. 202–14. See also Wilbur S. Gregory: "The Application of Teleonomic Description to the Diagnosis and Treatment of Emotional Instability and Personal and Social Maladjustment," *Character and Personality* (1945), March–June.

which John may be depended upon to behave in this way. For our purpose, the term "strong" is properly used in saying that John has a strong temper, meaning that when he becomes angry, he tends to be violently so, even though he may not become angry easily nor often.

Since stability is a measure of frequency, it depends upon the frequency, or stability, of the social situation of which the tinsit is a function. One does not have a tinsit to dislike oysters while singing hymns in church. Stability, then, refers to the degree of probability of a tinsit under stated conditions. In the paradigm "John is very likely to show a tinsit of violent anger at the boys when they tease him about girls," "very likely" refers to stability, "violent" refers to magnitude, "at the boys" indicates direction, and "when they tease him about girls" names the situation. The entire statement names and locates the tinsit.

A fourth property of a tinsit is *commonality*. This property, together with the others discussed, is a continuous variable; all are measured on a scale and are always thought of in the frame of "more or less." A fifth property of the tinsit is *form*. Behavior of any kind and of any thing is always a release of energy, and energy is always released in some form—heat, light, sound, or some other form of motion. The "forms" of a tinsit are not shapes, substances, or entities, but forms of motion and types of behavior. Their primary classification in this book is two-fold, *somatic* (organic) and *personic*.

Somatic Tinsits. This concept refers to all forms of behavior which pertain specifically to the body or soma, behavior generally referred to as organic or somatic. Such behavior includes all operations of the physiological processes, respiration, circulation, digestion, etc.: all movements of the neuro-muscular and skeletal structure. Some readers may at first have difficulty in thinking of such behavior as tinsits rather than general tendencies, because they are not accustomed to relate such operations to situations. This difficulty may be examined by referring to the example of the iron filings: "Do iron filings have a tendency to move in relation to a magnet when not moving in relation to a magnet?" By analogy, it might be asked: "Does the heart have a tendency to beat while not beating, the stomach to contract when not contracting?" These types of behavior, like all kinds of behavior, occur only under certain conditions, in certain situations. One of the conveniences of the concept tinsit is its applicability to behavior on all levels and to phenomena of all kinds, to every aspect of the universe. It is useful to, and cuts across, all sciences.

Personic Tinsits. When one is studying the behavior of human beings, one immediately encounters a form of behavior very different from that of any other aspect of the universe. There is, as it were, *a person in the body*.[7] The most difficult problems arise in the attempt to understand this person, or the configuration of probable behaviors which we herein call the person. To represent this behavior I have chosen the term *personic*. . . . Personic and somatic behaviors are distinguished from each other by the order of the stimuli to which they respond. Stimuli of the order $S \leftrightarrow R$ will be said to activate somatic behavior, while we shall say that personic behavior is activated by stimuli of the order $S \leftrightarrow M \leftrightarrow R$. Stimuli of the order $S \leftrightarrow R$ will, for us, represent bio-physical or physico-chemical occurrences; stimuli of the order $S \leftrightarrow M \leftrightarrow R$ will represent symbolic phenomena.[8]

[7] As an indication of the commonality of this thought, several years after this was written a book appeared with the title: *The Person in the Body, an Introduction to Psychosomatic Medicine*, by Leland E. Hinsie, M.D. New York: W. W. Norton & Co., Inc.; 1945.

[8] Personic and organic do not constitute a dichotomy in the sense of paired opposites; they constitute different levels of behavior.

7

The Presentation of Self in Everyday Life*

Erving Goffman

INTRODUCTION

When an individual enters the presence of others, they commonly seek to acquire information about him or to bring into play information already possessed. They will be interested in his general socio-economic status, his conception of self, his attitude toward them, his competence, his trustworthiness, etc. Although some of this information seems to be sought almost as an end in itself, there are usually quite practical reasons for acquiring it. Information about the individual helps to define the situation, enabling others to know in advance what he will expect of them and what they may expect of him. Informed in these ways, the others will know how best to act in order to call forth a desired response from him.

For those present, many sources of information become accessible and many carriers (or "sign-vehicles") become available for conveying this information. If unacquainted with the individual, observers can glean clues from his conduct and appearance which allow them to apply their previous experience with individuals roughly similar to the one before them or, more important, to apply untested stereotypes to him. They can also assume from past experience that only individuals of a particular kind are likely to be found in a given social setting. They can rely on what the individual says about himself or on documentary evidence he provides as to who and what he is. If they know, or know of, the individual by virtue of experience prior to the interaction, they can rely on assumptions

---

* From *The Presentation of Self in Everyday Life* by Erving Goffman. Copyright © 1959 by the author. Reprinted by permission of Doubleday & Company, Inc.

as to the persistence and generality of psychological traits as a means of predicting his present and future behavior.

However, during the period in which the individual is in the immediate presence of the others, few events may occur which directly provide the others with the conclusive information they will need if they are to direct wisely their own activity. Many crucial facts lie beyond the time and place of interaction or lie concealed within it. For example, the "true" or "real" attitudes, beliefs, and emotions of the individual can be ascertained only indirectly, through his avowals or through what appears to be involuntary expressive behavior. Similarly, if the individual offers the others a product or service, they will often find that during the interaction there will be no time and place immediately available for eating the pudding that the proof can be found in. They will be forced to accept some events as conventional or natural signs of something not directly available to the senses. In Ichheiser's terms,[1] the individual will have to act so that he intentionally or unintentionally *expresses* himself, and the others will in turn have to be *impressed* in some way by him.

The expressiveness of the individual (and therefore his capacity to give impressions) appears to involve two radically different kinds of sign activity: the expression that he *gives*, and the expression that he *gives off*. The first involves verbal symbols or their substitutes which he uses admittedly and solely to convey the information that he and the others are known to attach to these symbols. This is communication in the traditional and narrow sense. The second involves a wide range of action that others can treat as symptomatic of the actor, the expectation being that the action was performed for reasons other than the information conveyed in this way. As we shall have to see, this distinction has an only initial validity. The individual does of course intentionally convey misinformation by means of both of these types of communication, the first involving deceit, the second feigning.

Taking communication in both its narrow and broad sense, one finds that when the individual is in the immediate presence of others, his activity will have a promissory character. The others are likely to find that they must accept the individual on faith, offering him a

[1] Gustav Ichheiser, "Misunderstandings in Human Relations," Supplement to *The American Journal of Sociology*, LV (September, 1949), pp. 6–7.

just return while he is present before them in exchange for something whose true value will not be established until after he has left their presence. (Of course, the others also live by inference in their dealings with the physical world, but it is only in the world of social interaction that the objects about which they make inferences will purposely facilitate and hinder this inferential process.) The security that they justifiably feel in making inferences about the individual will vary, of course, depending on such factors as the amount of information they already possess about him, but no amount of such past evidence can entirely obviate the necessity of acting on the basis of inferences. As William I. Thomas suggested:

It is also highly important for us to realize that we do not as a matter of fact lead our lives, make our decisions, and reach our goals in everyday life either statistically or scientifically. We live by inference. I am, let us say, your guest. You do not know, you cannot determine scientifically, that I will not steal your money or your spoons. But inferentially I will not, and inferentially you have me as a guest.[2]

Let us now turn from the others to the point of view of the individual who presents himself before them. He may wish them to think highly of him, or to think that he thinks highly of them, or to perceive how in fact he feels toward them, or to obtain no clear-cut impression; he may wish to ensure sufficient harmony so that the interaction can be sustained, or to defraud, get rid of, confuse, mislead, antagonize, or insult them. Regardless of the particular objective which the individual has in mind and of his motive for having this objective, it will be in his interests to control the conduct of the others, especially their responsive treatment of him.[3] This control is achieved largely by influencing the definition of the situation which the others come to formulate, and he can influence

[2] Quoted in E. H. Volkart, editor, *Social Behavior and Personality*, Contributions of W. I. Thomas to Theory and Social Research (New York: Social Science Research Council, 1951), p. 5.

[3] Here I owe much to an unpublished paper by Tom Burns of the University of Edinburgh. He presents the argument that in all interaction a basic underlying theme is the desire of each participant to guide and control the responses made by the others present. A similar argument has been advanced by Jay Haley in a recent unpublished paper, but in regard to a special kind of control, that having to do with defining the nature of the relationship of those involved in the interaction.

this definition by expressing himself in such a way as to give them the kind of impression that will lead them to act voluntarily in accordance with his own plan. Thus, when an individual appears in the presence of others, there will usually be some reason for him to mobilize his activity so that it will convey an impression to others which it is in his interests to convey. Since a girl's dormitory mates will glean evidence of her popularity from the calls she receives on the phone, we can suspect that some girls will arrange for calls to be made, and Willard Waller's finding can be anticipated:

It has been reported by many observers that a girl who is called to the telephone in the dormitories will often allow herself to be called several times, in order to give all the other girls ample opportunity to hear her paged.[4]

Of the two kinds of communication—expressions given and expressions given off—this report will be primarily concerned with the latter, with the more theatrical and contextual kind, the non-verbal, presumably unintentional kind, whether this communication be purposely engineered or not. As an example of what we must try to examine, I would like to cite at length a novelistic incident in which Preedy, a vacationing Englishman, makes his first appearance on the beach of his summer hotel in Spain:

But in any case he took care to avoid catching anyone's eye. First of all, he had to make it clear to those potential companions of his holiday that they were of no concern to him whatsoever. He stared through them, round them, over them—eyes lost in space. The beach might have been empty. If by chance a ball was thrown his way, he looked surprised; then let a smile of amusement lighten his face (Kindly Preedy), looked round dazed to see that there *were* people on the beach, tossed it back with a smile to himself and not a smile *at* the people, and then resumed carelessly his nonchalant survey of space.

But it was time to institute a little parade, the parade of the Ideal Preedy. By devious handlings he gave any who wanted to look a chance to see the title of his book—a Spanish translation of Homer, classic thus, but not daring, cosmopolitan too—and then gathered together his beach-wrap and bag into a neat sand-resistant pile (Methodical and Sensible Preedy), rose

[4] Willard Waller, "The Rating and Dating Complex," *American Sociological Review*, II, p. 730.

slowly to stretch at ease his huge frame (Big-Cat Preedy), and tossed aside his sandals (Carefree Preedy, after all).

The marriage of Preedy and the sea! There were alternative rituals. The first involved the stroll that turns into a run and a dive straight into the water, thereafter smoothing into a strong splashless crawl towards the horizon. But of course not really to the horizon. Quite suddenly he would turn on to his back and thrash great white splashes with his legs, somehow thus showing that he could have swum further had he wanted to, and then would stand up a quarter out of water for all to see who it was.

The alternative course was simpler, it avoided the cold-water shock and it avoided the risk of appearing too high-spirited. The point was to appear to be so used to the sea, the Mediterranean, and this particular beach, that one might as well be in the sea as out of it. It involved a slow stroll down and into the edge of the water—not even noticing his toes were wet, land and water all the same to *him!*—with his eyes up at the sky gravely surveying portents, invisible to others, of the weather (Local Fisherman Preedy).[5]

The novelist means us to see that Preedy is improperly concerned with the extensive impressions he feels his sheer bodily action is giving off to those around him. We can malign Preedy further by assuming that he has acted merely in order to give a particular impression, that this is a false impression, and that the others present receive either no impression at all, or, worse still, the impression that Preedy is affectedly trying to cause them to receive this particular impression. But the important point for us here is that the kind of impression Preedy thinks he is making is in fact the kind of impression that others correctly and incorrectly glean from someone in their midst.

I have said that when an individual appears before others his actions will influence the definition of the situation which they come to have. Sometimes the individual will act in a thoroughly calculating manner, expressing himself in a given way solely in order to give the kind of impression to others that is likely to evoke from them a specific response he is concerned to obtain. Sometimes the individual will be calculating in his activity but be relatively unaware that this is the case. Sometimes he will intentionally and consciously express himself in a particular way, but chiefly because the tradition of his

[5] William Sansom, *A Contest of Ladies* (London: Hogarth, 1956), pp. 230–32.

group or social status require this kind of expression and not because of any particular response (other than vague acceptance or approval) that is likely to be evoked from those impressed by the expression. Sometimes the traditions of an individual's role will lead him to give a well-designed impression of a particular kind and yet he may be neither consciously nor unconsciously disposed to create such an impression. The others, in their turn, may be suitably impressed by the individual's efforts to convey something, or may misunderstand the situation and come to conclusions that are warranted neither by the individual's intent nor by the facts. In any case, in so far as the others act *as if* the individual had conveyed a particular impression, we may take a functional or pragmatic view and say that the individual has "effectively" projected a given definition of the situation and "effectively" fostered the understanding that a given state of affairs obtains.

There is one aspect of the others' response that bears special comment here. Knowing that the individual is likely to present himself in a light that is favorable to him, the others may divide what they witness into two parts; a part that is relatively easy for the individual to manipulate at will, being chiefly his verbal assertions, and a part in regard to which he seems to have little concern or control, being chiefly derived from the expressions he gives off. The others may then use what are considered to be the ungovernable aspects of his expressive behavior as a check upon the validity of what is conveyed by the governable aspects. In this a fundamental asymmetry is demonstrated in the communication process, the individual presumably being aware of only one stream of his communication, the witnesses of this stream and one other. For example, in Shetland Isle one crofter's wife, in serving native dishes to a visitor from the mainland of Britain, would listen with a polite smile to his polite claims of liking what he was eating; at the same time she would take note of the rapidity with which the visitor lifted his fork or spoon to his mouth, the eagerness with which he passed food into his mouth, and the gusto expressed in chewing the food, using these signs as a check on the stated feelings of the eater. The same woman, in order to discover what one acquaintance (A) "actually" thought of another acquaintance (B), would wait until B was in the presence of A but engaged in conversation with still another person (C). She would then covertly examine the facial expressions of A as he regarded B in conversation with C. Not being in conversation with B, and not being directly observed by him, A would sometimes relax usual constraints and tactful deceptions, and freely express what he was "actually" feeling about B. This Shetlander, in short, would observe the unobserved observer.

Now given the fact that others are likely to check up on the more controllable aspects of behavior by means of the less controllable, one can expect that sometimes the individual will try to exploit this very possibility, guiding the impression he makes through behavior felt to be reliably informing.[6] For example, in gaining admission to a tight social circle, the participant observer may not only wear an accepting look while listening to an informant, but may also be careful to wear the same look when observing the informant talking to others; observers of the observer will then not as easily discover where he actually stands. A specific illustration may be cited from Shetland Isle. When a neighbor dropped in to have a cup of tea, he would ordinarily wear at least a hint of an expectant warm smile as he passed through the door into the cottage. Since lack of physical obstructions outside the cottage and lack of light within it usually made it possible to observe the visitor unobserved as he approached the house, islanders sometimes took pleasure in watching the visitor drop whatever expression he was manifesting and replace it with a sociable one just before reaching the door. However, some visitors, in appreciating that this examination was occurring, would blindly adopt a social face a long distance from the house, thus ensuring the projection of a constant image.

This kind of control upon the part of the individual reinstates the symmetry of the communication process, and sets the stage for a kind of information game—a potentially infinite cycle of concealment, discovery, false revelation, and rediscovery. It should be added that since the others are likely to be relatively unsuspicious of the presumably unguided aspect of the individual's conduct, he can gain much by controlling it. The others of course may sense that the individual is manipulating the presumably spontaneous aspects of his behavior, and seek in this very act of manipulation some shading

---

[6] The widely read and rather sound writings of Stephen Potter are concerned in part with signs that can be engineered to give a shrewd observer the apparently incidental cues he needs to discover concealed virtues the gamesman does not in fact possess.

of conduct that the individual has not managed to control. This again provides a check upon the individual's behavior, this time his presumably uncalculated behavior, thus re-establishing the asymmetry of the communication process. Here I would like only to add the suggestion that the arts of piercing an individual's effort at calculated unintentionality seem better developed than our capacity to manipulate our own behavior, so that regardless of how many steps have occurred in the information game, the witness is likely to have the advantage over the actor, and the initial asymmetry of the communication process is likely to be retained.

When we allow that the individual projects a definition of the situation when he appears before others, we must also see that the others, however passive their role may seem to be, will themselves effectively project a definition of the situation by virtue of their response to the individual and by virtue of any lines of action they initiate to him. Ordinarily the definitions of the situation projected by the several different participants are sufficiently attuned to one another so that open contradiction will not occur. I do not mean that there will be the kind of consensus that arises when each individual present candidly expresses what he really feels and honestly agrees with the expressed feelings of the others present. This kind of harmony is an optimistic ideal and in any case not necessary for the smooth working of society. Rather, each participant is expected to suppress his immediate heartfelt feelings, conveying a view of the situation which he feels the others will be able to find at least temporarily acceptable. The maintenance of this surface of agreement, this veneer of consensus, is facilitated by each participant concealing his own wants behind statements which assert values to which everyone present feels obliged to give lip service. Further, there is usually a kind of division of definitional labor. Each participant is allowed to establish the tentative official ruling regarding matters which are vital to him but not immediately important to others, e.g., the rationalizations and justifications by which he accounts for his past activity. In exchange for this courtesy he remains silent or non-committal on matters important to others but not immediately important to him. We have then a kind of interactional *modus vivendi*. Together the participants contribute to a single over-all definition of the situation which involves not so much a real agreement as to what exists but rather a real agreement as to whose claims concerning what issues will be temporarily honored. Real agreement will also exist concerning the desirability of avoiding an open conflict of definitions of the situation.[7] I will refer to this level of agreement as a "working consensus." It is to be understood that the working consensus established in one interaction setting will be quite different in content from the working consensus established in a different type of setting. Thus, between two friends at lunch, a reciprocal show of affection, respect, and concern for the other is maintained. In service occupations, on the other hand, the specialist often maintains an image of disinterested involvement in the problem of the client, while the client responds with a show of respect for the competence and integrity of the specialist. Regardless of such differences in content, however, the general form of these working arrangements is the same.

In noting the tendency for a participant to accept the definitional claims made by the others present, we can appreciate the crucial importance of the information that the individual *initially* possesses or acquires concerning his fellow participants, for it is on the basis of this initial information that the individual starts to define the situation and starts to build up lines of responsive action. The individual's initial projection commits him to what he is proposing to be and requires him to drop all pretenses of being other things. As the interaction among the participants progresses, additions and modifications in this initial informational state will of course occur, but it is essential that these later developments be related without contradiction to, and even built up from, the initial positions taken by the several participants. It would seem that an individual can more easily make a choice as to what line of treatment to demand from and extend to the others present at the beginning of an encounter than he can alter the line of treatment that is being pursued once the interaction is underway.

[7] An interaction can be purposely set up as a time and place for voicing differences in opinion, but in such cases participants must be careful to agree not to disagree on the proper tone of voice, vocabulary, and degree of seriousness in which all arguments are to be phrased, and upon the mutual respect which disagreeing participants must carefully continue to express toward one another. This debaters' or academic definition of the situation may also be invoked suddenly and judiciously as a way of translating a serious conflict of views into one that can be handled within a framework acceptable to all present.

In everyday life, of course, there is a clear understanding that first impressions are important. Thus, the work adjustment of those in service occupations will often hinge upon a capacity to seize and hold the initiative in the service relation, a capacity that will require subtle aggressiveness on the part of the server when he is of lower socio-economic status than his client. W. F. Whyte suggests the waitress as an example:

> The first point that stands out is that the waitress who bears up under pressure does not simply respond to her customers. She acts with some skill to control their behavior. The first question to ask when we look at the customer relationship is, "Does the waitress get the jump on the customer, or does the customer get the jump on the waitress?" The skilled waitress realizes the crucial nature of this question. . . .
>
> The skilled waitress tackles the customer with confidence and without hesitation. For example, she may find that a new customer has seated himself before she could clear off the dirty dishes and change the cloth. He is now leaning on the table studying the menu. She greets him, says, "May I change the cover, please?" and, without waiting for an answer, takes his menu away from him so that he moves back from the table, and she goes about her work. The relationship is handled politely but firmly, and there is never any question as to who is in charge.[8]

When the interaction that is initiated by "first impressions" is itself merely the initial interaction in an extended series of interactions involving the same participants, we speak of "getting off on the right foot" and feel that it is crucial that we do so. Thus, one learns that some teachers take the following view:

> You can't ever let them get the upper hand on you or you're through. So I start out tough. The first day I get a new class in, I let them know who's boss . . . You've got to start off tough, then you can ease up as you go along. If you start out easy-going, when you try to get tough, they'll just look at you and laugh.[9]

Similarly, attendants in mental institutions may feel that if the new

---

[8] W. F. Whyte, "When Workers and Customers Meet," Chap. VII, *Industry and Society*, ed. W. F. Whyte (New York: McGraw-Hill, 1946), pp. 132–33.

[9] Teacher interview quoted by Howard S. Becker, "Social Class Variations in the Teacher-Pupil Relationship," *Journal of Educational Sociology*, XXV, p. 459.

patient is sharply put in his place the first day on the ward and made to see who is boss, much future difficulty will be prevented.[10]

Given the fact that the individual effectively projects a definition of the situation when he enters the presence of others, we can assume that events may occur within the interaction which contradict, discredit, or otherwise throw doubt upon this projection. When these disruptive events occur, the interaction itself may come to a confused and embarrassed halt. Some of the assumptions upon which the responses of the participants had been predicated become untenable, and the participants find themselves lodged in an interaction for which the situation has been wrongly defined and is now no longer defined. At such moments the individual whose presentation has been discredited may feel ashamed while the others present may feel hostile, and all the participants may come to feel ill at ease, nonplussed, out of countenance, embarrassed, experiencing the kind of anomy that is generated when the minute social system of face-to-face interaction breaks down.

In stressing the fact that the initial definition of the situation projected by an individual tends to provide a plan for the cooperative activity that follows—in stressing this action point of view—we must not overlook the crucial fact that any projected definition of the situation also has a distinctive moral character. It is this moral character of projections that will chiefly concern us in this report. Society is organized on the principle that any individual who possesses certain social characteristics has a moral right to expect that others will value and treat him in an appropriate way. Connected with this principle is a second, namely that an individual who implicitly or explicitly signifies that he has certain social characteristics ought in fact to be what he claims he is. In consequence, when an individual projects a definition of the situation and thereby makes an implicit or explicit claim to be a person of a particular kind, he automatically exerts a moral demand upon the others, obliging them to value and treat him in the manner that persons of his kind have a right to expect. He also implicitly forgoes all claims

---

[10] Harold Taxel, "Authority Structure in a Mental Hospital Ward" (unpublished Master's thesis, Department of Sociology, University of Chicago, 1953).

to be things he does not appear to be[11] and hence forgoes the treatment that would be appropriate for such individuals. The others find, then, that the individual has informed them as to what is and as to what they *ought* to see as the "is."

One cannot judge the importance of definitional disruptions by the frequency with which they occur, for apparently they would occur more frequently were not constant precautions taken. We find that preventive practices are constantly employed to avoid these embarrassments and that corrective practices are constantly employed to compensate for discrediting occurrences that have not been successfully avoided. When the individual employs these strategies and tactics to protect his own projections, we may refer to them as "defensive practices"; when a participant employs them to save the definition of the situation projected by another, we speak of "protective practices" or "tact." Together, defensive and protective practices comprise the techniques employed to safeguard the impression fostered by an individual during his presence before others. It should be added that while we may be ready to see that no fostered impression would survive if defensive practices were not employed, we are less ready perhaps to see that few impressions could survive if those who received the impression did not exert tact in their reception of it.

In addition to the fact that precautions are taken to prevent disruption of projected definitions, we may also note that an intense interest in these disruptions comes to play a significant role in the social life of the group. Practical jokes and social games are played in which embarrassments which are to be taken unseriously are purposely engineered.[12] Fantasies are created in which devastating exposures occur. Anecdotes from the past—real, embroidered, or fictitious—are told and retold, detailing disruptions which occurred, almost occurred, or occurred and were admirably resolved. There seems to be no grouping which does not have a ready supply of these games, reveries, and cautionary tales, to be used as a source of

---

[11] This role of the witness in limiting what it is the individual can be has been stressed by Existentialists, who see it as a basic threat to individual freedom. See Jean-Paul Sartre, *Being and Nothingness*, trans. by Hazel E. Barnes (New York: Philosophical Library, 1956), pp. 365ff.

[12] Goffman, *op. cit.*, pp. 319–27.

humor, a catharsis for anxieties, and a sanction for inducing individuals to be modest in their claims and reasonable in their projected expectations. The individual may tell himself through dreams of getting into impossible positions. Families tell of the time a guest got his dates mixed and arrived when neither the house nor anyone in it was ready for him. Journalists tell of times when an all-too-meaningful misprint occurred, and the paper's assumption of objectivity or decorum was humorously discredited. Public servants tell of times a client ridiculously misunderstood form instructions, giving answers which implied an unanticipated and bizarre definition of the situation.[13] Seamen, whose home away from home is rigorously he-man, tell stories of coming back home and inadvertently asking mother to "pass the fucking butter." [14] Diplomats tell of the time a near-sighted queen asked a republican ambassador about the health of his king.[15]

To summarize, then, I assume that when an individual appears before others he will have many motives for trying to control the impression they receive of the situation. This report is concerned with some of the common techniques that persons employ to sustain such impressions and with some of the common contingencies associated with the employment of these techniques. The specific content of any activity presented by the individual participant, or the role it plays in the interdependent activities of an on-going social system, will not be at issue; I shall be concerned only with the participant's dramaturgical problems of presenting the activity before others. The issues dealt with by stagecraft and stage management are sometimes trivial but they are quite general; they seem to occur everywhere in social life, providing a clear-cut dimension for formal sociological analysis.

It will be convenient to end this introduction with some definitions that are implied in what has gone before and required for what is to follow. For the purpose of this report, interaction (that is, face-to-face interaction) may be roughly defined as the reciprocal

[13] Peter Blau, "Dynamics of Bureaucracy" (Ph.D. dissertation, Department of Sociology, Columbia University, forthcoming, University of Chicago Press), pp. 127–29.

[14] Walter M. Beattie, Jr., "The Merchant Seaman" (unpublished M.A. Report, Department of Sociology, University of Chicago, 1950), p. 35.

[15] Sir Frederick Ponsonby, *Recollections of Three Reigns* (New York: Dutton, 1952), p. 46.

influence of individuals upon one another's actions when in one another's immediate physical presence. *An* interaction may be defined as all the interaction which occurs throughout any one occasion when a given set of individuals are in one another's continuous presence; the term "an encounter" would do as well. A "performance" may be defined as all the activity of a given participant on a given occasion which serves to influence in any way any of the other participants. Taking a particular participant and his performance as a basic point of reference, we may refer to those who contribute the other performances as the audience, observers, or coparticipants. The pre-established pattern of action which is unfolded during a performance and which may be presented or played through on other occasions may be called a "part" or "routine."[16] These situational terms can easily be related to conventional structural ones. When an individual or performer plays the same part to the same audience on different occasions, a social relationship is likely to arise. Defining social role as the enactment of rights and duties attached to a given status, we can say that a social role will involve one or more parts and that each of these different parts may be presented by the performer on a series of occasions to the same kinds of audience or to an audience of the same persons.

SUGGESTED READINGS

HOWARD S. BECKER and ANSELM STRAUSS. Careers: Personality and Adult Socialization, *American Journal of Sociology*, *62*: 253–263, 1956.

EDGAR F. BORGATTA. The Structure of Personality Characteristics, *Behavioral Science*, *9*: 8–17, 1964.

HUGH D. DUNCAN. *Communication and Social Order*, Bedminster Press, 1962.

GEORGE C. HOMANS. *Social Behavior: Its Elementary Forms*, Harcourt, Brace, and World, New York, 1961.

MANFORD H. KUHN and THOMAS S. MCPARTLAND. An Empirical Investigation of Self-Attitudes, *American Sociological Review*, *19*: 68–76, 1954.

ALFRED R. LINDESMITH and ANSELM L. STRAUSS. *Social Psychology*, revised edition, Holt, Rinehart and Winston, New York, 1956.

[16] For comments on the importance of distinguishing between a routine of interaction and any particular instance when this routine is played through, see John von Neumann and Oskar Morgenstern, *The Theory of Games and Economic Behaviour* (2nd ed.; Princeton: Princeton University Press, 1947), p. 49.

Jerome G. Manis and Bernard N. Meltzer (Eds.). *Symbolic Interaction*, Allyn and Bacon, Boston, 1967.

Arnold M. Rose (Ed.). *Human Behavior and Social Processes*, Houghton Mifflin Company, 1962.

Tamotsu Shibutani. *Society and Personality*, Prentice-Hall, Englewood Cliffs, N.J., 1961.

Part III

Unifying Concepts in Personality Theory

Because the concept of role is so interwoven with the concept of personality, any distinction between role theory and personality theory cannot help but be an arbitrary one, and in instances a misleading one as well. In this volume role is part of the writings of Parsons, Mead, Goffman, albeit the meanings bear little relationship to each other.

It is recognized that the role concept serves as a bridge between personality and social structure, one author contending that ". . . role is as essential to the understanding of groups as to that of the individual personality." [1] *However, the fact that there is little agreement as to the definition of role makes its linkage to personality and social systems difficult to state with any degree of explicitness. Periodic calls for the clarification of the concept and the introduction of new vocabularies for the concept of role and derived terms (role taking, role playing, role conflict, role consensus, etc.) do little to help resolve the most basic question: In what ways does role contribute to the study and understanding of personality? This question can be approached by recognizing that the relationship between role and personality is a function of the particular ways in which the role concept happens to be employed. Miyamoto, in his examination of the research uses of role, provides a taxonomy which creates a clearer perspective.*

Of the many concepts around which personality theory has been built, the reference group concept has been one of the most useful to sociologists. As commonly used, the term refers to groups whose presumed perspectives are used by persons as a frame of reference for the organization of cognitive fields. Various groups may serve as reference groups, although membership is not essential—orientation is sufficient. All kinds of social aggregates may serve as reference groups—ready identification or degree of structure is unimportant.

[1] Theodore M. Newcomb, "Role Behaviors in the Study of Individual Personality and Groups," in H. Brand (Ed.), *The Study of Personality*, John Wiley and Sons, New York, 1954, p. 340.

Their essential feature is that they are entities, real or imagined, to which certain social values are imputed. But in all cases they constitute important sources of social control, functioning as sources of values selected by an individual for the guidance of his behavior or attitude system, and in some instances through the direct exertion of social influence. In the paper "Reference Groups as Perspectives," Shibutani reviews the history of the term and examines the theoretical and empirical contexts in which it appears. As the article develops, it becomes clear that one reason the reference group concept has enjoyed enduring popularity is because it throws into relief the part played by the other in personality functioning.

The social act is a unifying concept for the study of the individual because virtually all human behavior, be it personality, role, or communication, is implicated in social acts. The social act has various connotations. In a general sense, it refers to any action taking place in a social setting, but in a specific sense it refers to a set of act-react sequences of mutually related individuals. It is with aspects of the latter meaning that the Miyamoto article is primarily concerned. Miyamoto traces the usage of the phrase from its origins to contemporary social psychological theory and research. He contends that the consequences of employing the social act as a central analytic concept can be severalfold. A number of phenomena, including the self-concept, could be investigated in their natural settings. Such an approach would also help arrive at a solution to the problem of the generalized as opposed to the situationally specific aspects of the self-concept. In addition, the study of social acts and their consequences on self-conceptions and roles could contribute significantly to the understanding of organized social processes.

8

The Impact on Research of Different Conceptions of Role*

S. FRANK MIYAMOTO

Considering the size and complexity of the literature on role, it is impossible in a short paper to do more than indicate the main currents of thought which appear to have guided these writings and sketch some of the specific influences upon research which these ideas have had. Fortunately, Gross, Mason, and McEachern in their well-known work on role analysis give a discussion of role theory that serves admirably as background for the present article.[1]

At the outset it is necessary to draw distinctions between the key term *role* and two related terms, status (or position) and role behavior. Almost all definitions of role specify two components, (1) status or position, and (2) behavior pattern; that is, role is defined as the behavior pattern characteristic of persons in a given position. In addition, as Gross and associates indicate,[2] the behavior pattern in question is viewed from either of two standpoints. (a) Role may refer to normatively expected behavior, the behavior that a person in a given position should engage in. So conceived, role is necessarily a conceptual or definitional thing, and is distinguished from role behavior which refers to the actual behavior of a person fulfilling a role. (b) Role is sometimes defined as the behavior predicted for a person in a given position, but in this case no clear distinction is maintained between the terms role and role behavior. When the

---

* From S. Frank Miyamoto, "The Impact on Research of Different Conceptions of Role," *Sociological Inquiry, 33:* 114–123, 1963. By permission of the editor, *Sociological Inquiry.*

[1] Neal Gross, W. S. Mason, and A. W. McEachern, *Explorations in Role Analysis*, New York: John Wiley and Sons, 1958.

[2] *Ibid.*, pp. 11–18.

latter usage is followed, the expectations of behavior are often said to reside in the status or position, but not in the role.

When role is defined as normatively expected behavior, a problem arises of distinguishing it from status, for the latter also implies expectations. Nevertheless, semantic justification may be offered for retaining both terms. For example, the two questions, "What is his marital status?" and "What is his marital role?" imply different meanings although both may refer to expectations. The first implies the determination of a person's position among a set of related positions; the latter implies the determination of a person's behavior in a given position. In addition, the first requires the specification of only those expectations which will suffice to distinguish among related positions; the second requires the specification of those expectations which will explain a person's behavior in a given position. In such usage, status and role represent two perspectives on the same reference object. Studies of status are necessarily closely linked to studies of role, but in this paper only incidental attention is given to the subject of status.

Certain developing trends of usage, reflected for example in a current introductory text,[3] also deserve mention. It has been suggested that the term *status* be reserved for use in designating degrees of prestige, and *position* be employed for indicating location among a set of interrelated roles. Furthermore, *role requirement* is offered as a general term to cover two subtypes of normative role definitions: *role prescriptions*, which refer to formal rules and official role designations, and *role expectations*, which refer to informal rules and informal role definitions. These suggestions have merit, but they are not followed in the present discussion because the studies which are reviewed here generally did not observe such refinements.

There are many ways in which the different conceptions of role may be classified. For the present purpose, the following three basic points of view are distinguished: those which emphasize (1) the cultural maintenance function of role, (2) the social interactional function of role, and (3) the personal adjustmental function of role. The scheme of classification is admittedly imperfect, and certainly it is not novel. Sargent, for example, has pointed out that roles "have ingredients of cultural, of personal, and of social determina-

[3] G. A. Lundberg, C. C. Schrag, and O. N. Larsen, *Sociology* (Third Edition), New York: Harper and Row, 1963, p. 12 and pp. 146–164.

tion. But never is a role *wholly* cultural, *wholly* personal, or *wholly* situational." [4]

The quotation from Sargent suggests two problems of the classification method. First, writers often recognize the influence of all three ingredients in role determination. However, in any given study there is a tendency to emphasize one or another of these factors, with important consequences for the nature of the study, as we shall try to show. Second, Sargent speaks of role as being determined by cultural, social, and personal influences, while other writers speak of role as serving to maintain these processes. There is no necessary contradiction in the two points of view, however, for in seeking to maintain a system, the system may exert a determinative influence upon behavior.

Finally, our phrasing "the function of a role" should cause no surprise, for a role bespeaks a function; indeed, the main cause for alarm may be the possible redundancy in the expression.

THE CULTURE MAINTENANCE FUNCTION OF ROLE

Ralph Linton has given the classic definition of this conception of role where he says, "Role will be used to designate the sum total of the culture patterns associated with a particular status . . . role is the dynamic aspect of a status: what the individual has to do in order to validate his occupation of the status." [5]

The dominant features of this conception of role are: (1) The role is a cultural given; that is, it is culturally or institutionally defined and is therefore widely recognized within the culture or subculture as the normative prescription of behavior for a person in a given position. (2) A cultural system is maintained by the coordination of various roles, and the requirements of system maintenance therefore exert pressures upon those holding positions within the system to conform to role expectations. (3) Because a cultural system is made up of several subsystems of relations in each of which a person may

---

[4] S. Stanfeld Sargent, "Conceptions of Role and Ego in Contemporary Psychology," in J. H. Rohrer and M. Sherif (eds.), *Social Psychology at the Crossroads*, New York: Harper and Brothers, 1951, p. 359.

[5] Ralph Linton, *The Cultural Background of Personality*, New York: D. Appleton-Century Company, 1945.

hold a distinct position, the same person generally incorporates many roles within himself.

Linton, of course, was not the first to call attention to the significance of the role concept although he doubtless deserves credit for formalizing and giving prominence to it.[6] The interest of sociologists in the concept stemmed from their prior interest in status differentiation and its consequences to behavior.[7] The prototype of role analysis, therefore, consisted of identifying a culturally or institutionally recognized status—for example, the father, mother, and child in the family, the bureaucrat, the waitress, the delinquent, and the professional thief [8]—and of characterizing the typical behavior patterns associated with the given status.

While this conception of role is a part of the older tradition of sociology, publications continue to appear which elaborate the view. Thus, studies of relatively recent date may be found which discuss the role of the Protestant clergy,[9] the business executive,[10] the spouse,[11] and the academic man.[12] Klapp's studies of social types[13] —for example, of the fool, the villain, and the hero—suggest the

[6] Ralph Linton, *The Study of Man*, New York: D. Appleton-Century Company, 1936, pp. 105–114.

[7] Everett C. Hughes, "Personality Types and the Division of Labor," *American Journal of Sociology*, 33 (March, 1928), pp. 754–768.

[8] See, for example, H. H. Gerth and C. W. Mills, *From Max Weber: Essays in Sociology*, New York: Oxford University Press, 1946, pp. 186–194 and pp. 196–204, where some of Weber's contributions are presented. Also, E. W. Burgess, "The Study of the Delinquent as a Person," *American Journal of Sociology*, 28 (May, 1923), pp. 657–680; and Frances R. Donovan, *The Saleslady*, Chicago: The University of Chicago Press, 1929.

[9] Warren O. Hagstrom, "The Protestant Clergy as a Profession: Status and Prospects," *Berkeley Publications in Social Institutions*, 3 (Spring, 1957), pp. 1–12.

[10] William E. Henry, "The Business Executive: The Psycho-Dynamics of a Social Role," *American Journal of Sociology*, 54 (January, 1949), pp. 286–291.

[11] Annabelle B. Motz, "The Role Conception Inventory: A Tool for Research in Social Psychology," *American Sociological Review*, 17 (August, 1952), pp. 465–470.

[12] J. G. Manis, "A Quantitative Note on the Academic Role," *American Sociological Review*, 16 (December, 1951), pp. 837–839.

[13] Orrin E. Klapp, *Heroes, Villains, and Fools*, Englewood Cliffs, New Jersey: Prentice-Hall, Inc., 1962.

endless number of topics to which this mode of analysis may be applied.

The idea of the culturally fixed role that is related to a given status has been used in another way. In several studies, subjects are classified into certain standard categories, such as male-female or husband-wife, behavior correlates of these categories are found, and the behavior is then interpreted as resulting from the role expectations associated with the status, although role itself is not actually treated as a variable.[14] These studies, in fact, would be much improved if the roles themselves were identified and analyzed as variables.

If role is conceived as "what the individual has to do in order to validate his occupation of the status," that is, if the status exerts pressures on the individual to conform to role requirements, a number of additional problems are suggested. For example, how may personality types and personal motives be adapted to role requirements; how does the individual adjust when confronted simultaneously by two or more role requirements; and how does the individual respond when a given role develops internal contradictions due to cultural change? These problems of role conflict, role contradiction, and role strain have, in fact, received the largest amount of attention in the literature on role.

Hughes was one of the first to interest himself in the relationship between personality and status requirements,[15] and also the contradictions of status which lead to role conflicts.[16] In a series of studies both he and his students have used the typical approach of singling out some occupational position, such as that of the realtor,[17] the foreman,[18] the public school teacher,[19] the dance band musician,[20]

[14] Eugene A. Wilkening, "Joint Decision-Making in Farm Families as a Function of Status and Role," *American Sociological Review*, 23 (April, 1958), pp. 187–192.

[15] E. C. Hughes, *op. cit.*

[16] E. C. Hughes, "Dilemmas and Contradictions of Status," *American Journal of Sociology*, 50 (March, 1945), pp. 353–359.

[17] E. C. Hughes, *The Growth of an Institution: The Chicago Real Estate Board*, Chicago: Society for Social Research, 1931.

[18] Donald E. Wray, "Marginal Men of Industry: The Foreman," *American Journal of Sociology*, 54 (January, 1949), pp. 298–301.

[19] Howard S. Becker, "The Career of the Chicago Public School Teacher," *American Journal of Sociology*, 57 (March, 1952), pp. 470–477.

[20] Howard S. Becker, "The Professional Dance Band Musician and His

the boxer,[21] and the janitor,[22] and of describing the institutional expectations of these positions. But the primary attention of these studies is upon the contradictions and strains inherent in the prescribed role, and the techniques of social adaptation which are therefore employed to meet these strains. What emerges is a picture of the contingencies and contradictions characteristic of the formal status system, and the sub-culture of adjustmental techniques which are nurtured in each status group in response to these strains.

Studies addressed specifically to questions of role conflict appeared earliest in the investigation of marital and sex roles. Kirkpatrick's pioneer study of 1936 entitled "Inconsistency in Marriage Roles and Marriage Conflict," foreshadowed many of the main approaches to and conceptions of role conflict which are reflected in later studies.[23] He defined three culturally recognized roles of married women which he found to be conflicting: the wife-and-mother role (traditional role), the companion role, and the partner (or shared responsibility) role. He further defined four types of role conflict: (1) choice between incompatible roles, (2) inability to choose because of the confusion and multiplicity of roles, (3) opposition of role expectations between husband and wife, and (4) role or ethical contradictions arising from the simultaneous choice of incompatible roles. Conceiving of role conflict as a problem of choice among roles, Kirkpatrick devised an instrument requiring his subjects, husbands and wives separately, to choose one or both of incompatibly paired situational statements representing the three feminine role types. Space does not permit discussion of the findings, but the significant fact is that the main conceptions underlying later role conflict studies were largely outlined in this early investigation. In a recent study of marital adjustment, Hurvitz introduced a variation by distinguishing between role expectation and role behavior for both husband and wife and offers evidence that role

---

Audience," *American Journal of Sociology*, 57 (September, 1951), pp. 136–144.

[21] S. Kirson Weinberg and H. Arond, "The Occupational Culture of the Boxer," *American Journal of Sociology*, 57 (March, 1952), pp. 460–469.

[22] Ray Gold, "Janitors Versus Tenants: A Status-Income Dilemma," *American Journal of Sociology*, 57 (March, 1952), pp. 486–493.

[23] Clifford Kirkpatrick, "Inconsistencies in Marriage Roles and Marriage Conflict," *International Journal of Ethics*, 46 (1936), pp. 444–460.

conflicts at the level of expectations may lead to different consequences than those at the level of behavior.[24]

In these studies the role conflict is assumed to stem almost wholly from the circumstances of the external cultural system: the uneven development of institutional expectations under cultural change or the overlapping of institutional demands. This is true, for example, of Komarovsky's study of cultural contradictions in the female role, in which the "feminine" role traceable to traditional views is seen as contradicting the "modern" role of equalitarian expectations with men.[25] The focus of attention is therefore upon the question of how the individual is to adjust to the external contradiction. Similarly, in Burchard's study of the military chaplain, the role conflict is seen as arising from the contradiction between the goals of the military and religious institutional systems, and the problem investigated is again the one of adjustmental methods in the face of this conflict.[26]

The overwhelming interest in the study of role conflicts has resulted in the slighting of the equally important question of the structural integration of roles, a question to which Benedict,[27] Parsons,[28] and others gave attention in earlier writings. Referring to one aspect of the latter problem, Parsons has remarked, "Age and sex categories constitute one of the main links of structural continuity in terms of which structures which are differentiated in other respects are articulated with each other. . . ."[29] That is, such differentiated systems as the family, education, occupations, and community participation are articulated with each other by the appropriate interweaving of age-sex roles. This view of the articulation of roles, it may be noted, is different from the conception of adjusting conflicting roles. Merton's conception of the *role set*, which

---

[24] Nathan Hurvitz, "The Measurement of Marital Strain," *American Journal of Sociology*, 65 (May, 1960), pp. 610–615.

[25] Mirra Komarovsky, "Cultural Contradictions and Sex Roles," *American Journal of Sociology*, 52 (November, 1946), pp. 184–189.

[26] W. W. Burchard, "Role Conflicts of Military Chaplains," *American Sociological Review*, 19 (October, 1954), pp. 528–535.

[27] Ruth Benedict, "Continuities and Discontinuities in Cultural Conditioning," *Psychiatry*, 1 (May, 1938), pp. 161–167.

[28] Talcott Parsons, "Age and Sex in the Social Structure of the United States," *American Sociological Review*, 7 (October, 1942), pp. 604–620.

[29] *Ibid.*, p. 604.

cannot be discussed here in the manner that it deserves, appears to provide a theoretical formulation that permits systematic research on the question of the articulation of roles.[30]

THE SOCIAL INTERACTIONAL FUNCTION OF ROLE

In contrast to the cultural maintenance function of role, the viewpoint emphasizing the social interactional function is characterized by the following distinguishing features. (1) The role is regarded, not as a cultural given, but as a product of a social interactional process and as a matter for subjective interpretation and definition. (2) The emphasis is placed upon the function of role in facilitating interaction between persons, or of offering lines of action in situations where the cultural requirements of behavior are not fully specified.

Cottrell, in the article "The Adjustment of the Individual to His Age and Sex Roles,"[31] concerns himself with the cultural roles of age and sex, but his formulation indicates a transition from the strictly culturological conception of role. In defining role he says, "I shall be using the term role to refer to an internally consistent series of conditioned responses by one member of a social situation which represents the stimulus pattern for a similarly internally consistent series of conditioned responses of the other(s) in that situation."[32] In this statement, not only is role cast in an interactional setting, but role in some degree becomes a matter for adjustmental responses. Thus, adjustment to the role, it is hypothesized, will hinge upon the influence of such variables as the clarity of the role, consistency of the response of others, compatibility of several related roles, identification with others, and the importance of the given role.

Stouffer's study of role conflict,[33] which undoubtedly stimulated a

[30] Robert K. Merton, "The Role Set Problem in Sociological Theory," *British Journal of Sociology*, 8 (1957), pp. 106–126.

[31] Leonard S. Cottrell, "The Adjustment of the Individual to His Age and Sex Roles," *American Sociological Review*, 7 (October, 1942), pp. 617–620.

[32] *Ibid.*, p. 617.

[33] Samuel A. Stouffer, "An Analysis of Conflicting Social Norms," *American Sociological Review*, 14 (December, 1949), pp. 707–717.

revival of interest in the subject, illustrates an investigation of the problem posed by Cottrell, of how an individual selects among several role possibilities. As in the earlier studies of role conflict, the conflict investigated was a dilemma of choice between two culturally defined role expectations. His student subjects, it will be remembered, were asked to decide what they would do if, as proctors at an examination, they observed a student cheating. The potentially conflicting role expectations of school authorities and fellow students were built into the situation described. The distinctive features of this study—the features distinguishing it from prior studies of role conflict—were the investigation of the hypotheses that (1) the subject's perception of role expectations will vary with the situation—for example, where the cheater in the story is an "ordinary friend" versus a "roommate-friend"; (2) the range of role expectations will vary both within the individual and between subjects; and (3) the role behavior which the subject says he would choose is dependent upon both the situation and the range of role expectations. From this point of view, role conflict is not merely a confrontation of a person by a cultural contradiction, but the role expectations underlying the conflict are themselves subject to interpretation by the actors in the situation.

The initial study by Stouffer spawned a number of others which have investigated such influences on role conflict resolution as personality types,[34] personal needs, and the perception of the role expectations,[35] culminating in the interesting theoretical model of conflict resolution by Gross, Mason, and McEachern.[36] Turner's study of the function of roles in moral judgment,[37] which bears a distinct kinship to the Stouffer research, emphasizes more strongly than the others the function of the self-other relationship in determining role expectations, and he accordingly emphasizes such variables as role-taking and the role standpoint as primary influences upon role.

The conception of role as functioning to facilitate social inter-

[34] Elliot G. Mishler, "Personality Characteristics and the Resolution of Role Conflicts," *Public Opinion Quarterly*, 17 (Spring, 1953), pp. 115–135.

[35] J. W. Getzels and E. G. Guba, "Role, Role Conflict and Personality," *American Sociological Review*, 19 (April, 1954), pp. 164–175.

[36] Gross, Mason, and McEachern, *op. cit.*, pp. 244–318.

[37] Ralph H. Turner, "Moral Judgment, a Study in Roles," *American Sociological Review*, 17 (February, 1952), pp. 70–77.

action is most clearly seen in the studies of roles in small group settings. Morton Deutsch,[38] with Benne and Sheats,[39] observed a variety of roles in problem-solving groups which they found to be classifiable into three main groupings, the roles which facilitate the task, the group maintenance, and the personal needs satisfaction functions of the group. The general theme of this notion has been documented by the studies of Bales and Slater[40] in which they found that two role types, the "idea man" and the "best-liked man," tended to emerge in their problem-solving situations, the first fulfilling functions in the task area and the second fulfilling functions in the socio-emotional area of the group. Landsberger,[41] in an application of the Bales-Slater hypothesis to the study of the role of mediators in labor-management disputes, found distinct patterns of activity in the task and socio-emotional leadership areas which could be accounted for by the peculiar requirements of the mediator role. The study is suggestive of the kind of nexus which may be found between the culturally defined roles, such as that of collective bargaining mediators, and roles which emerge from social interactional process.

We cannot close this section without a reference to the effect of the social interactional conception upon the role analysis of school superintendents by Gross, Mason, and McEachern. The main problem investigated concerned the validity of the culturological assumption that the role expectations attached to a given status have an unambiguous, common meaning for members of a society. They, in fact, demonstrated that the degree of role consensus varies greatly with the role item, by position and between positions, and that the variations in role consensus occur with respect to intensity as well as direction. The fact of variations in role consensus became the key to their further analyses, for it then was possible to inquire into

---

[38] Morton Deutsch, "The Effects of Cooperation and Competition upon Group Process," in D. Cartwright and A. Zander, *Group Dynamics*, Evanston: Row Peterson and Company, 1953, p. 336.

[39] K. D. Benne and P. Sheats, "Functional Roles and Group Members," *Journal of Social Issues*, 4 (1948), pp. 41–49.

[40] P. E. Slater, "Role Differentiation in Small Groups," *American Sociological Review*, 20 (June, 1955), pp. 300–310.

[41] Henry A. Landsberger, "Interaction Process Analysis of Professional Behavior: A Study of Labor Mediators in Twelve Labor-Management Disputes," *American Sociological Review*, 20 (October, 1955), pp. 566–575.

the factors determining the variations, the factors contributing to consensus, and the consequences of consensus and variation of role expectations upon criteria behavior.

As long ago as the study of the J-Curve Hypothesis by Floyd Allport there has been a suggestion in the literature of the invalidity of assuming a homogeneity of meanings with respect to norms of behavior. The study by Gross, Mason, and McEachern has given clear evidence of the utility of discarding the postulate of consensus and of the possibilities for the systematic investigation of role that results from the treatment of role expectations as a variable rather than as a constant.

Yet, an implication may be read into their work that would be misleading. It may not be assumed, on the basis of their study, that there is no such thing as consensus with respect to a role. If a random sample of adult Americans were asked what behavior might be expected of a school superintendent, it seems certain that there would be a high degree of agreement regarding a large area of excluded behavior, agreement about certain gross forms of expected and approved behavior, and varying degrees of consensus regarding the details of the role. The suggestion is that the method of Gross and associates may equally be applied to the determination of the cultural definitions of a role, those on which a high degree of consensus exists, as well as to measure the variations. The problem may then be investigated of the interconnection between the levels of definition.

THE PERSONAL ADJUSTMENTAL FUNCTION OF ROLE

In this last category of role studies, emphasis is placed upon the function of role in facilitating personal adjustment. The issue, it will be noted, is related to but distinguished from the problem of adjustment to a role. There are several variations of this conception, two of which may be illustrated.

Roles learned under one circumstance and appropriate in that situation may be applied in other situations, whether appropriately or inappropriately, for adjustmental reasons. The inappropriate applications, of course, provide the more vivid illustrations. Perhaps the first study bearing on the adjustmental function of role was that by Cottrell [42] in which he investigated sex roles in marital adjustment. He there reported the case of a young man who, as a younger brother to two domineering and overprotective sisters, acquired a highly dependent role and disastrously carried the role into his married life. The implication is, of course, that roles learned early in life have persistence and tend to be employed in meeting problems of later life. Robert E. L. Faris' [43] discussion of the "neurotic role" makes somewhat the same point. He suggested that persons confronted by insoluble personal conflicts often adapt such inappropriate roles as that of the sick, the weak, or the overburdened. To this writer's knowledge, few studies have been done pursuing this idea.

Another kind of adjustmental problem is presented when an institutional system, by its definition of a person's role, brings into play modes of adjustment which were unintended in the institutional goals. The studies of the "sick role" and "patient role" illustrate the problem. Hospitals, for example, have traditionally encouraged sick persons to define themselves accordingly and assume the patient role, but there is increasing evidence that the assumption of the sick role and patient role may, in fact, be inimical to the hospital's aim of curing the patient.[44] In these studies, self-conception is often treated as an intervening variable. That is, the interactional situation is perceived as leading a person to develop a certain kind of self-conception, and the role played is then considered to be his means of representing himself in the image of the self-concept.

CONCLUSIONS

We have suggested that role studies are classifiable by their emphasis upon the culture maintenance, social interactional, or personal adjustmental function which the role is presumed to perform. As between the cultural and social interactional conceptions,

[42] Leonard Cottrell, "Roles and Marital Adjustment," *Publications of the American Sociological Society*, 27 (May, 1933), pp. 107–112.

[43] R. E. L. Faris, *Social Psychology*, New York: Ronald Press Company, 1952, pp. 309–328.

[44] K. T. Erikson, "Patient Role and Social Uncertainty: A Dilemma of the Mentally Ill," *Psychiatry*, 20 (1957), pp. 263–274.

our own bias is to favor the latter, for as Gross and associates have indicated, many more researchable problems are suggested from the latter point of view. Nevertheless, role unquestionably has its cultural aspects, and a specialist in role studies would be misguided if he were to overlook the possibilities of research in that area. The application of the role concept to the fields of personal adjustment and social problems appears to have been barely tapped, and it seems predictable that increased interest in this approach will develop in those fields.

Reference Groups as Perspectives*

TAMOTSU SHIBUTANI

Although Hyman coined the term scarcely more than a decade ago, the concept of reference group has become one of the central analytic tools in social psychology, being used in the construction of hypotheses concerning a variety of social phenomena. The inconsistency in behavior as a person moves from one social context to another is accounted for in terms of a change in reference groups; the exploits of juvenile delinquents, especially in interstitial areas, are being explained by the expectations of peer-group gangs; modifications in social attitudes are found to be related to changes in associations. The concept has been particularly useful in accounting for the choices made among apparent alternatives, particularly where the selections seem to be contrary to the "best interests" of the actor. Status problems—aspirations of social climbers, conflicts in group loyalty, the dilemmas of marginal men—have also been analyzed in terms of reference groups, as have the differential sensitivity and reaction of various segments of an audience to mass communication. It is recognized that the same generic processes are involved in these phenomenally diverse events, and the increasing popularity of the concept attests to its utility in analysis.

As might be expected during the exploratory phases in any field of inquiry, however, there is some confusion involved in the use of this concept, arising largely from vagueness of signification. The available formal definitions are inconsistent, and sometimes formal definitions are contradicted in usage. The fact that social psychologists can understand one another in spite of these ambiguities, however, implies an intuitive recognition of some central meaning, and

---

* Reprinted from "Reference Groups as Perspectives" by Tamotsu Shibutani, *American Journal of Sociology*, 60: 562–569, 1955. Copyright 1955 by the University of Chicago.

an explicit statement of this will enhance the utility of the concept as an analytic tool. The literature reveals that all discussions of reference groups involve some identifiable grouping to which an actor is related in some manner and the norms and values shared in that group. However, the relationship between these three terms is not always clear. Our initial task, then, is to examine the conceptions of reference groups implicit in actual usage, irrespective of formal definitions.

One common usage of the concept is in the designation of that group which serves as the point of reference in making comparisons or contrasts, especially in forming judgments about one's self. In the original use of the concept Hyman spoke of reference groups as points of comparison in evaluating one's own status, and he found that the estimates varied according to the group with which the respondent compared himself. Merton and Kitt, in their reformulation of Stouffer's theory of relative deprivation, also use the concept in this manner; the judgments of rear-echelon soldiers overseas concerning their fate varied, depending upon whether they compared themselves to soldiers who were still at home or men in combat. They also propose concrete research operations in which respondents are to be asked to compare themselves with various groups. The study of aspiration levels by Chapman and Volkmann, frequently cited in discussions of reference-group theory, also involves variations in judgment arising from a comparison of one's own group with others.[1] In this mode of application, then, a reference group is a standard or check point which an actor uses in forming his estimate of the situation, particularly his own position within it. Logically, then, *any* group with which an actor is familiar may become a reference group.

A second referent of the concept is that group in which the actor aspires to gain or maintain acceptance; hence, a group whose claims are paramount in situations requiring choice. The reference group of the socially ambitious is said to consist of people of higher strata

[1] H. H. Hyman, "The Psychology of Status," *Archives of Psychology*, XXXVIII (1942), 15; R. K. Merton and A. Kitt, "Contributions to the Theory of Reference Group Behavior," in R. K. Merton and P. F. Lazarsfeld (eds.), *Studies in the Scope and Method of "The American Soldier"* (Glencoe, Ill.: Free Press, 1950), pp. 42–53, 69; D. W. Chapman and J. Volkmann, "A Social Determinant of the Level of Aspiration," *Journal of Abnormal and Social Psychology*, XXXIV (1939), 225–38.

whose status symbols are imitated. Merton and Kitt interpret the expressions of willingness and felt readiness for combat on the part of inexperienced troops, as opposed to the humility of battle-hardened veterans, as the efforts of newcomers to identify themselves with veterans to whom they had mistakenly imputed certain values.[2] Thus, the concept is used to point to an association of human beings among whom one seeks to gain, maintain, or enhance his status; a reference group is that group in which one desires to participate.

In a third usage the concept signifies that group whose perspective constitutes the frame of reference of the actor. Thus, Sherif speaks of reference groups as groups whose norms are used as anchoring points in structuring the perceptual field,[3] and Merton and Kitt speak of a "social frame of reference" for interpretations.[4] Through direct or vicarious participation in a group one comes to perceive the world from its standpoint. Yet this group need not be one in which he aspires for acceptance; a member of some minority group may despise it but still see the world largely through its eyes. When used in this manner, the concept of reference group points more to a psychological phenomenon than to an objectively existing group of men; it refers to an organization of the actor's experience. That is to say, it is a structuring of his perceptual field. In this usage a reference group becomes any collectivity, real or imagined, envied or despised, whose perspective is assumed by the actor.

Thus, an examination of current usage discloses three distinct referents for a single concept: (1) groups which serve as comparison points; (2) groups to which men aspire; and (3) groups whose perspectives are assumed by the actor. Although these terms may be related, treating together what should be clearly delineated as generically different can lead only to further confusion. It is the contention of this paper that the restriction of the concept of reference group to the third alternative—that group whose perspective constitutes the frame of reference of the actor—will increase its usefulness in research. Any group or object may be used for comparisons, and one need not assume the role of those with whom

---

[2] *Op. cit.*, pp. 75–76.

[3] M. Sherif, "The Concept of Reference Groups in Human Relations," in M. Sherif and M. O. Wilson (eds.), *Group Relations at the Crossroads* (New York: Harper & Bros., 1953), pp. 203–31.

[4] *Op. cit.*, pp. 49–50.

he compares his fate; hence, the first usage serves a quite different purpose and may be eliminated from further consideration. Under some circumstances, however, group loyalties and aspirations are related to perspectives assumed, and the character of this relationship calls for further exploration. Such a discussion necessitates a restatement of the familiar, but, in view of the difficulties in some of the work on reference groups, repetition may not be entirely out of order. In spite of the enthusiasm of some proponents there is actually nothing new in reference-group theory.

CULTURE AND PERSONAL CONTROLS

Thomas pointed out many years ago that what a man does depends largely upon his definition of the situation. One may add that the manner in which one consistently defines a succession of situations depends upon his organized perspective. A perspective is an ordered view of one's world—what is taken for granted about the attributes of various objects, events, and human nature. It is an order of things remembered and expected as well as things actually perceived, an organized conception of what is plausible and what is possible; it constitutes the matrix through which one perceives his environment. The fact that men have such ordered perspectives enables them to conceive of their ever changing world as relatively stable, orderly, and predictable. As Reizler puts it, one's perspective is an outline scheme which, running ahead of experience, defines and guides it.

There is abundant experimental evidence to show that perception is selective; that the organization of perceptual experience depends in part upon what is anticipated and what is taken for granted. Judgments rest upon perspectives, and people with different outlooks define identical situations differently, responding selectively to the environment. Thus, a prostitute and a social worker walking through a slum area notice different things; a sociologist should perceive relationships that others fail to observe. Any change of perspectives—becoming a parent for the first time, learning that one will die in a few months, or suffering the failure of well-laid plans—leads one to notice things previously overlooked and to see the familiar world in a different light. As Goethe contended, history is continually rewritten, not so much because of the discovery of new documentary evidence, but because the changing perspectives of historians lead to new selections from the data.

Culture, as the concept is used by Redfield, refers to a perspective that is shared by those in a particular group; it consists of those "conventional understandings, manifest in act and artifact, that characterize societies."[5] Since these conventional understandings are the premises of action, those who share a common culture engage in common modes of action. Culture is not a static entity but a continuing process; norms are creatively reaffirmed from day to day in social interaction. Those taking part in collective transactions approach one another with set expectations, and the realization of what is anticipated successively confirms and reinforces their perspectives. In this way, people in each cultural group are continuously supporting one another's perspectives, each by responding to the others in expected ways. In this sense culture is a product of communication.

In his discussion of endopsychic social control Mead spoke of men "taking the role of the generalized other," meaning by that that each person approaches his world from the standpoint of the culture of his group. Each perceives, thinks, forms judgments, and controls himself according to the frame of reference of the group in which he is participating. Since he defines objects, other people, the world, and himself from the perspective that he shares with others, he can visualize his proposed line of action from this generalized standpoint, anticipate the reactions of others, inhibit undesirable impulses, and thus guide his conduct. The socialized person is a society in miniature; he sets the same standards of conduct for himself as he sets for others, and he judges himself in the same terms. He can define situations properly and meet his obligations, even in the absence of other people, because, as already noted, his perspective always takes into account the expectations of others. Thus, it is the ability to define situations from the same

---

[5] R. Redfield, *The Folk Culture of Yucatan* (Chicago: University of Chicago Press, 1941), p. 132. For a more explicit presentation of a behavioristic theory of culture see *The Selected Writings of Edward Sapir in Language, Culture and Personality*, ed. D. G. Mandelbaum (Berkeley: University of California Press, 1949), pp. 104–9, 308–31, 544–59.

standpoint as others that makes personal controls possible.[6] When Mead spoke of assuming the role of the generalized other, he was not referring to people but to perspectives shared with others in a transaction.

The consistency in the behavior of a man in a wide variety of social contexts is to be accounted for, then, in terms of his organized perspective. Once one has incorporated a particular outlook from his group, it becomes his orientation toward the world, and he brings this frame of reference to bear on all new situations. Thus, immigrants and tourists often misinterpret the strange things they see, and a disciplined Communist would define each situation differently from the non-Communist. Although reference-group behavior is generally studied in situations where choices seem possible, the actor himself is often unaware that there are alternatives.

The proposition that men think, feel, and see things from a standpoint peculiar to the group in which they participate is an old one, repeatedly emphasized by students of anthropology and of the sociology of knowledge. Why, then, the sudden concern with reference-group theory during the past decade? The concept of reference group actually introduces a minor refinement in the long familiar theory, made necessary by the special characteristics of modern mass societies. First of all, in modern societies special problems arise from the fact that men sometimes use the standards of groups in which they are *not* recognized members, sometimes of groups in which they have never participated directly, and sometimes of groups that do not exist at all. Second, in our mass society, characterized as it is by cultural pluralism, each person internalizes several perspectives, and this occasionally gives rise to embarrassing dilemmas which call for systematic study. Finally, the development of reference-group theory has been facilitated by the increasing interest in social psychology and the subjective aspects of group life, a shift from a predominant concern with objective social structures to an interest in the experiences of the participants whose regularized activities make such structures discernible.

---

[6] G. H. Mead, "The Genesis of the Self and Social Control," *International Journal of Ethics*, XXXV (1925), 251–77, and *Mind, Self and Society* (Chicago: University of Chicago Press, 1934), pp. 152–64. Cf. T. Parsons, "The Superego and the Theory of Social Systems," *Psychiatry*, XV (1952), 15–25.

A reference group, then, is that group whose outlook is used by the actor as the frame of reference in the organization of his perceptual field. All kinds of groupings, with great variations in size, composition, and structure, may become reference groups. Of greatest importance for most people are those groups in which they participate directly—what have been called membership groups—especially those containing a number of persons with whom one stands in a primary relationship. But in some transactions one may assume the perspective attributed to some social category—a social class, an ethnic group, those in a given community, or those concerned with some special interest. On the other hand, reference groups may be imaginary, as in the case of artists who are "born ahead of their times," scientists who work for "humanity," or philanthropists who give for "posterity." Such persons estimate their endeavors from a postulated perspective imputed to people who have not yet been born. There are others who live for a distant past, idealizing some period in history and longing for "the good old days," criticizing current events from a standpoint imputed to people long since dead. Reference groups, then, arise through the internalization of norms; they constitute the structure of expectations imputed to some audience for whom one organizes his conduct.

THE CONSTRUCTION OF SOCIAL WORLDS

As Dewey emphasized, society exists in and through communication; common perspectives—common cultures—emerge through participation in common communication channels. It is through social participation that perspectives shared in a group are internalized. Despite the frequent recitation of this proposition, its full implications, especially for the analysis of mass societies, are not often appreciated. Variations in outlook arise through differential contact and association; the maintenance of social distance—through segregation, conflict, or simply the reading of different literature—leads to the formation of distinct cultures. Thus, people in different social classes develop different modes of life and outlook, not because of anything inherent in economic position, but because similarity of occupation and limitations set by income level dispose them to certain restricted communication channels. Those in different ethnic groups form their own distinctive cultures because their identifications incline them to interact intimately with each other and to maintain reserve before outsiders. Different intellectual traditions within social psychology—psychoanalysis, scale analysis, *Gestalt*, pragmatism—will remain separated as long as those in each tradition restrict their sympathetic attention to works of their own school and view others with contempt or hostility. Some social scientists are out of touch with the masses of the American people because they eschew the mass media, especially television, or expose themselves only condescendingly. Even the outlook that the *avant-garde* regards as "cosmopolitan" is culture-bound, for it also is a product of participation in restricted communication channels—books, magazines, meetings, exhibits, and taverns which are out of bounds for most people in the middle classes. Social participation may even be vicarious, as it is in the case of a medievalist who acquires his perspective solely through books.

Even casual observation reveals the amazing variety of standards by which Americans live. The inconsistencies and contradictions which characterize modern mass societies are products of the multitude of communication channels and the ease of participation in them. Studying relatively isolated societies, anthropologists can speak meaningfully of "culture areas" in geographical terms; in such societies common cultures have a territorial base, for only those who live together can interact. In modern industrial societies, however, because of the development of rapid transportation and the media of mass communication, people who are geographically dispersed can communicate effectively. Culture areas are coterminous with communication channels; since communication networks are no longer coterminous with territorial boundaries, culture areas overlap and have lost their territorial bases. Thus, next-door neighbors may be complete strangers; even in common parlance there is an intuitive recognition of the diversity of perspectives, and we speak meaningfully of people living in different social worlds—the academic world, the world of children, the world of fashion.

Modern mass societies, indeed, are made up of a bewildering variety of social worlds. Each is an organized outlook, built up by people in their interaction with one another; hence, each communication channel gives rise to a separate world. Probably the greatest sense of identification and solidarity is to be found in the various communal structures—the underworld, ethnic minorities, the social elite. Such communities are frequently spatially segregated, which isolates them further from the outer world, while the "grapevine" and foreign-language presses provide internal contacts. Another common type of social world consists of the associational structures —the world of medicine, of organized labor, of the theater, of café society. These are held together not only by various voluntary associations within each locality but also by the periodicals like *Variety*, specialized journals, and feature sections in newspapers. Finally, there are the loosely connected universes of special interest—the world of sports, of the stamp collector, of the daytime serial— serviced by mass media programs and magazines like *Field and Stream*. Each of these worlds is a unity of order, a universe of regularized mutual response. Each is an area in which there is some structure which permits reasonable anticipation of the behavior of others, hence, an area in which one may act with a sense of security and confidence.[7] Each social world, then, is a culture area, the boundaries of which are set neither by territory nor by formal group membership but by the limits of effective communication.

Since there is a variety of communication channels, differing in stability and extent, social worlds differ in composition, size, and the territorial distribution of the participants. Some, like local cults, are small and concentrated; others, like the intellectual world, are vast and the participants dispersed. Worlds differ in the extent and clarity of their boundaries; each is confined by some kind of horizon, but this may be wide or narrow, clear or vague. The fact that social worlds are not coterminous with the universe of men is recognized; those in the underworld are well aware of the fact that outsiders do not share their values. Worlds differ in exclusiveness and in the extent to which they demand the loyalty of their participants. Most important of all, social worlds are not static entities; shared perspectives are continually being reconstituted. Worlds come into existence with the establishment of communication channels; when life conditions change, social relationships may also change, and these worlds may disappear.

[7] Cf. K. Riezler, *Man: Mutable and Immutable* (Chicago: Henry Regnery Co., 1950), pp. 62–72; L. Landgrebe, "The World as a Phenomenological Problem," *Philosophy and Phenomenological Research*, I (1940), 38–58; and A. Schuetz, "The Stranger: An Essay in Social Psychology," *American Journal of Sociology*, XLIX (1944), 499–507.

Every social world has some kind of communication system—often nothing more than differential association—in which there develops a special universe of discourse, sometimes an argot. Special meanings and symbols further accentuate differences and increase social distance from outsiders. In each world there are special norms of conduct, a set of values, a special prestige ladder, characteristic career lines, and a common outlook toward life—a Weltanschauung. In the case of elites there may even arise a code of honor which holds only for those who belong, while others are dismissed as beings somewhat less than human from whom bad manners may be expected. A social world, then, is an order conceived which serves as the stage on which each participant seeks to carve out his career and to maintain and enhance his status.

One of the characteristics of life in modern mass societies is simultaneous participation in a variety of social worlds. Because of the ease with which the individual may expose himself to a number of communication channels, he may lead a segmentalized life, participating successively in a number of unrelated activities. Furthermore, the particular combination of social worlds differs from person to person; this is what led Simmel to declare that each stands at that point at which a unique combination of social circles intersects. The geometric analogy is a happy one, for it enables us to conceive the numerous possibilities of combinations and the different degrees of participation in each circle. To understand what a man does, we must get at his unique perspective—what he takes for granted and how he defines the situation—but in mass societies we must learn in addition the social world in which he is participating in a given act.

LOYALTY AND SELECTIVE RESPONSIVENESS

In a mass society where each person internalizes numerous perspectives there are bound to be some incongruities and conflicts. The overlapping of group affiliation and participation, however, need not lead to difficulties and is usually unnoticed. The reference groups of most persons are mutually sustaining. Thus, the soldier who volunteers for hazardous duty on the battlefield may provoke anxiety in his family but is not acting contrary to their values; both his family and his comrades admire courage and disdain cowardice. Behavior may be inconsistent, as in the case of the proverbial office tyrant who is meek before his wife, but it is not noticed if the transactions occur in dissociated contexts. Most people live more or less compartmentalized lives, shifting from one social world to another as they participate in a succession of transactions. In each world their roles are different, their relations to other participants are different, and they reveal a different facet of their personalities. Men have become so accustomed to this mode of life that they manage to conceive of themselves as reasonably consistent human beings in spite of this segmentalization and are generally not aware of the fact that their acts do not fit into a coherent pattern.

People become acutely aware of the existence of different outlooks only when they are successively caught in situations in which conflicting demands are made upon them, all of which cannot possibly be satisfied. While men generally avoid making difficult decisions, these dilemmas and contradictions of status may force a choice between two social worlds. These conflicts are essentially alternative ways of defining the same situation, arising from several possible perspectives. In the words of William James, "As a man I pity you, but as an official I must show you no mercy; as a politician I regard him as an ally, but as a moralist I loathe him." In playing roles in different social worlds, one imputes different expectations to others whose differences cannot always be compromised. The problem is that of selecting the perspective for defining the situation. In Mead's terminology, which generalized other's role is to be taken? It is only in situations where alternative definitions are possible that problems of loyalty arise.

Generally such conflicts are ephemeral; in critical situations contradictions otherwise unnoticed are brought into the open, and painful choices are forced. In poorly integrated societies, however, some people find themselves continually beset with such conflicts. The Negro intellectual, children of mixed marriages or of immigrants, the foreman in a factory, the professional woman, the military chaplain—all live in the interstices of well-organized structures and are marginal men.[8] In most instances they manage to make

[8] Cf. E. C. Hughes, "Dilemmas and Contradictions of Status," *American Journal of Sociology*, L (1945), 353–59, and E. V. Stonequist, *The Marginal Man* (New York: Charles Scribner's Sons, 1937).

their way through their compartmentalized lives, although personal maladjustments are apparently frequent. In extreme cases amnesia and dissociation of personality can occur.

Much of the interest in reference groups arises out of concern with situations in which a person is confronted with the necessity of choosing between two or more organized perspectives. The hypothesis has been advanced that the choice of reference groups—conformity to the norms of the group whose perspective is assumed—is a function of one's interpersonal relations; to what extent the culture of a group serves as the matrix for the organization of perceptual experience depends upon one's relationship and personal loyalty to others who share that outlook. Thus, when personal relations to others in the group deteriorate, as sometimes happens in a military unit after continued defeat, the norms become less binding, and the unit may disintegrate in panic. Similarly, with the transformation of personal relationships between parent and child in late adolescence, the desires and standards of the parents often become less obligatory.

It has been suggested further that choice of reference groups rests upon personal loyalty to significant others of that social world. "Significant others," for Sullivan, are those persons directly responsible for the internalization of norms. Socialization is a product of a gradual accumulation of experiences with certain people, particularly those with whom we stand in primary relations, and significant others are those who are actually involved in the cultivation of abilities, values, and outlook.[9] Crucial, apparently, is the character of one's emotional ties with them. Those who think the significant others have treated them with affection and consideration have a sense of personal obligation that is binding under all circumstances, and they will be loyal even at great personal sacrifice. Since primary relations are not necessarily satisfactory, however, the reactions may be negative. A person who is well aware of the expectations of significant others may go out of his way to reject them. This may account for the bifurcation of orientation in minority groups, where some remain loyal to the parental culture while others seek desperately to become assimilated in the larger world. Some who withdraw from the uncertainties of real life may establish loyalties to

[9] H. S. Sullivan, *Conceptions of Modern Psychiatry* (Washington, D.C.: W. H. White Psychiatric Foundation, 1947), pp. 18–22.

perspectives acquired through vicarious relationships with characters encountered in books.[10]

Perspectives are continually subjected to the test of reality. All perception is hypothetical. Because of what is taken for granted from each standpoint, each situation is approached with a set of expectations; if transactions actually take place as anticipated, the perspective itself is reinforced. It is thus the confirming responses of other people that provide support for perspectives.[11] But in mass societies the responses of others vary, and in the study of reference groups the problem is that of ascertaining *whose* confirming responses will sustain a given point of view.

THE STUDY OF MASS SOCIETIES

Because of the differentiated character of modern mass societies, the concept of reference group, or some suitable substitute, will always have a central place in any realistic conceptual scheme for its analysis. As is pointed out above, it will be most useful if it is used to designate that group whose perspective is assumed by the actor as the frame of reference for the organization of his perceptual experience. Organized perspectives arise in and become shared through participation in common communication channels, and the diversity of mass societies arises from the multiplicity of channels and the ease with which one may participate in them.

Mass societies are not only diversified and pluralistic but also continually changing. The successive modification of life-conditions compels changes in social relationships, and any adequate analysis requires a study of these transformational processes themselves. Here the concept of reference group can be of crucial importance. For example, all forms of social mobility, from sudden conversions

---

[10] Cf. R. R. Grinker and J. P. Spiegel, *Men under Stress* (Philadelphia: Blakiston Co., 1945), pp. 122–26; and E. A. Shils and M. Janowitz, "Cohesion and Disintegration in the Wehrmacht in World War II," *Public Opinion Quarterly*, XII (1948), 280–315.

[11] Cf. G. H. Mead, *The Philosophy of the Act* (Chicago: University of Chicago Press, 1938), pp. 107–73; and L. Postman, "Toward a General Theory of Cognition," in J. H. Rohrer and M. Sherif (eds.), *Social Psychology at the Crossroads* (New York: Harper & Bros., 1951), pp. 242–72.

to gradual assimilation, may be regarded essentially as displacements of reference groups, for they involve a loss of responsiveness to the demands of one social world and the adoption of the perspective of another. It may be hypothesized that the disaffection occurs first on the level of personal relations, followed by a weakening sense of obligation, a rejection of old claims, and the establishment of new loyalties and incorporation of a new perspective. The conflicts that characterize all persons in marginal roles are of special interest in that they provide opportunities for cross-sectional analyses of the processes of social change.

In the analysis of the behavior of men in mass societies the crucial problem is that of ascertaining how a person defines the situation, which perspective he uses in arriving at such a definition, and who constitutes the audience whose responses provide the necessary confirmation and support for his position. This calls for focusing attention upon the expectations the actor imputes to others, the communication channels in which he participates, and his relations with those with whom he identifies himself. In the study of conflict, imagery provides a fertile source of data. At moments of indecision, when in doubt and confusion, who appears in imagery? In this manner the significant other can be identified.

An adequate analysis of modern mass societies requires the development of concepts and operations for the description of the manner in which each actor's orientation toward his world is successively reconstituted. Since perception is selective and perspectives differ, different items are noticed and a progressively diverse set of images arises, even among those exposed to the same media of mass communication. The concept of reference group summarizes differential associations and loyalties and thus facilitates the study of selective perception. It becomes, therefore, an indispensable tool for comprehending the diversity and dynamic character of the kind of society in which we live.

10

The Social Act: Re-Examination of a Concept*

S. Frank Miyamoto

The interactionist point of view in social psychology was for some time mainly a framework of suggestive concepts, but as a result of recent studies of status and roles, the self, interpersonal perception, communication, and consensus, the framework is now acquiring the kind of connective tissue that was long wanting. While these studies have brought notable advances and their continuation should yield important consequences for social psychology, it is a curious fact that current investigations tend to ignore the concept which originally was considered the keystone of the interactionist approach. I wish to clarify what I consider this lacuna to be.

Although the exaggeration does some injustice, one is tempted to say that much of current research in this area is less concerned with social interaction itself than with the components of interaction, or with its consequences. Furthermore, in those studies which focus upon interaction, the process tends to be conceived as a mechanistic interplay of actions, selves, roles, and norms, thus eliminating the need to consider the meaningful context of interaction.

For the earlier writers who were largely responsible for initiating the interactionist view, however, the socially meaningful context of interaction was of primary significance and was, indeed, the foundation idea upon which their analyses were constructed. Thus, W. I. Thomas clearly implied that the *definition of the situation* provides the frame of reference of social interaction, and that organized social relations presuppose the existence of a body of common definitions among the group members. Park and Burgess referred to the cooperative (that is, corporate) nature of social relations within which

---

* By permission, from S. Frank Miyamoto, "The Social Act: Re-Examination of a Concept," *Pacific Sociological Review*, 2: 51–55, 1959.

individual behavior is implicated. Finally, G. H. Mead repeatedly emphasized that the interactional processes with which he was concerned occur within the context of the social act, that is, within the context of a goal-oriented, organized group action.

Mention of this classical background may cause you to wonder "what all the shooting is about" for no one to my knowledge questions the import of the concepts referred to, and a generation of social psychologists have been trained to think in these terms. The concern here, however, is with the gap between theory and research, with the fact that what is explicit in the theoretical statement is reduced to the status of the implicit in empirical research. The latter assertion is again an exaggeration for a few have attempted to deal explicitly with the context of interaction as a variable. Leonard Cottrell, in particular, has stressed *the situation* as a neglected area of interaction studies.[1] In a series of publications he and his students have foreshadowed many of the ideas offered here, so much so that I may often be dangerously close to plagiarism. The justification for this presentation is the hope that, as in musical composition, a variation on a theme may be considered provocative and as offering new meanings.

Although a number of different concepts with similar meanings have been used in reference to the aspect of the social process under discussion, for reasons I shall clarify later, special attention is given to Mead's notion of the social act. The latter term is familiar to many, but to make sure that our ideas about it correspond, a little space is devoted to its explication.

THE SOCIAL ACT

The term "social act" has been used with two different meanings. Loosely employed, it refers to any act occurring in a social context; that is, any act having a social object as referent. In Mead's usage, however, it refers to a group action; specifically, to an organized action of two or more individuals that is directed toward some

---

[1] Leonard S. Cottrell, Jr., "The Analysis of Situational Fields in Social Psychology," *American Sociological Review*, 7 (June, 1942), pp. 370–382; and his, "Some Neglected Problems in Social Psychology," *American Sociological Review*, 15 (December, 1950), pp. 705–712.

common goal. It is the latter meaning with which we are concerned.

Virtually all meaningful human behavior is implicated within social acts. As I sit in my office writing this paper, I am implicated in that social act called the annual meeting of the Pacific Sociological Society. The annual meeting is in fact a social act that covers a rather long time span, and is composed of those manifold coordinated actions of many persons which occur in the planning, preparation, and carrying out of the meeting. My writing is interrupted by a student who wishes to discuss some problems related to my course which he is taking, and now I am implicated in a social act that represents a segment of the academic process. Even with regard to that self-destructive behavior of stopping to smoke a cigarette, a case can be made out for its implication within a social act.

Illustrations are readily offered, but the attempt to define the concept technically reveals its ambiguities. Ignoring the ambiguities for the moment, however, some of the general features of the social act may be indicated. First, the concept refers to an abstraction from a continuous social process. Most social acts are intricately interwoven with many other acts and it is only by abstraction that a given instance may be singled out for observation. Second, a social act is conceived as having a beginning and ending even though it is difficult to define these boundaries in specific cases. Third, social acts may be subsumed within larger social acts and in certain respects it is arbitrary as to which segment one chooses to give attention.

Fourth and most important is the assumption that the social act is goal-directed or functional for the group and that individual acts will tend to be coordinated toward the fulfilment of the function. It is further assumed that people are capable of recognizing the social act which each situation implies as well as their respective role in each act. Alternatively, it is assumed that if the definition of the social act is not pre-established, but interaction continues, the participants will seek to define the social act. Viewed in this way, the social process is constituted not of a network of individual behaviors but of a network of social acts within which individual behaviors are organized.

Beyond these basic notions there are some important variations of conception. Mead said little or nothing about changes in the social act which may be induced by the accompanying social interaction, assuming rather its prior organization in a relatively stable form. By contrast, it seems clear that Blumer regards social acts as representing highly fluid situations in which the coordination of action is something attained rather than something given.[2] A distinction thus arises between the structured as opposed to fluid conception of social acts.

In discussing these same problems, Cottrell has expressed a preference for the concept of *the situation* over that of the social act,[3] perhaps because the former is more general in meaning covering all the variations that may come to mind. There are two reasons why we have reversed the choice. The problems which we find interesting concern those interpersonal relations in which the participants adapt, or attempt to adapt, their behavior to each other in an effort to move along some directionally oriented course. The concept of the situation fails to suggest the idea of joint action and is also a more diffuse reference that may imply non-social as well as social situations. On the other hand, the social act, as an analogy to the idea of the individual act, implies both motivation and coordination of group action. Second, if the concept of the social act is often unsatisfactory because of its ambiguities, one may solve the problem by wielding Occam's Razor. There are many social acts which are relatively well organized and stable, and where the ambiguities of definition are minimal. Initially, observation may be restricted to these relatively clearly defined instances. Social psychology may perhaps first learn to walk by solving interaction problems in these relatively uncomplex settings, and later learn to run.

IMPLICATIONS

The question of why anyone should interest himself in the concept still remains for consideration. Three examples are cited of how this way of viewing interaction problems may yield interesting consequences.

[2] See, for example, Herbert Blumer, "Psychological Import of the Human Group," in Muzafer Sherif and M. O. Wilson (eds.), *Group Relations at the Crossroads*, New York: Harper and Brothers, 1953, pp. 193–197.

[3] Cottrell, "Some Neglected Problems in Social Psychology," *op. cit.* p. 711f.

If the assumption is accepted that socially meaningful relations generally take place within the context of social acts, it would seem that such processes as self-conceptualization, role definition, and definition of expectations, which are usually considered significant aspects of interactional processes, must be affected by the specific social acts within which these defining processes occur. There is, in fact, one area of social psychological research in which the latter view has come to be accepted. Leadership studies of an earlier day concentrated on generalized personal traits or personality types which might be found associated with leadership. The inconclusive findings of these studies, plus the impact of other investigations which showed that a leader in one situation might turn out a nonleader in another, has led to the currently accepted proposition that leadership is a function of the situation.[4] Probably a better formulation of the proposition remains to be stated. Nevertheless, there appears to be a fair amount of validity to the proposition that, to put the matter in our terms, leadership is functionally related to the social act.

This kind of interpretation, however, has to date made relatively little impress upon other areas of interaction research. For example, Gough in his use of the adjective check-list for defining the self-concept takes account of situational variations in self-definition, but the primary aim of his research seems directed toward determining the generalized self-conception of each of his subjects.[5] Similarly, Dymond in her study of empathic ability implies a generalized empathic ability,[6] but the example of an American trying to empathize with a Chinese in Peiping should suggest the element of situational specificity in empathic ability. That is, to my knowledge there is at present no widely held view that self-conception, empathic ability, role definitions, and other components of social interaction are functions of the situation. Indeed, the research evidence with which to accept or reject such a proposition is lacking. If the

[4] Cecil A. Gibb, "Leadership," in Gardner Lindzey (ed.), *Handbook of Social Psychology, Vol. II*, Cambridge, Mass.: Addison-Wesley Publishing Co., 1954, especially pp. 913–917.

[5] Harrison G. Gough, *Reference Handbook for the Gough Adjective Check-list*, Berkeley: The University of California Institute of Personality Assessment and Research (Mimeographed), April, 1955.

[6] Rosalind F. Dymond, "A Scale for the Measurement of Empathic Ability," *Journal of Consulting Psychology*, 13 (April, 1949), pp. 127–133.

proposition is true, however, it may account for a good deal of the unexplained variance often found in correlations between self-concept or empathic ability and certain criterion variables. Our suggestion is that the problem of the generalized as opposed to the situationally specific aspects of the self-concept, roles, and norms may be solved by research on these phenomena within the context of defined social acts.

Research on the social act should also illuminate a type of problem to which Theodore Newcomb has given attention in his article "The Communicative Act."[7] Using a communication model involving two persons, A and B, and an object of reference, X, Newcomb derives an hypothesis such as the following:

> The stronger the forces toward A's co-orientation in respect to B and X, (a) the greater A's strain toward symmetry with B in respect to X; and (b) the greater the likelihood of increased symmetry as a consequence of one or more communicative acts.[8]

The proposition is difficult to express more simply, for the term "co-orientation" is not clearly defined. Symmetry may be translated readily to mean agreement, but co-orientation refers to some meaning such as interdependence. Hence, the proposition may be interpreted to mean that the greater the interdependence between A, B, and X, the greater the strain toward agreement between A and B with respect to X, where communication occurs. Newcomb's main concern is to derive other hypotheses regarding symmetry from this basic postulate.

Newcomb seems fully aware that the concept of co-orientation is necessary to his model, yet he remains inordinately vague regarding the meaning of the term. We would suggest that the most significant way in which co-orientation occurs is by the joint definition by a number of persons of a social act situation. When people participate in a social act there is interdependence of the members as well as pressure to communicate, both of which are implied in the idea of co-orientation. Furthermore, where Newcomb speaks of the "forces toward co-orientation" we might substitute the idea

[7] Theodore M. Newcomb, "An Approach to the Study of Communicative Acts," *Psychological Review*, 60 (November, 1953), pp. 393–404.
[8] *Ibid.*, p. 396.

of forces toward participating in given social acts. If a typology of social acts can be established, it would be possible to determine for a given group those social acts in which the forces for participation are strong and those for which the forces are weak. In short, it seems possible to reduce the vagaries of Newcomb's model by specifying social acts as the context of communicative acts.

Finally, with regard to social organization, the central subject matter of sociology, one could elaborate at length on a conception of social organization as a network of social acts. However, I prefer to devote the limited space to a quick look at the related topic of social disorganization. In the framework of the present discussion, the obvious conception of social disorganization that comes to mind is that of a situation in which a group of people are unable to carry out social acts; that is, there is insufficient coordination of action to maintain organized social relations. For example, we speak of mental disorder and alcoholism as disorganizing in a family because they interfere with the coordination of member actions for the fulfilment of normal family expectations. Social disorganization may also be viewed in another way. The non-social and erratic behavior of the mentally disordered and the alcoholic are often the products of an organized social process. That is, there are social acts by which people become intoxicated and there are others by which people become personally disorganized. There are also those intriguing instances of social acts called intergroup conflict in which the actions of one group produce predictable and, in a sense, coordinate but opposed responses on the part of the other. One suspects that the appropriate formulation of disorganization problems in terms of social acts may lead to added understanding of the organized processes which yield social disorganization.

SOME PROBLEMS FOR INVESTIGATION

If social acts are to be studied profitably, it will be necessary to have some method of identifying them and an appropriate conceptual scheme for their analysis. Unfortunately, I have no ready-made scheme to offer. My purpose, therefore, will be to indicate some of the directions in which I believe the answers are to be found.

The basic assumption regarding social acts is that they represent organized social processes with respect to which people orient their behavior and coordinate their actions. This leads us to assume, further, that people must be able to arrive at common definitions of social acts.

The assumption of common definitions of situations, however, seems contradicted by the studies of perception variability and particularly by the findings in the recent study of role consensus by Gross, McEachern, and Mason.[9] In their study of role definitions among school superintendents and school board members in Massachusetts, the authors emphasize the variability of role definitions which occur within each group as well as between them. That variability of situational definitions occurs seems undeniable. It is consistent with the present argument to expect differences of definition as situations vary. However, these studies do not exclude the possibility that in the organized relations of people certain common perceptions and common definitions will be found present. Reversing the problem of variability of consensus posed by Gross and associates, we ask whether a minimal consensual basis will be found wherever people are engaged in a social act.

Fritz Heider in his recent work, *The Psychology of Interpersonal Relations*, deals with problems which, although primarily psychological in formulation, bear directly on these issues.[10] Heider, whose forte is perception psychology, begins by pointing to the fact of perception constancy. He would say, for example, that this sheet of paper which I hold before you is seen by you as a rectangular sheet, 8½ by 11 inches in size, but that if you were responding only to the light stimuli reaching you at your respective positions most of you could not possibly see it as a rectangle nor as anything so large. That is, psychologically we impose invariances upon the variability of stimuli which reach us, and those attributes of objects which dispose them to manifest themselves as invariant and predictable he calls "psychological dispositional properties." Size, shape and color are among the invariant properties of physical objects. Heider's concern in this work is to ascertain the psychological dispositional

---

[9] Neal Gross, Ward S. Mason, and Alexander McEachern, *Explorations in Role Analysis: Studies of the School Superintendency Role*, New York: John Wiley & Sons, 1957.

[10] Fritz Heider, *The Psychology of Interpersonal Relations*, New York: John Wiley & Sons, 1958.

properties in interpersonal relations. Using common-sense psychology for data and what Newcomb calls "a cultivated naivete," Heider searches out the psychological dispositional properties of such everyday concepts as *can, trying, wanting, suffering, sentiment, belonging,* and *ought.*

The cultivated naivete of Heider's work is too sophisticated for summary presentation here, but the implications of his study for our discussion may be obvious. Social acts are historical events and as with history we might say that "a social act never repeats itself." Moreover, a social act may possess incredible complexity and variability. Nevertheless, people are able to coordinate action in even very complex social acts. We assume that this is possible because of a sufficient consensual basis for joint action. We further assume that the sufficient consensual basis will be found in the dispositional properties of social acts and of interpersonal relations.

Heider, unfortunately, deliberately set aside consideration of sociological problems and therefore provides no blueprint of the dispositional properties of social acts. His method, however, may be directly applicable to our problem. He took common sense words, grammatical structure, and ways of thinking as primary data, and then looked for invariant properties among them. Similarly, social acts may perhaps be studied by examining the common sense verbal identifications which are made of them and by searching for the psychological dispositional properties (or perhaps we should say "sociological dispositional properties") to be found in the verbal characterizations of social acts.

To take a simple illustration, we generally have little difficulty distinguishing between communicative acts which are very hostile from those which are friendly. We should like to know what the psychological dispositional properties are by which these two situations are distinguished.

The obvious answer may be that communications which are very hostile employ entirely different words from those used in friendly social relations and that the difference of meaning is readily apprehended. There are occasions of social conversation, however, when people jokingly speak and act as if they were very hostile, but despite the antagonistic format of the communicated matter, there may be no doubt that the statement is made as a friendly gesture. Pursuing this line of inquiry, one would be led into a Heiderian type of analysis with regard to the psychological dispositional properties in the intentions of communicators, the segment of life space which the act occupies, the sentiments and values expressed, and so on. What may result from such a mode of analysis cannot be foreseen, but one suspects that by treating social acts as perceptual objects in the commonsense field, a fruitful application may be made of Heider's method.[11]

If it is possible to identify social acts we should then be able to solve another problem, namely, the typing of social acts. The idea of typologizing social acts and identifying their invariant properties is not at all new. Some years ago LaPiere in his *Collective Behavior* devoted major attention to classifying and describing the basic characteristics of the cultural, recreational, control, and escape types of social interaction and their subtypes.[12] His work still remains the most comprehensive treatment of the subject.

Typologies, however, prove sterile when their relevance for problems fails to be demonstrated. To help insure relevance, two things might be done. First, instead of employing an objectively derived scheme of classification, types recognized in common sense might be used. Second, the typology of social acts should be developed with respect to defined social settings, such as the family, industry, or any setting in which fairly definite group objectives may occur. It then becomes meaningful to ask what function each type of social act serves. For example, although the typology developed by Slater[13] distinguishing the "idea men" and "best-liked men" in small group relations has more to do with the differentiation of roles than of social acts, his study suggests analogically that social acts of the task variety as opposed to those emphasizing socio-emotional reactions may serve related but different functions within a given social process. Typologies of this type may be limited but

---

[11] For examples of work in this direction see Roger G. Barker and Herbert F. Wright, *Midwest and Its Children*, Evanston, Ill.: Row, Peterson and Co., 1955, and Nelson Foote, "Concept and Method in the Study of Human Development," in Muzafer Sherif and M. O. Wilson (eds.), *Emerging Problems in Social Psychology*, Norman, Oklahoma: Institute of Group Relations, University of Oklahoma, 1957, pp. 29–49.

[12] Richard T. LaPiere, *Collective Behavior*, New York: McGraw-Hill Book Co., 1938.

[13] Philip E. Slater, "Role Differentiation in Small Groups," *American Sociological Review*, 20 (June, 1955), pp. 300–310.

they have the virtue of relevance in research and should in time provide the basis for more inclusive schemes.

Finally, the main purpose in studying social acts is to permit a less segmented approach to the study of social interaction. The basic idea underlying this paper is the belief that when social acts are identified as distinct entities the accompanying interaction then can be carefully observed from beginning to end, as Bales has done. Unlike Bales, however, it would be necessary to inquire how the participants defined the situation and to inquire further how this perception affects their action in the given context.

In addition, instead of studying self-conceptions, role definitions, and empathizing in the abstract, they would be investigated in their native habitat, within the social act. In particular, inquiry would be directed at the question of how these components are affected by the particular kind of social act within which they occur. Nor would the approach preclude the possibility that generalized aspects of self-conception, role definitions, and the like might be uncovered, but the generalization would not be brought into existence by fiat and the generalized conception would have a known relationship to the situationally specific aspects of these components.

The suggested approach should be acceptable even for those who emphasize, as does Nelson Foote, "The uncertainty of every outcome . . . (the) exploratory, formulative, creative in every observable episode." [14] Even highly fluid social acts must be held together by some bonds and our guess is that these bonds have their basis in the invariant properties which we have hypothesized. The question then concerns the relationship between the invariant properties and the variable conditions.

SUMMARY

The modest aim of this paper has been to emphasize again the need for research on the organized character of the interactional process. It has suggested that the social process can, with some arbitrariness to be sure, be divided into definable units which some have called "interaction episodes." More than this, however, this paper urges the development of methods by which to identify the

[14] Foote, *op. cit.*, p. 36.

definitions of social acts which we assume occur phenomenally in people. It then should be possible to determine how such definitions affect, or fail to affect, roles, self-concept, and other apparatus of interaction; and this kind of knowledge, it would seem, might give us some fairly basic understanding of organized social process.

It will be obvious to you that the ideas expressed here are extremely traditional. What is suggested, however, is that a number of lines of thinking—including those of Leonard Cottrell, Nelson Foote, R. E. L. Faris, Robert F. Bales, Theodore Newcomb, Fritz Heider, and Barker and Wright—appear to be converging again upon this traditional problem. There is this difference, however, that in the intervening period since the classical writings a slow but certain accumulation of social psychological knowledge has taken place that provides us with new ideas and instruments with which to explore the area. One wonders if the time may not be ripe to launch a thorough re-exploration of this traditional problem.

SUGGESTED READINGS

ORVILLE G. BRIM, JR. Personality Development as Role-Learning, in Ira Iscoe and Harold W. Stevenson (Eds.), *Personality Development in Children*, University of Texas Press, Austin, Tex., 1960, pp. 127–159.

WALTER COUTU. Role-playing vs. Role-taking: An Appeal for Clarification, *American Sociological Review*, 16: 180–184, 1951.

NEIL GROSS, WARD S. MASON, and ALEXANDER W. McEACHERN. *Exploration in Role Analysis*, John Wiley and Sons, Inc., New York, 1958.

MANFORD H. KUHN. The Reference Group Reconsidered, *Sociological Quarterly*, 5: 6–21, 1964.

DANIEL J. LEVINSON. Role, Personality, and Social Structure in the Organizational Setting, *Journal of Abnormal and Social Psychology*, 58: 170–180, 1959.

THEODORE M. NEWCOMB. An Approach to the Study of Communicative Acts, *Psychological Review*, 60: 393–404, 1953.

MICHAEL S. OLMSTED. Character and Social Role, *American Journal of Sociology*, 63: 49–57, 1958.

SAMUEL STOUFFER and JACKSON TOBY. Role Conflict and Personality, *American Journal of Sociology*, 56: 395–406, 1951.

RALPH H. TURNER. Role-taking, Role Standpoint, and Reference-Group Behavior, *American Journal of Sociology*, 61: 316–328, 1956.

Part IV

Issues and Problems

In this section, Turner raises some basic issues regarding the sociological study of personality. He considers the consequences of building theory and basing research on the assumption that society activates a latent personality structure that evolves along predetermined dimensions as opposed to the assumption that society actually creates the dimensions along which personality varies. Turner also raises the question of what distinguishes personality from other forms of behavior and presents several criteria for personality classification. The question of the relationship between society and personality, which was raised in a number of other selections in this volume, is also explored in detail.

The paper by Yinger is concerned with the distinction between personality theories from a sociological standpoint and from a psychological standpoint. It is Yinger's contention that progress in the development of an adequate sociological theory of personality has been hampered by the tendency to extend the concepts and research designs of psychology and sociology rather than to develop concepts on a level intermediate to these disciplines. His aim is to describe a multidisciplinary approach to personality and to indicate its value in certain situations, especially those prevailing in changing and heterogeneous societies. The approach is designed so that it takes account simultaneously of individual tendencies and structural influences.

The final paper, by Spitzer and Swanson, presents a brief history of the development of sociological thought on personality and reviews some of the major directions that contemporary theory and research in sociology are taking.

11

The Problem of Social Dimensions in Personality*

RALPH H. TURNER

CLOSED AND OPEN SYSTEM MODELS

No one today seriously discounts the impact of culture and society in the formation of personality, nor denies the fruitfulness of a search for differences in modal personality types among cultures and subcultures. There is dispute over the extent and nature of such differences and the character of the causal principles linking personality to society, but the relationship itself has become axiomatic.

Nevertheless, in the study of sociocultural determinants of personality an implicit assumption is frequently made which precludes what might be the sociologist's major contribution to the field. Personality is treated as a psychogenically closed system which society activates but does not structure. Social environment selects from among the predetermined ways in which the organism can function and determines the rate of function. Because societies activate the several dimensions of personality at varying rates, there is considerable range in modal configurations. The differences are nevertheless reducible to varying combinations of rates for the same set of personality variables.

The closed system model resembles a piece of machinery which is designed to perform a set of tasks and each of which tasks is controlled by specific intake devices. At any given moment an organism can be usefully regarded as such a closed system, capable only of a repertoire of responses and capable of being activated only by

---

* By permission, from Ralph Turner, "The Problem of Social Dimension in Personality," *Pacific Sociological Review*, 4: 57–62, 1961. Paper presented at the annual meeting of the American Sociological Association, St. Louis, 1961.

stimuli which are suited to its activators. But such sociological and anthropological study of personality assumes that the character of the closed system is independent of culture, especially with respect to the dimensions of functioning, if not of intake. From the early studies in the ecology of mental disorders to recent research in social psychiatry the problem has been defined as discovering a relationship between a sociological variable and a preestablished psychiatric type. Culture-personality studies and research into personality characteristics of social classes and age and sex subcultures have likewise sought a fit between a group dimension and a pre-validated personality classification. The social science investigator typically employs an instrument which has been designed to measure or classify personalities according to some established psychological school of thought.[1] The sociologist, who cannot claim competency in deciding which psychological theories of personality are correct, must nevertheless choose, running the risk that his own work will be rendered irrelevant when the tides of thought in psychology change.

The point of our discussion can best be grasped by considering the accomplishment and limitation of the modal character approach to culture-personality study. Investigations which compare the frequency of given personality configurations in various societies depend upon the assumption that their types or variables are equally valid in each of the societies. Implicitly denied from the start is the assumption that what societies do is to *organize* the complex of behavior in distinctive ways. The personalities of the Zuni looked amazingly uniform to Ruth Benedict, leading her to describe a modal type which probably reflected her experience with variation inside of American culture.[2] The apparent uniformity may have been an artifact of the failure of Zuni society to differentiate personality into the types and along the dimensions most common in Western society. At the same time, Zuni society may have differentiated personality along other dimensions to which the western observer was not sensitized by his own culture. The modal personal-

---

[1] Daniel Miller phrases the approach in typical fashion when he suggests that the problem in cross-cultural investigation is to know which of the systems to select from a standard psychological text on personality. Cf. "Personality and Social Interaction," in *Studying Personality Cross-Culturally*, Bert Kaplan, ed., Evanston, Ill.: Row, Peterson, 1961, p. 271.

[2] *Patterns of Culture*, Boston: Houghton Mifflin, 1934.

ity approach then diverts attention from the possibility that culture may create the dimensions along which personality varies, because of its preoccupation with finding one or more dimensions on which societies can be compared.

An instructive example is supplied by Thomas and Znaniecki's discussion of the Philistine, Bohemian, and Creative types of social character.[3] While these types are offered as products of a universal socialization process, the authors comment, "An unavoidable consequence of the now prevalent social organization is that the immense majority of individuals is forced either into Philistinism or Bohemianism." The competition among many rival complexes for the individual's conformity violates the requirements of personal integrity. The individual then either adheres to one scheme hypocritically, or continually passes from one unsatisfactory system to another. Thus Thomas and Znaniecki describe a type of society in which people tend to be differentiated along a Philistine-Bohemian dimension, leaving unstated the implication that in a differently ordered society character structures might be organized along other dimensions. In light of their speculation it might be more fruitful to compare societies in which the Bohemian-Philistine differentiation is marked with those in which there is little consistent differentiation of this kind, than to compare societies according to the degree of Bohemianism and Philistinism.

Confusion about the proper dependence upon ultimately psychological and neuropsychological concepts sometimes derives from failure to distinguish between the study of elementary psychological processes and the organization of personality. The study of personality is distinctive chiefly because its object is the *organization* of behavior in individuals. One could hardly defend a conception of infinite malleability which denies a set of common human psychological processes. But organization at the *person* level—the characteristic orientations of persons toward social objects—cannot be inferred directly from a knowledge of elementary neural properties, and consequently need not be uniform from society to society.

Our object in this paper is to suggest that sociologists can make a useful contribution by testing the assumption which is normally implicit. In order to test the assumption, investigators must formu-

[3] Edmund H. Volkart, ed., *Social Behavior and Personality*, New York: Social Science Research Council, 1951, p. 185.

late hypotheses which precede from the opposite axiom, and from some conception of the social processes of personality organization. If such hypotheses are consistently refuted, the model of the psychogenically closed system may be followed with greater assurance. If the hypotheses are confirmed, an extensive area of investigation will have been opened up. Beginning with an examination of the criteria by which we identify dimensions and type of personality we shall suggest clues to probable relationships between social structure and the nature of personality organization.

THE BASES FOR PERSONALITY CLASSIFICATION

Treatment of personality always takes its reference from behavior, observed or hypothesized. But personality study looks at behavior in a distinctive fashion which supplies the criteria for useful classifications of personality. First, a personality variable or type refers to some observable *consistency* in behavior. An unrepeated type of action is not in itself made the basis for establishing a dimension or type of personality, and the dimensions we make the basis of personality theory reflect areas in which considerable behavioral consistency has been noted on the part of large segments of the population.

Second, categories of personality incorporate interrelatednesses of behavior. A *constellation* of behaviors is implied, such that if you observe one or two elements of the constellation in an individual you also expect to find the others. A concept such as the authoritarian personality, for example, would be totally without justification except for the assumption that its various elements are predictable from one another.[4]

A third criterion for a category in personality analysis is that it must *differentiate* people.

Fourth, we apply a criterion of *significance* to the behavior whose consistency, interrelatednesses, and interpersonal differentiation are the bases for a personality category. From time to time the Sunday supplements amuse us by noting that we probably are consistent

[4] Theodore Adorno, et al., *The Authoritarian Personality*, New York: Harper, 1950, esp. pp. 224–241.

about which sock we put on first, and that this is related to how we get into an automobile, etc. But we do not make such regularities a basis for personality study because the behavior is not of a kind which has much effect on the behavior of other people. We study authoritarianism, introversion, ego-strength, because they denote configurations of behavior which make a difference in interaction with others. Significant behavior is behavior which others notice, consider important, and characteristically respond to by an adjustment in their own behavior.

Fifth, we distinguish between personality and mere conformity to the norms of position. For example, on a ritual occasion two military officers may display equally commanding behavior, but we discount this as concealing true personality differences, and look to their behavior when they are off their ceremonial guard. This criterion is merely an extension of the requirement that personality categories differentiate persons rather than positions, but is worthy of special stress because it leads us to some crucial observations about the social sources of personality organization.

There is a rather simple moral from this list of criteria for categories of personality. The study of personality should be in large part the study of sources and processes of organization of behavior. If we are to search for the dynamics which account for the peculiar structure which personality exhibits, we must look for them in the sources of consistency, interrelatedness of behavior, differentiation among individuals, and significance. If we can locate important causes of consistency in behavior, we shall have discovered some of the dynamic factors accounting for the organization of personality. The same observation applies to the other criteria.

SOCIAL SOURCES OF PERSONALITY ORGANIZATION

Cultural choice and personality

The fifth criterion for personality classification is a good starting point for specifying probable relationships. When we discounted ceremonial behavior as an indicator of personality, saying that one soldier was a decisive and commanding sort of person and the other a weak person underneath the surface, we assumed that there were other occasions when such differences would be reflected in behavior. But a society in which there is considerable achieved status may be necessary for such a notion of personality as the *real*, the *underlying tendency*, to emerge. When human behavior is dominated by ascribed status the opportunities for a person to behave in non-ritual circumstances in a way which can be recognized as weakness or strength will be fewer and less important than in American society. The opportunity to undergo systematic learning of a pattern of behavior inconsistent with the ascribed role will be less well developed and a conception of the "real self" or "real personality" hidden behind public behavior is likely to be less salient than it is in our theorizing about personality.

The foregoing observation suggests one determinant of personality organization. Personality dimensions form about areas of choice, where the culture is permissive, either by explicit value or by default. Stated another way, personality dimensions are related to the lines of slack in the social order. Where the culture is entirely compelling and behavior is defined precisely, the possibility for personality dimensions to arise is severely limited.

An example which may be germane to this principle is the importance of the domination-submission theme in the study of personality in the United States and some western societies. Almost every system for the study of personality devised in the United States has emphasized variations of some sort about the idea of domination among its major variables. In Winch's study of mate selection the "needs" which conform to the complementarity hypothesis are generally those related to a dimension of assertiveness and receptiveness.[5] But the variable of ascendance, dominance, assertiveness, etc. may be less crucial in personality differentiation in other societies. There may be less consistency along this dimension outside of ritual situations, fewer other variables may cluster about it, it may be a less significant variable in interaction. The preoccupation with questions of relative dominance in the family and in marital relations in the American family is likewise exceptional, and arises from the undefined character of dominance. The result is that instead of the individual moving smoothly according to cultural dictate between situations demanding dominance and situ-

[5] Robert Winch, *Mate Selection*, New York: Harper, 1958.

ations demanding submission in his relations with different categories of people, he learns a predominantly dominant or predominantly submissive orientation which becomes his characteristic stance to such a degree that it impinges upon his ability to perform in situations where the proper dominance is unambiguously defined.[6]

Organization of Socializing Experiences

The first criterion of personality organization which we suggested was consistency of behavior. The most general social and cultural sources of consistency are of two kinds. One of these is exposure to a consistent sequence of socializing experiences, but experiences which are consistently different from those of some other persons. The second is the presence of cultural values which sensitize self and other disproportionately to some facets of behavior. These sources supply further clues to the social correlates of personality differentiation.

Socialization takes place through a succession of many experiences in many relationships. If the result is some personal consistency the explanation must be that threads of consistency run through these experiences. The parent-child relationship may be as important as we suppose it is chiefly because of its continuity in the life of the individual. The social organization helps to determine which aspects of the socializing relationship between parent and child will be most consistent and which least consistent, which elements of the relationship will be grouped, and what the major alternative groupings will be. The socializing agent's relationship to the socializee is shaped in large part by what responsibilities he performs outside of the socializing relationship and the timing of these activities. Consistencies, then, will be determined by the alternative patterns of extra-socializing tasks and by the alternative systems of combining the tasks with the socialization relationship.

The axes of consistency will also vary according to the concentra-

[6] Margaret Mead has noted a difference of this sort in Samoa. "Such a man does not develop a fixed response to others which is definitely either dominance or submission, leadership or discipleship, authoritarian insistence or meek compliance, exhibitionism or refusal to play any public part; the multiplicity and contrast between his roles prevent any commitment to one personality type from developing." *Cooperation and Competition Among Primitive Peoples*, New York: McGraw-Hill, 1937, p. 296.

tion or dispersion of socializing responsibility, and the generality or specialization in socializing relationships. Many anthropologists have called attention to the difference in modal personality produced in the extended family relationship as compared with the nuclear system.[7] But a systematic exploration of alternate modes of adaptation by the child to each of the two kinds of family relationship might supply the framework for discovering different axes of personality organization. A family system such as the Trobriand Islanders, which makes a sharp differentiation between the indulgent father and the stern uncle, might be examined from this standpoint.

Major Values and Self-Conception

The idea of a self-conception which brings some order into personality on the basis of self-other relationships is commonplace for sociologists. Sociologists are also aware that it is not only an internal strain for consistency which is at work.[8] Only if the individual's behavior is sufficiently orderly that others can make minimal predictions will the responses of the others be sufficiently predictable to the individual that he can exercise some control over his social environment. Because ability to control others depends upon being sufficiently predictable oneself, the individual early acquires some consistent organized orientations toward social objects. The orderliness in behavior of which we speak is designated by values. The interactive pressures toward consistency are therefore organized according to the major types of value differentiation made in a society. In accordance with the predominant modal personality approach we have excellent studies which attempt to relate dominant value to modal personality, but few to the internal differentiation of personality types in response to specific values.[9]

The range of deviant personality types is relevant here. Margaret Mead in a pioneering study called attention to the absence of the

[7] Cf. Dorothea Leighton and Clyde Kluckhohn, *Children of the People*, Cambridge: Harvard University Press, 1947, pp. 42–49.

[8] Prescott Lecky, *Self-Consistency: A Theory of Personality*, New York: Island Press, 1951.

[9] Among the interesting exceptions to this observation is Raymond A. Bauer's discussion of two alternate forms of adaptation in "The Psychology of the Soviet Middle Elite: Two Case Histories," in *Personality in Nature, Society, and Culture*, eds., Clyde Kluckhohn and Henry A. Murray, New York: Knopf, 1953, pp. 633–650.

type of homosexuality with which we are acquainted in American society in some of the primitive groups she studied.[10] One notable feature of the berdache appears to be the absence of polarization into active and passive roles among homosexuals to which we are accustomed. Here may be an example of a type of personality differentiation which arises out of one way of valuing and treating homosexuality which does not arise out of another.

Many of our classifications of personality convey implicitly a favorable or unfavorable valuation. This frequently embarrassing observation may not stem from tendencies in the investigator to import his values into the investigation, but from the impact of values upon the formation of consistencies and clusters of behavior during socialization. If socialization serves chiefly to make the individual predictable, if the major basis of predictability is personal consistency, and if the most important axes of predictability are major values, there is good reason to expect useful personality dimensions to be value-loaded.

Major Divisions of Labor

In discussing the two previous facets of social structure we have emphasized the sources of consistency in behavior. We can also uncover clues from the sources of tendencies for behavior to form constellations. The major divisions of labor supply an important basis for linkages of behavior. While the more refined specialties of labor may not appear until adolescence or adulthood, there are some pervasive divisions for which children are prepared early in life. Each such division separates a large variety of behavior into a few sets, creating the expectation with supporting social pressure that an individual will pattern his behavior principally from one of the clusters rather than randomly from all.

A review of correlational studies would undoubtedly reveal that a large proportion of the dimensions and types employed in personality analysis are associated with the sex of the individual. As long as the personality variables are assumed to derive their structure from the psychogenic properties of the organism, interpretation of such relationships is the conventional problem of understanding

[10] *Sex and Temperament in Three Primitive Societies*, New York: William Morrow & Co., 1934, pp. 290–309.

correlations between two independent variables. But alternatively, such correlations may reveal that social definitions of sex roles have helped to account for the organization of behavior into the clusters which are being employed in the personality analysis. The more pervasive the division of labor between the sexes the wider the range of behaviors which will be associated and the more strongly they will be associated with the sex division.

Thorsten Veblen, in *The Instinct for Workmanship*, develops the theory that the dominant type of occupation in any era created a general outlook on life and approach to the natural and social world.[11] These dominant occupations also probably establish a fundamental set of dimensions which serve as a reference in the organization of personality. Again, the discovery that many personality characteristics bear some correlation with occupation may be partly the discovery of one of the sources of the prevailing differentiations of personality.

Instrumental Consequences of Roles

The other important way in which social organization leads to the grouping of behaviors is through attaching instrumental consequences to the performance of various roles. A highly speculative account of how such linking of characteristics might take place can be suggested, not for its intrinsic merit but as an example of the kinds of possibilities worth exploring. The introversion-extraversion dimension is one which rests empirically upon the clustering of several kinds of tendencies. The extravert, for example, prefers sociability to solitude, prefers action to reflection, and is insensitive to minor slights and unfavorable reactions. While Jungian theory interrelates these and other elements on the basis of the psychogenic character of the organism, there is room for alternate hypotheses. The last few centuries in western civilization have been a period in which traditional social controls have been weakened so that the individual who is moderately insensitive to disapproval from others is a "favored" type. Because of the reward structure, such an individual develops self-confidence and is prepared to act readily and is comfortable in the presence of others. In a society in which sensitivity to others was an asset rather than a liability, the same cor-

[11] *The Instinct for Workmanship*, New York: B. W. Huebsch, 1918.

relations might be lacking. If American society is swinging, as Reisman proposes, from inner direction to other direction, the interrelationship among these elements should be altered in the process. The change would mean not principally that introversion or extraversion would become less common, but that the clustering of forms of behavior necessary to justify the use of such a concept would be altered.

The object of offering these five points has been to demonstrate that a plausible case can be made for the position that the dimensions along which personality is organized may vary with the society. The five general relationships can serve as a starting point for hypotheses which can be used to test whether the usual axiom or the alternative view best fits actual situations.

RELATIONSHIP BETWEEN SOCIOGENIC AND PSYCHOGENIC

Separation Between Levels

At this point account must be taken of criticisms lodged against excessive social determinism by such writers as Inkeles[12] and Wrong.[13] Wrong's criticisms apply largely to an overly simplistic conception of socialization as a process whereby individuals are fitted into a cultural mold, rather than learning to take account of society and culture systematically in their behavior. Inkeles asserts that some psychological theory must be assumed in the sociological study of personality. Both of these criticisms indicate that sociological studies of personality cannot merely ignore the psychogenic system of organization in personality. The presence of two levels of organization means that behavior will never be wholly predictable on the basis of socio-cultural personality variables. We have approached the problem of this paper by searching for the sources of consistency, interrelatedness, and significance in behavior; clearly

[12] "Personality and Social Structure," in *Sociology Today*, eds., Robert K. Merton, Leonard Broom, and Leonard S. Cottrell, Jr., New York: Basic Books, 1959, pp. 249–276.
[13] "The Oversocialized Conception of Man in Modern Sociology," *American Sociological Review*, 26 (April, 1961), pp. 183–193.

there are such sources in the nature of the organism as well as in social structure. The knotty problem is therefore the nature of the relationship between the levels of organization, and what account must be taken of each in study of the other.

One approach to this problem is to show that processes at the two levels correspond so as to produce the same set of dimensions. Talcott Parsons' examination of the differentiation of roles during socialization is a monumental effort to establish such a relationship.[14] While such careful logic cannot easily be discounted, the solution seems too easy. It seems improbable that the dynamics of one level should correspond to those at another unless one is merely an extension of the other.

Earlier Ernest Burgess dealt with this problem imaginatively in his distinction between the psychogenically determined "personality type" and the sociogenically determined "social type."[15] While the two levels do not correspond, the effective adoption of a social type depends upon its supplying avenues for expression of the personality type. Thus the psychogenic is causally prior and less flexible, and while it does not determine directly the sociogenic level it sets limits within which sociogenic processes must operate. The problem in Burgess' analysis, however, is that the psychogenic includes too much and the sociogenic too little. The sociogenic is limited to the adoption of culturally identified roles, and the psychogenic includes such obviously social learning as a characteristic reaction to authority and supervision. With a more comprehensive conception of the sociogenic, the Burgess hypothesis remains a highly promising approach to this problem.

Whatever the functioning relationship between the levels of personality, the recognition of intrinsically social dimensions of organization suggests the principle that homogeneity at one level may correspond to heterogeneity at the other. This principle can be most simply illustrated through the generalizing effect of culture. The "favored personality" concept indicates that attitudes which have one dynamic in the individual who serves as model may be

[14] Talcott Parsons and Robert F. Bales, *Family, Socialization and Interaction Process*, Glencoe, Ill.: Free Press, 1955, pp. 35–257.

[15] "Discussion," in Clifford R. Shaw, *The Jackroller*, Chicago: University of Chicago Press, 1930, pp. 184–197.

emulated by others who lack these dynamics.[16] The parent who has a set of attitudes because of her own unique psychological dynamics may transmit them to her children without the original dynamics. Thus the system of orientations toward social objects may be homogenous but the psychogenic constellations heterogeneous.

An interesting correspondence can be found between Horney's neurotic with his need to be loved and to control and Riesman's other-directed man.[17] The two sets of symptomatic descriptions are largely variations on a common theme. But Horney calls her type neurotic and discovers its dynamics in a reaction to the sense of isolation and powerlessness which arises in consequence of competitiveness. Reisman's type, on the other hand, is assertedly functional to our society and arises through the normal processes of social transmission. Is it possible that the two views accurately reflect the situation as it prevailed two decades apart. Perhaps the pattern developed first as Horney specifies, and then became subject to the generalizing impact of culture so that it now may be acquired with or without the dynamics described by Horney. If this were so we could reasonably observe that the socially homogeneous other-directed personality type need not correspond to any strictly psychological type. By this reasoning the discovery of small correlations, such as those in the monumental authoritarian personality studies, need not supply any clue to the determination of a socially important personality type.

Perhaps such observations can help to shed light on the debate over Durkheim's famous assertion that a social fact must always be explained by a social fact.[18] Durkheim's social facts correspond to the organization of behavior at the sociogenic level. The organization of behavior at this level bears a stable relationship only to causes at that level. Relationships to other levels are fortuitous and impermanent, though none-the-less important while they exist. Theory always posits some kind of closed system in which relationships are

---

[16] Cf. Don Martindale and Elio Monachesi, *Elements of Sociology*, New York: Harper, 1951, pp. 312–378.

[17] Karen Horney, *The Neurotic Personality of Our Time*, New York: W. W. Norton, 1937; David Riesman, *The Lonely Crowd*, New Haven: Yale University Press, 1950.

[18] Emile Durkheim, *Les Regles de la Methode Sociologique*, Paris: Librairie Felix Alcan, 1927, pp. 120–137.

necessary rather than fortuitous, and theory can consequently be developed only within such a level.[19] But theory and the prediction of actual behavior are different matters. Theory at any one level gives only a partial accounting for behavior. Hence, Durkheim himself was forced to work with broad correlations, on the assumption that relationships at other levels were random with respect to the social level he was studying.

CONCLUSION

The import of the foregoing is not to detract from the many exciting achievements of the standard approaches to personality study. It is rather to call attention to the dilemma of the sociologist who depends for his theory upon the psychologist or the anthropologist, and to urge the fruitfulness of another line of inquiry which has received scant attention.

It is of interest to note that sociology made a vigorous start in the area of culture-personality study in the work of Durkheim, Thomas, and others, but in recent years has largely abdicated to anthropologists and psychologists. Psychologists who had devised the instruments and the concepts for the study of personality, and anthropologists who had refined the techniques for summarizing cultures, monopolized the skills required in the conventional approaches to culture and personality. The sociologist, whose forte lay in elaborating the processes and differentiation within a society could enter the area only by abandoning his interest in social structure for the anthropologist's interest in culture, or by simplifying his conceptions of social structure in order to note rough associations between the psychologists' categories and broad subcultures. But the problem of how a given society supplies unique patterns of organization for personality, corresponding to the differentiating processes at work within that society, calls for precisely the skills of the analysis of social structure which are nearest to the sociologist's stock in trade.

It is time to rejuvenate the sociological field of study once called

[19] Cf. Ralph H. Turner, "The Quest for Universals in Sociological Research," *American Sociological Review*, 18 (December, 1953), pp. 604–611.

"social differentiation." But in rejuvenating it we should add an important dimension. Differentiation is not only the elaboration of social structure; it may also be the source of a major level of organization in individual personality. Because societies differentiate their populations differently, they may also provide different organizing frameworks for personality. The study of more profound relationships between social structure and personality organization may well be the most promising next step after culture-personality. And such traditional sociological types as Thomas' types of immigrants,[20] Park's marginal man,[21] and Strong's social types of Negroes,[22] need not be disparaged because they have not been translated into a set of psychological variables.

[20] Robert E. Park and Herbert A. Miller, *Old World Traits Transplanted*, Chicago: Society for Social Research, 1925, pp. 81ff.

[21] Robert E. Park, "Human Migration and the Marginal Man," *American Journal of Sociology*, 33 (May, 1928), pp. 881–893.

[22] Samuel M. Strong, "Social Types in a Minority Group: Formulation of a Method," *American Journal of Sociology*, 48 (March, 1943), pp. 563–573.

12

Research Implications of a Field View of Personality*

J. MILTON YINGER

Perhaps in no other area of research is the student of human behavior so likely to be caught in the grip of his own concepts as in personality theory. That "personality" is simply a word, a construct in our heads, not a reality "out there," is a difficult position to maintain. Because it is a term that can readily be attached to the observable individuals whose behavior we seek to understand, we tend to reify personality. This is the more serious because of the limiting influence of theoretical perspectives. Inevitably our concepts and our research procedures reflect the psychological, psychiatric, sociological, and social-psychological theories of personality to which they are related.

It is the purpose of this paper to show how research is influenced by the selective attention to variables that results from different perspectives. Thereafter, the aim is to describe a multidisciplinary approach to personality and to indicate its peculiar value as a construct in certain situations, particularly those that prevail in changing and heterogeneous societies. There is no need to deny either the possibility or the value of purely psychological or purely sociological theories of personality, so long as the nature of their abstractions is kept fully in mind. But I believe it can be shown that a social-psychological construct is a more powerful analytic tool.

For certain kinds of problems we can afford to accept the Newtonian view of the physical world. Modifications of our notions of time and space and changes in the mechanical conception of the stable structure of matter become necessary, however, when our

---

* Reprinted from "Research Implications of a Field View of Personality" by J. Milton Yinger, *American Journal of Sociology*, *68:* 580–592, 1963. Copyright 1962, 1963 by the University of Chicago.

curiosity leads us to explore outward to the reaches of the universe or inward to variations in processes inside the atom.

By analogy, a purely sociological view of personality, designed largely to study "social structure," "culture and personality," and "role," and a purely psychological view of personality, concerned primarily with the isolation and measurement of inner "traits" and their configuration, can contribute to the solution of some kinds of problems. Under conditions in which sociocultural structure and individual experience are relatively stable and repetitive, *either* a purely sociological *or* psychological approach to personality is useful. The constructs of each are likely to be adequate *indexes* of the variables studied by the other. Thus definition of personality and prediction of behavior in terms of cultural norms and role requirements approximate the results obtained by analysis of the internal structure of the person, under conditions of stability. Oppositely, and somewhat paradoxically, under such conditions definition of personality and prediction of behavior in terms of inner traits and their configurations approximate the results obtained by a purely sociological approach to the same questions. Each discipline can partly afford to disregard the variables of interest to the other because of their relative stability. (One can afford to disregard the influence of altitude—or more generally, air pressure—on the boiling point of water if he seeks prediction at one altitude only.) The variables being neglected are no less operative because of their stability, but since their influence is constant it can be disregarded for purposes of prediction.

Under conditions of social change and mobility, however, the situation is quite different. If the psychologist seeks prediction simply by exploration of variation of inner "traits" (honesty, gregariousness, authoritarianism, aggressiveness, anxiety, persuasibility), he has to contend with the wide variation in situations within which these inner forces express themselves. And the sociologist or anthropologist who thinks of personality primarily in terms of cultural norms and roles is confronted, in changing societies, with wide variation in the extent and manner of their internalization. <u>Under such conditions, a unit of analysis that is simultaneously psychological and sociological becomes essential.</u> The terms "psychology" and "sociology" are used here in their widest meaning to refer to the study of biopsychological tendencies and sociocultural structures. For some purposes, elaboration of a four-level model may be preferable. In fact, each of the levels is a *system* of multiple variables. Personality tendencies related to aspiration and motivation, for example, may converge or diverge, with very different results for behavior.[1]

There is nothing startling or new about this point of view. It is close to the perspective of those sociologists who emphasize social interaction and those social psychologists who speak in terms of a field view.[2] But only rarely do we find social psychological research designed to handle simultaneously the variables that derive from inner tendencies and those that stem from the influences of the social situation. A great deal has been learned, of course, by the efforts to develop purely sociological or purely psychological models. Difficulty arises when these models are used directly as guides to research on social-psychological problems, that is, are used to predict *behavior* of the individual in the social setting, which is the social-psychological task. Strictly speaking, the interest of psychology is not in behavior, but in the inner tendency system of the individual and how it is produced.[3] More obviously, sociology is not concerned

---

[1] For some studies of the interaction of two or more variables on the personality level see Bernard Rosen, "The Achievement Syndrome: A Psychocultural Dimension of Social Stratification," *American Sociological Review*, XXI (April, 1956), 203–11 and his "Race, Ethnicity, and the Achievement Syndrome," *American Sociological Review*, XXIV (February, 1959), 47–60; and Loren Chapman and Donald Campbell, "The Effect of Acquiescence Response-Set upon Relationships among the F Scale, Ethnocentrism, and Intelligence," *Sociometry*, XXII (June, 1959), 153–61.

[2] See, e.g., Kurt Lewin, *A Dynamic Theory of Personality* (New York: McGraw-Hill Book Co., 1935); Alfred R. Lindesmith and Anselm L. Strauss, *Social Psychology* (rev. ed.; New York: Dryden Press, 1956); Gardner Murphy, *Personality* (New York: Harper & Bros., 1947), chaps. xxxviii and xxxix; Talcott Parsons and Edward Shils (eds.), *Toward a General Theory of Action* (Cambridge, Mass.: Harvard University Press, 1951); Alex Inkeles, "Personality and Social Structure," in *Sociology Today*, ed. Robert Merton, Leonard Broom and Leonard Cottrell, Jr. (New York: Basic Books, 1959), chap. xi; Theodore M. Newcomb, *Social Psychology* (New York: Dryden Press, 1950); and a valuable but somewhat neglected book by Walter Coutu, *Emergent Human Nature* (New York: Alfred A. Knopf, Inc., 1949).

[3] This statement conflicts with the view of earlier "behaviorists" of the Watson school and with some contemporary experimental psychologists, Skinner, for example, who have no interest in the internal tendency

with the behavior of individuals, but with sociocultural systems and how they are produced.[4] Few of us are content to work on these levels of abstraction, however. The ultimately intriguing problem for most of us is: Why do human beings behave as they do? When we approach this question, the vital point is that behavior is always simultaneously situational and personal. We cannot answer the question by use of the constructs derived from either psychology or sociology, nor by adding attention to a few variables derived from the discipline that is not our main starting point. Social psychology has an essentially different unit of analysis: individual behavior in the social context.

There are doubtless several reasons why sociologists and psychologists frequently move into social psychological problems without reformulating the unit of study. Two factors seem most important: Even when we are concerned with purely psychological or sociological questions, we must study behavior, from which alone we can *infer* the inner structure of the person or the patterns of the sociocultural system. It is scarcely surprising that we should sometimes confuse our inferences with the behavior from which they are derived. But

---

system—Watson's "mystery box." In their research, attention is paid only to a S → R formula, not to the usual S → O → R formula of much psychological study. The behaviorist in this sense undertakes a different type of abstraction from psychology as I have defined it. He seeks to isolate the results of a stimulus on behavior, all other things being equal. The emphasis on response and behavior may obscure the abstract quality of his research. This leads the experimentalist to disregard, and sometimes to disdain, the influence of variables studied by his fellow psychologists who are interested in the organism and those studied by sociologists, who insist that both stimuli and the response-setting are often social. There is no reason to object to Skinner's approach, provided the nature of the abstraction is kept in mind. It is only necessary to state that it is no substitute for personality psychology and that it certainly does not deal with the variables of interest to sociology. But perhaps most importantly for this paper—because of the identification of experimental psychology with behavior, and therefore the possibility of confusion—experimental psychology is no substitute for social psychology, with its more complicated unit of analysis.

[4] This is in disagreement with Franz Adler, "A Unit Concept for Sociology," *American Journal of Sociology*, LXV (January, 1960), 356–64, where it is suggested that behavior is the basic unit for both psychological and sociological analysis. In other respects, Adler's interpretation, despite this disagreement, seems to be in harmony with that developed here.

the results, as I shall try to show below, are poor understanding and prediction. A second source of the tendency to use sociological or psychological models to structure social-psychological questions is the pattern of academic training. Most of us have had our training in either psychology or sociology. Few are willing to depart far from "home" territory, because there we find the colleague group, the sources of prestige or promotion, the main reference group, and perhaps most important, there we find the continuing work being guided by the same models by means of which we have learned to look at our data. Under such conditions, we are proud of, and are rewarded in proportion to, the "purity" of our research model.

Whatever the causes, there is a widespread tendency to absorb social psychology into one of the "parent" disciplines, with, I am convinced, unfortunate results. Whether we declare with Krech and Crutchfield that "social psychology does not differ in any fundamental way from psychology in general," [5] or with Strauss that "Social psychology . . . should have much to offer its sister fields, but only insofar as its practitioners can self-consciously tie their work back to the social organizational heart of sociology and anthropology," [6] we are led to an inadequate formulation of the analysis of the individual behaving in the group.[7]

The difficulty in achieving a social-psychological view of personality is shown even in the pioneering work of Lewin, whose interpretation of the field view did not entirely successfully incorporate personal and situational forces into the unit of analysis. In describing Lewin's work, Deutsch writes:

Psychology must take into account physical and social facts which obey nonpsychological laws and which determine the external events that will impinge upon the perceptual motor regions of the person. . . .

[5] David Krech and Richard S. Crutchfield, *Theory and Problems of Social Psychology* (New York: McGraw-Hill Book Co., 1948), p. 7.

[6] Anselm Strauss, *Mirrors and Masks: The Search for Identity* (Glencoe, Ill.: Free Press, 1959), p. 11.

[7] It is perhaps significant that some of the basic theoretical work in social psychology has come from persons who were neither sociologists nor psychologists. It has come from philosophers, who easily disregard boundaries, from anthropologists, whose work is usually near the descriptive level and thus more readily focused on behavior, and from psychiatrists, many of whom are primarily concerned with the total behaving individual, not with abstracted segments.

A FIELD VIEW OF PERSONALITY

The nonpsychological milieu cannot have direct effects upon behavior because its parts are alien to psychological environments, except as its parts get transformed into goals, barriers, and other psychological facts through perception. However, as Wright and Barker point out:

"It is nonetheless true that the nonpsychological milieu affects behavior indirectly. It provides the physical and social raw materials for psychological habitats; and by supplying these resources it goes far to determine just what behavior shall and shall not be possible for all who live within it."[8]

This statement well represents Lewin's dominant, if not his only, interpretation of the field approach. What is not said, however, and what prevents the Lewinian view from being fully field theoretical is that *the psychological environment cannot have direct effects on behavior either;* it must be conjoined with a facilitating non-psychological milieu, as Deutsch calls it. And in the same sense, the system of psychological tendencies provides the raw materials capable of being influenced by the environment and thus "goes far to determine just what behavior shall and shall not be possible," to use the phrase from Wright and Barker. It is one thing to take account of environmental forces as limiting conditions, as most psychologically trained field theorists do. It is another thing to incorporate personality variables and environmental variables into the very unit of analysis, with full attention to the fact that neither by itself has "direct effects upon behavior"—that is, has effects that are not mediated through the other system of influences.

In Lewin's work, field means "psychological field"—that part of the total series of forces that is perceived by an individual. It seems reasonable to a psychologically trained person to say that an individual cannot be influenced by a force of which he is unaware. (We will not here explore the several possible levels of perception.) "For all practical purposes," the author of a recent book writes, "this perceptual field is reality to the person doing the perceiving . . . ; it may not be in accord with the external observer's perceptions, but it and it alone determines behavior."[9] What is missed by this kind of observation is recognition that a person's

---

[8] Morton Deutsch in *Handbook of Social Psychology*, ed. Gardner Lindzey (Cambridge, Mass.: Addison-Wesley Publishing Co., 1954), I, 193.

[9] Otto Strunk, Jr., *Religion: A Psychological Interpretation* (Nashville, Tenn.: Abingdon Press, 1962).

perceptions are a function not only of his sensitivities but also of the available stimuli, many of them derived from culture and social structure. Priority in determining behavior can be assigned neither to the sensitivities of the person nor to the facilitating forces in the environment, because both are always involved in the equation.

It is perhaps not surprising that psychologists should sometimes fail to recognize the influence of social structure independent of the individuals' perceptions of it. That sociologists should fall into the same error is more puzzling. Thus Gross, Mason, and McEachern, in an otherwise first-rate study, deal with role conflict only in terms of the perceptions of position incumbents.[10] But lack of consensus on the part of the members of the role set, whether or not that lack is perceived, affects the structure within which interaction takes place and the alternatives available to an actor, and thus influences his behavior. Perception of these facts by an actor is an additional variable; but the personality fact must be distinguished from the social fact.

THE FIELD VIEW OF PERSONALITY ABNORMALITY

The tendency to shift, without due notice, from an abstract sociological or psychological model to an interpretation of behavior can be found in almost every research area. Studies of delinquency, of discrimination, of creativity, of leadership have often treated either personal tendencies or situations as limiting conditions, not as causal forces. Insofar as the aim of research is to isolate, by analysis, the influence of one set of variables, this procedure is valid; but the persistent error is the practice of shifting from analysis on the inner-tendency system level or the sociocultural system level to the interpretation of behavior, which always involves influences from both levels. Consider this illustration of the "fallacy of misplaced concreteness": "whatever be the element of social disintegration we

[10] Neal Gross, Ward Mason, and Alexander McEachern, *Explorations in Role Analysis* (New York: John Wiley & Sons, 1958), p. 248. More commonly, of course, sociologists emphasize precisely the distinct effects of social structure, individual differences held constant. See Peter M. Blau, "Structural Effects," *American Sociological Review*, XXV (April, 1960), 178–93.

are concerned with, its influence makes itself felt only on a *selected group of individuals*. It must therefore be the physical and mental makeup of offenders, as compared with nonoffenders, that presents the crucial and practical issue in the study of crime causation."[11] On the other side, some sociologists emphasize subcultural norms, the influence of the group and community patterns as the "crucial and practical issues." They tend to overlook the problem associated with the fact that only some of those exposed to the crime-supporting situation engage in crime.[12]

It is a commonplace for students of human behavior to point out that "economic man" does not exist, that it is simply an idea, useful to varying degrees in the effort to understand economic behavior. No more does "sociological man" or "psychological man" exist. This can best be illustrated perhaps by examining some aspects of abnormal behavior, because the tendency to take certain causal forces for granted may be weakened by observing departures from the norm. When Durkheim sought an explanation of suicide, for example, he examined various theories, one by one, finding each inadequate until he came to the influences of the social structure. No psychopathic state, he found, "bears a regular and indisputable relation to suicide." Nor did the analysis of "normal psychological states"

---

[11] "Crime Causation," in *National Probation and Parole Association Yearbook* (1941), p. 90. Note how precisely this reverses Durkheim's perspective, discussed below.

[12] Walter B. Miller, "Lower Class Culture as a Generating Milieu of Gang Delinquency," *Journal of Social Issues*, XIV, No. 3 (1958), 5–19. Many recent studies, of course, qualify excessively psychological or sociological views of crime and work toward an integrated theory. See Lewis Yablonsky, "The Delinquent Gang as a Near-Group," *Social Problems*, VII (Fall, 1959), 108–17; Gresham Sykes and David Matza, "Techniques of Neutralization: A Theory of Delinquency," *American Sociological Review*, XXII (December, 1957), 664–70; Albert Cohen, *Delinquent Boys* (Glencoe: Free Press, 1955); Solomon Kobrin, "The Conflict of Values in Delinquency Areas," *American Sociological Review*, XVI (October, 1951), 653–661; John Kitsuse and David Dietrick, "Delinquent Boys: A Critique," *American Sociological Review*, XXIV (April, 1959), 208–15; William McCord and Joan McCord, *Origins of Crime: A New Evaluation of the Cambridge-Somerville Youth Study* (New York: Columbia University Press, 1959); Marshall Clinard in Merton, Broom, and Cottrell (eds.), *op. cit.*, pp. 509–36; J. Milton Yinger, "Contraculture and Subculture," *American Sociological Review*, XXV (October, 1960), 625–35.

prove of value, although he recognized differences in aptitude for suicide "permitting but not necessarily implying suicide and therefore giving no explanation for it." [13]

For decades this study has been used, with good reason, as a prime example of sociological research. There is often the tendency, however, to think of it not as an attempt to isolate the social structural aspect of suicide causation but as a complete theory of suicide. Durkheim does get near to a blending of individual and social factors.[14] He notes that individual tendency is a necessary if not a sufficient cause (although he does not use these terms). What he fails to make clear is that the sociocultural forces are also necessary but insufficient. His development of the idea of "productive cause" (*la cause productrice*) gives primacy to the social structural factor; but this is meaningful only in the explanation of a social *rate* of suicide, not in the social psychological task of explaining the behavior of the individual in the group setting. To restate the brief quotation from Durkheim, one can with as much justice say that an anomic setting "permits but does not necessarily imply suicide." Not everyone in such settings commits suicide. Durkheim helped to eliminate an excessively individualistic theory by demonstrating the influence of sociological factors in a dramatic way. As an illustration of the new light that can be thrown on old facts by the use of a sociological perspective, *Le Suicide* is a masterpiece. It is when we try to use the study as a social-psychological theory that we get into difficulty, for it is no more adequate as an explanation of behavior than the individualistic interpretations it so successfully attacked.[15]

The social-psychological point of view can be described in simple mathematical terms by putting the familiar concepts of "predisposing" factors (located in the individual) and "precipitating" factors (located in the situation)[16] into scales. Assume that values

---

[13] Emile Durkheim, *Suicide* (Glencoe, Ill.: Free Press, 1951), p. 103.

[14] See *ibid.*, pp. 102–3 and 323–24, for example.

[15] On this question see Inkeles, *op. cit.*; George Simpson's Preface to his translation of Durkheim's *Suicide;* Talcott Parsons, *The Structure of Social Action* (New York: McGraw-Hill Book Co., 1937), p. 326; Maurice Halbwachs, *Les Causes du suicide* (Paris: F. Alcan, 1930); and A. F. Henry and J. F. Short, *Suicide and Homicide* (Glencoe, Ill.: Free Press, 1954).

[16] See, e.g., E. Gartly Jaco, "The Social Isolation Hypothesis and Schizophrenia," *American Sociological Review*, XIX (October, 1954).

can range from zero to ten, which would represent the theoretically limiting cases. The likelihood of suicide (or of any other act being interpreted by the use of this scheme) is measured by the product of the values on these two presumed scales; if either is zero, the act will not occur no matter how high the score on the other measure. Thus a person caught in a thoroughly anomic situation and surrounded by other social forces strongly precipitating him toward suicide will have no likelihood of performing the act if his "predisposal" score is zero. Similarly, if he is as thoroughly predisposed as is theoretically imaginable, but is surrounded by a situation that contains no precipitating influences whatsoever, suicide will not occur.

To think in terms of empirically more likely cases, we can hypothesize a "score" of 50 as the point at which suicide is likely to occur. A person with a "predisposal" score of 1 to 4 will be immune even in the most powerfully precipitating context, as anomic and stressful as one can imagine. If his score rises to 5, however, he becomes vulnerable in situations with the highest possible score. One can successfully predict a high *rate* (that is, a group measure) when such precipitating influences as anomie are strong (let us say, arbitrarily, above 7), because the product scores of a large number are brought above the assumed critical point of 50. A precipitating score of 5 will affect only those with a predisposal score of 10; but if the former score rises to 7, all those above 7 in the latter measure are affected.[17] Knowledge of anomie, therefore, may allow us better to predict rates but is of no value in the social psychological task of understanding how particular individuals will behave in the social context. This statement can be reversed, of course: knowledge of individual tendencies tells us who is vulnerable but does not indicate the likelihood of a given act, which is always situationally influenced. The situation may be so constant that we have learned to take it for granted; but that is no indication of its irrelevance.

567–77; and T. A. C. Rennie, "The Yorkville Community Mental Health Research Study," in *Interrelations between the Social Environment and Psychiatric Disorders* (New York: Milbank Memorial Fund, 1953), pp. 213ff.

[17] In this greatly oversimplified scheme, I have assumed two arithmetic scales and precision in measurement. I have also disregarded the question of functionally equivalent types of behavior.

And as we seek to extend our propositions in time and space we are inevitably confronted with variation in situational influence.

This same approach can guide our study of the more general problems of the social psychology of abnormality. The field view states that mental illness as behavior is not something *in* the person; it is a process that results from the interaction of the person with the situation. Two persons, equally burdened by doubt and guilt, equally torn by mutually contradictory inclinations, equally confused by ego-alienating desires (or however one may want to describe the abnormality-prone individual) are not necessarily equally likely to express these tendencies by abnormal behavior. One person may live in a supportive environment that blunts the edge of his anxieties or furnishes socially approved and ego-approved outlets for their expression. Another may be caught in a situation that compounds his anxieties. The task of sociology is to isolate the sociocultural conditions that minimize and those that maximize the likelihood of abnormal behavior (normlessness, or contradictory norms, or stressful socialization). The task of psychology is to isolate those conditions that establish tendency systems immune to or vulnerable to "abnormality-prone" environments. Social psychology, then, is concerned with the behavior of the individual in the situation. These are, of course, highly abstract distinctions. Many research studies and many scientists operate on two or more of these levels. It is essential, however, that the levels be kept analytically distinct in our minds, as they often are not, lest we assume that measures of normlessness or measures of inner stress can lead directly to prediction of behavior.

A psychogenic theory alone cannot explain abnormality both because there are alternative ways of expressing the inner tendencies and also because there is variation in the strength of precipitating forces. The positions one occupies, his class environment, the total situation of which he is a part all help to account for the path that he will follow. A sociogenic theory alone cannot explain abnormality because different inner-tendency systems respond differently to the same sociocultural circumstances. It is true that among persons equally anxious, one may become delinquent, another neurotic or a drug addict, another deeply religious, depending upon situational variation. Oppositely, however, the same situation may precipitate neurosis in one, delinquency in another, and unusual effort in a third, because of different "selector systems" within the individual.

When we conceive of personality as process, not as a system of inner traits, the study of abnormality takes on new dimensions. It is one thing to say that a given individual *is paranoiac;* it is another to say that he behaves paranoiacally under certain conditions. The latter statement leads us, with Cameron, for example, to seek out the precipitating conditions. If the suspicions, threats, and aggressive actions of the paranoia-prone individual heighten the anxiety of those around him, "he inevitably arouses defensive and retaliatory hostility in others." [18] This response seems to confirm his interpretation of the situation and promotes his aggressive tendencies. If, however, hostility-promoting responses are lacking, if a neutral therapist serves as a bridge to reality, the paranoia-prone individual "can begin to entertain doubts and consider alternative interpretations." [19]

Certainly an excessively situational approach to personality would lead to error: not all persons are equally liable to delusional responses. For some, only the most favorable conditions imaginable can prevent hostile behavior. It is less obvious that research which disregards the conditions under which behavior occurs, which studies only inner "traits," also leads to error. Such research yields good prediction for extreme cases under the usual range of conditions. If the predisposal score is high, most situations will precipitate abnormal behavior. The difficulty in this approach, however, is that it tends to support a conception of personality that yields poor prediction in dealing with persons with lower predisposal scores or in unusual conditions (in a different culture, for example, or in the neutral and supportive context of therapy). If I may speak in analogical terms again, if one lives in an environment that never falls below $0°$ C. or goes above $100°$ C. he can afford to predict solely on the basis of the "traits" of H_2O that it is a liquid. This is an adequate way of saying that H_2O, a compound with certain potentialities, is liquid under certain conditions which, being constant, can be disregarded. That does not mean, however, that the conditions are not always involved in producing the results.

The point of view being developed here requires a more drastic

[18] Norman Cameron, "The Paranoid Pseudo-Community Revisited," *American Journal of Sociology*, LXV (July, 1959), p. 58.
[19] *Ibid.*, p. 58.

departure from disciplinary perspectives than is sometimes realized. To say that social interactional and cultural factors are involved in the origins of mental illness is not the same as saying that the situation in which a person with abnormal tendencies behaves *now* affects the likelihood and the forms of abnormal responses. Quite traditional psychiatry can accept the former statement, particularly if reference is to the social experiences in early life. Field view takes a more "radical" position when it argues that abnormality is a function of the current situation as well as of current tendencies.

This distinction can be illustrated by reference to the complicated problem of class variation in rates of schizophrenia. It is probably true that the rate is higher among the lower classes. (One can say only probably true, both because the total incidence is not the same as the detected or the hospitalized incidence, and also because later detection or treatment of cases in the lower classes may lead to greater severity, longer hospitalization or persistence, and hence to greater incidence at any given time.) There is good evidence that class subcultures and variation in patterns of interaction are among the causes of this differential. Persons vulnerable to schizophrenia are more likely to develop in lower-class contexts, according to this view, because of the frustrations, the subculturally allowable responses to frustrations, the family patterns, and other social facts more characteristic of lower-class than of middle- or upper-class experience. But field theory goes further: rates among the lower classes are higher, not only because of tendency differences laid down in the individuals but also because the contemporary situations facilitate different types of response. If two groups, one lower and one middle class, with equal predispositions, were compared, the lower-class group may have a higher rate, not because of what is in them (tendencies having been matched), but because of differences in precipitating forces: The responses of families and communities to illness and treatment vary by class; therapeutic demands are to some degree class-oriented; functionally alternative forms of response are not equally available. These may be among the situational ingredients that facilitate a schizophrenic response more frequently in one group than in another.

A field view requires redefinition of abnormality, not only in the sense that cultural and subcultural norms as well as contradictions within the person are taken into account, but more drastically in the sense that abnormality can be defined only in the process of interaction. Fried and Lindemann, for example, suggest this operational definition for extreme mental ill health: Impulses break through the regulations of the ego and superego; behavior cannot be controlled by the usual regulatory agencies—family, peers, work colleagues—and thus a crisis is precipitated; efforts to support the ego-superego system by the usual agencies of control fail, endangering the normal institutional structure and patterns of interaction; extraordinary institutional resources are drawn in.[20] This is no mere adding together of individual and group factors; it is a *process* definition that requires simultaneous attention to the various levels of influence.

If both tendencies and situations are involved in the causation of abnormal behavior, they must both be considered in programs of therapy. During World War II, persons removed from the front lines because of neurotic or psychotic symptoms had a much higher rate of recovery if they were treated in the combat zone than if they were taken to a hospital far from battle.[21] A conception of personality that leads one to think in terms of neurotic or psychotic persons as separate entities cannot easily interpret such observations. When we conceive of personality as behavior, however, and speak of tendencies toward neurosis under certain conditions, the full range of facts can be accounted for.

The only modification of the field view required here is recognition of the fact that *from the point of view of strategy* one or another of the causal forces may be more accessible to change. It may be most efficient to disregard the tendencies of mildly disturbed children and to concentrate on changing their situations. On the other hand, it may be necessary to take the social structures and cultural values as fairly fixed, as far as a deeply disturbed person is concerned, so that therapy must concentrate on the modification of his tendencies. Such strategic decisions, however, should not be permitted to obscure the continuing presence of both sets of forces in the causal

---

[20] Marc Fried and Erich Lindemann, "Sociocultural Factors in Mental Health and Illness," *American Journal of Orthopsychiatry*, XXXI (January, 1961), 87–101.

[21] See John Clausen in Merten, Broom, and Cottrell (eds.), *op. cit.*, p. 503.

equation. Continuous awareness of their interaction is necessary not only for theory but also for therapy. This is shown in an interesting way by group therapy, in which the effort is made to modify abnormal tendencies by experience in an artifically created and temporary social system with a somewhat unique subculture. Assuming success in this effort, one may be faced with the possibility that the individual, on returning to the dominant social world, will find himself too uninhibited or outspoken.[22] His former symptoms, however painful and awkward, were not wholly out of joint with the social system of which they were a part; they were indeed efforts to struggle with it. This is not to argue against therapy, of course, but only to stress the need for attention to the entire field of forces. Beck, who notes the possible dysfunctional consequences of group therapy, indicates that this is not typically a serious problem. Therapy ends short of full transformation of the person; the outside world continues to restrain him, and the restraints may be more acceptable if therapy has lowered self-deprecation and rigidities; and if the group processes in the therapeutic situation have taught patients to see social clues better, they may interact more adequately with the group.[23]

CONTINUITY OF PERSONAL TENDENCY

It is sometimes supposed that field theory eliminates or minimizes the idea that there is continuity to personality. Attention to the importance of situational influences can be interpreted, by both opponents and proponents, to mean that the individual is a creature of all the outside forces playing upon him at a given moment. His tendencies are so numerous and so lacking in structure that the facilitating and inhibiting forces of the environment become the crucial variables. In emphasizing the ahistorical nature of science, for example (only those influences at work in the contemporary field can affect behavior; their histories are not directly relevant), Lewin challenged the importance of continuity of personality.

[22] See Dorothy Beck, "The Dynamics of Group Psychotherapy as Seen by a Sociologist," *Sociometry*, XXI (June, 1958 and September, 1958), 98–129, 180–97.
[23] *Ibid.*, pp. 191–95.

Past events are precipitates of present behavior tendencies

A careful statement of field theory, however, does not in fact deny personality continuity. It does require a reinterpretation of the concept. Certainly an emphasis on the supreme importance of experiences in infancy and childhood as determining forces in behavior is challenged. Whether it be William James's idea of individual habit as "the enormous fly-wheel of society," or Freud's conception of character structure, or the emphasis of much contemporary learning theory on the canalization of response through reward and punishment—presumably to the end of stable response patterns—any theory that focuses on internal forces operating independently of any context seems inadequate. Yet each of these points of view can be made consonant with a field approach. When habits, character structure, or canalized responses are interpreted as a readiness to act, not as behavior, they need not clash with a field view. If it is true that an individual never behaves in a vacuum, it is equally true that the sociocultural and physical environments never call out behavior in a tendencyless individual.

When he described the ahistorical quality of science, Lewin did not deny the significance of past events. He simply noted that they could be significant for behavior only insofar as there were precipitates of these events in present tendencies. Stated in this way, the extent of tendency continuity becomes an empirical problem for investigation. There are good grounds for hypothesizing substantial continuity of personality. The bringing of the past into the present through memory, the continuity of the body, the very meaning of "self" and the insightful if not definitive construct of self-consistency all suggest the usefulness of the idea. Clinical insight into the way a neurotic person clings to his symptoms, evidence that prejudices often persist even in the face of powerful challenging facts, knowledge that propaganda messages can be twisted around by a perceiver to support his established views, and the vivid impression that most persons have of a strong lifeline connecting them with their own past all support the idea of continuity. For each such support, however, there are also contrary evidences: neurotic symptoms sometimes change or disappear, prejudices shift or are eliminated, communications may change attitudes, and individuals sometimes have the pleasant or unpleasant sense of drastic changes in themselves.

It is necessary to speak tentatively on this question because a definitive test of personality continuity is difficult to design. There may be substantial agreement among persons of widely differing theoretical perspectives on these propositions: Individuals vary in the extent to which they experience personality change as adults; some are "chameleons" and some are "beavers," to use Eugene Lerner's terms, and most are in between. Societies vary in the proportions of chameleons and beavers they produce, or in the extent to which they promote inner- and other-directedness. Some aspects of personality are more malleable than others; judgments may change more readily than opinions, opinions more readily than attitudes, attitudes than values, and values than self-image—to put the issue in overly simple terms. Personality changes are least likely to occur when the group structures with which the individual is involved remain stable.

This last statement, based on a field perspective, has received unusually stringent tests in recent years in the efforts to manipulate human beings. These efforts have ranged from verbal communications designed to change opinions and closely linked actions to major campaigns to "brainwash" military captives and transform their basic values and allegiances. By stating the issue from a field point of view, we can see the problem of the consistency of personality from the opposite perspective, that is, the "inconsistency of personality."[24]

Systematic efforts to crush resistance and to remake the value hierarchies of individuals in concentration camps and prisoner-of-war camps provide a severe test of the degree to which persons can be manipulated. There are difficult problems involved in the interpretation of the evidence, for it can be read in several different ways.

---

[24] For evidence on this question see, e.g., Bruno Bettelheim, "Individual and Mass Behavior in Extreme Situations," *Journal of Abnormal and Social Psychology*, XXXVIII (October, 1943), 417–52; Albert Biderman and Herbert Zimmer, *The Manipulation of Human Behavior* (New York: John Wiley & Sons, 1961); E. A. Cohen, *Human Behavior in the Concentration Camp* (New York: W. W. Norton & Co., 1953); I. E. Farber, Harry F. Harlow, and Louis J. West, "Brainwashing, Conditioning and DDD (Debility, Dependency, Dread)," *Sociometry*, X (December, 1957), 271–85; Czeslaw Milosz, *The Captive Mind* (New York: Alfred A. Knopf, Inc., 1953); Edgar H. Schein, "The Chinese Indoctrination Program for Prisoners of War: A Study of Attempted 'Brainwashing,'" *Psychiatry*, LXI (May, 1956), 149–72.

An observer who is convinced that personality is a fairly stable organization of traits, the result of early experience acting upon a unique inheritance, will view evidence of drastic changes as temporary products of unusual situations. The "real" personality will reappear when conditions return to "normal." From the perspective of this paper, this is an inadequate formulation. If earlier personality tendencies manifest themselves again when an agency of manipulation is removed, after having been inhibited by that agency, it is not only because they have remained in the personality, but also because the situation that encourages them has returned. By this statement I do not want to contradict the principles stated above: some persons change less readily than others (their tendencies persist over a wider range of situations); and some personality tendencies are less malleable than others. I simply want to emphasize also that some social structures change less readily than others (allow a narrower range of alternatives among which personality tendencies may "select"), and that some aspects of the structure are less malleable than others. A situationalist view that treats individual variations as bothersome exceptions is just as inadequate as a personalist or traitist view that treats situational variations as bothersome exceptions.

From the point of view of field theory, the degree to which human beings can be manipulated involves the interaction of variables on several levels. Analysis of the influence of drugs, lack of sleep, injury, and illness requires physiochemical research. The task is to discover how much the variance in behavior can be accounted for by the effects of drugs, for example, when personality, cultural, and group variables have been controlled. On the personality level, fear, anxiety, ability to withstand pain, and knowledge of issues are illustrative variables. Knowledge of cultural values and roles is also valuable for prediction: Turkish soldiers captured by the Chinese during the Korean War may have been less easily manipulated than some American soldiers, perhaps because there is much greater consensus on the role "soldier" and on the values of toughness in Turkish culture. On the level of social structure, the need is to study the ways in which efforts to manipulate behavior are affected by group processes. The Chinese Communists systematically destroyed the group structure among prisoners: leaders were removed, informing on one's fellows was rewarded, a sense of alienation from home support was promoted by allowing only unhappy letters to come through. Thus they sought a radical alienation from the sustaining influence of the group.

CONCLUSION

A field approach demands that we make our research designs even more complicated than they are; but it will yield correspondingly more satisfying results in any attempt to understand or predict behavior. Physicists and biologists are well aware of the need for this perspective. In the words of Jennings: "What any particular cell of the individual produces is largely determined by the surroundings of that cell—by the cells in contact with it, and by the hormones that bathe it; in short, by the 'internal environment'—so that the same set of genes produces different results in different cases."[25] One can, of course, add that the same environment produces different results when it influences cells with different potentialities.

Such a view would drastically alter the theoretical perspective of such research as that reported by Hovland and Janis in *Personality and Persuasibility*.[26] They are looking for elements in the person that will explain persuasibility, presumably regardless of the content of the message, the medium of communication, the communicator, or any other situational factor. They are looking, in short, for what they call the "unbound" trait of persuasibility. This is a possible construct, yielding prediction under some conditions. But as a general theory it seems to me to be quite inadequate; to try to predict from "trait" alone is to run into difficulty when a repetitive and consistent situation changes. Some of their hypotheses are borne out only because conditions vary over a narrow part of the imaginable range of messages, media, and communicators, and because they have isolated those persons for study who tend to be persuaded by a wide variety of communicators or messages. Again let me put the argument in simple mathematical terms. Assume that a score of 24 or more will produce persuasion of a given indi-

[25] H. S. Jennings, *The Biological Basis of Human Nature* (New York: W. W. Norton & Co., 1930), p. 122.

[26] Carl Hovland, and Irving Janis (eds.), *Personality and Persuasibility* (New Haven, Conn.: Yale University Press, 1959).

vidual by a given message in a particular situation. Assume further that individuals vary from 0 to 10 in persuasibility tendency (not an "unbound" trait) and that situations (the message-communicator complex) have the same possible range in influence. Persons with a persuasibility score of 8 will be persuaded by all situations with a score of 3 or higher, but those with a score of 3, only by communications with an influence score of 8 or higher.[27] Hovland and Janis, by discovering those persons with a high tendency score, could afford to disregard message content, medium of communication, and other situational aspects and still get good prediction, because a large proportion of situations would have the requisite influence. It is often true that a fairly simple concept seems quite good when applied to extreme cases. (Paradoxically, an opposite theory may seem equally good. I suspect a Durkheim could develop a usable theory of "situation and persuasion," disregarding individual differences entirely.) A sterner test of a theory's adequacy, however, is its ability to interpret the behavior of persons along the whole range of tendencies toward persuasibility. For such a task, what is needed is not the isolation of presumed traits, but the specification of the conditions under which various tendencies are expressed.

If a "trait" approach is inadequate, it is equally true that our understanding is limited if we are excessively situationist, overlooking variations in individual tendency system. When Lewin, Lippitt, and White vary "group atmosphere" and process, in their studies of boys' clubs,[28] they add significantly to our knowledge by isolating the influence of strictly social forces. They could predict certain *rates* of behavior without paying any attention to differences in individual propensity. But again, their success is partly a result of the fact that the tendencies of the boys involved varied over a narrow part of the imaginable range. Systematic variation in age, cultural and subcultural values, tendencies toward hostility, and the

[27] The simple product model here is doubtless inadequate. It is quite possible that a 24 produced by a 3×8 combination has a different meaning from one produced by a 6×4 combination.

[28] See Kurt Lewin, Ronald Lippitt, and Ralph White, "Patterns of Aggressive Behavior in Experimentally Created 'Social Climates,'" *Journal of Social Psychology*, X (1939), 271–99; and Lippitt and White, "An Experimental Study of Leadership and Group Life," in *Readings in Social Psychology*, ed. Theodore Newcomb and Eugene Hartley (New York: Henry Holt & Co., 1947), pp. 314–30.

like, is necessary for knowledge of who will respond in various ways to "democratic" and "autocratic" group situations. Do six-year-olds respond in the same way as sixteen-year-olds? Do insecure and self-confident boys react differently? Would results be the same in Japan, Russia, and the United States?

It is not my intent to argue against the possibility or the desirability of a purely sociological or purely psychological approach to the study of personality, in each instance with the variables crucial to the other approach being controlled. It is vitally necessary, however, that those variables truly be controlled, not simply disregarded. And we must realize that our "victories" will be in the world of abstraction of our own creation. On the behavioral level, these variables are not controlled, but fully operative, and their influence must be taken into account. <u>The function of psychological and sociological research on personality is to isolate one set of variables for more precise measurement.</u> When we forget this function and attempt to make one or the other approach serve as a total theory of behavior, we weaken our understanding, despite good prediction under some circumstances. A social-psychological theory, building on the discoveries of the more abstract disciplines, is a more adequate guide to rese rch that seeks to understand behavior.

13

Sociological Perspectives on the Person*

STEPHAN P. SPITZER AND ROBERT M. SWANSON

The readings in this volume illustrate some of the major sociological contributions to the area of personality. However, the readings should not be construed as a complete compilation, since we were able to include only a representative sampling from the total number of important contributions available. This summary chapter endeavors to (1) describe various changes that the sociology of personality has undergone, and (2) point toward some recent trends and developments in the sociology of personality.

THE INDIVIDUAL AS A TOPIC FOR SOCIOLOGICAL INVESTIGATION

Even more than now, sociology at the turn of the century was a discipline concerned with the organization of society, the study of social institutions, and the study of groups. Thus, one of the first questions that should be raised is why sociologists felt it necessary to make any assumptions about man's nature, or even to consider the individual as a unit of analysis.

One reason that the individual was introduced as a unit of analysis was to help explain how society is possible. Early theories of social organization listed characteristics of society in a detailed manner, but neglected to account for how society came to be, or how society is held together.[1] One plausible approach that avoided undue dependence upon abstract conceptualizations was to study the

---

* Written especially for this Insight Book.

[1] A notable exception is found in the work of Emile Durkheim who posited that society is possible because of common values which impart cohesiveness to the group. See *Division of Labor*, Free Press, Glencoe, Ill., 1947.

individuals making up societies. Secondly, sociologists were concerned with problems of men, because the rapid industrialization at the turn of the century was disruptive both to the individual and society. Concern with the effects of social change was beginning to take a place in social thought. Such men as Tönnies, Weber, Marx, and Booth focused upon these problems.

As sociologists became interested in personality, a major issue consistently arose between nominalists and realists about the proper locus of sociological investigation. The nominalists argued that the individual organism was the solid reality which constituted the unit of social life, and depreciated society to the status of an abstraction. From this position society could be nothing more than the sum of the individual members composing it. In opposition, the realists maintained that society was an entity *sui generis*, and thus social phenomena could not be adequately understood as long as attention was concentrated exclusively on the individual. From this position the culture of a group could be regarded as something more than and different from the summated characteristics of individuals.

In the course of time it became evident that no satisfactory solution could be arrived at as long as the issue was stated in terms of an either/or dichotomy.[2] A number of theorists began to emphasize that the individuals who participate in the activities that bring a social group into being also beome part of the product that they helped to create as group members. Here, neither the individual nor the group is adequate to comprise all the aspects of the life of man in society. As Cooley pointed out:

A separate individual is an abstraction unknown to experience, and so likewise is society when regarded as something apart from individuals. The real thing is Human Life, which may be considered either in an individual aspect or in a social, that is to say a general aspect; but it is always . . . both individual and general. In other words, "society" and "individuals"

[2] For an account of the development and eventual demise of the nominalist/realist controversy, see Louis Wirth, "Social Interaction: The Problem of the Individual and the Group," *American Journal of Sociology*, 44: 965–979, 1939; see also Charles K. Warriner, "Groups are Real: A Reaffirmation," *American Sociological Review*, 21: 549–554, 1956.

do not denote separable phenomena, but are simply collective and distributive aspects of the same thing. . . .[3]

Consequently, the nominalist/realist issue is rarely raised in sociology. Cooley's position is taken for granted.

Some theorists associated with the Social Structure approach have built into their contentions the notion that societies and individuals can be regarded as separate although interdependent levels of analysis. Others have been unconcerned with positing separate levels of analysis, tacitly assuming that neither society nor the individual were ultimate entities, and maintaining rather that the task of sociology is simply to identify and examine the linkages between society and the individual. For analytic purposes, one may regard society as an independent variable and personality as a dependent variable, or conversely personality as an independent variable and society as a dependent variable. But in so doing, it is assumed that neither one of these entities has greater concreteness nor reality than the other.

Whether the individual or society is the real or appropriate unit for analysis does not present a problem to those individuals associated with the Interactionist approach. Symbolic interaction, upon which much of this approach is based, regards society as the product of individual personalities and individual personalities as the product of society. Any division would be both artificial and inappropriate.

Another reason that the question ceased to be an issue was the growing recognition that social phenomena could be analyzed as complexes of meaningfully oriented actions of persons reciprocally related to one another. This approach is based upon the assumption that society as well as personality exists whenever a number of persons engage in interaction. Simmel's insistence that social interaction be the focus of sociological inquiry not only helped lay to rest the sterile individual-group controversy but also led to a marked advance in our understanding of the relationship between personality and society.[4]

[3] Charles H. Cooley, *Human Nature and the Social Order*, Schocken Books, New York, 1964, pp. 36–37 (originally published 1902).
[4] Georg Simmel, *Conflict and the Web of Group Affiliations* (translated by Kurt Wolff and Reinhard Bendix), Free Press, New York, 1966.

ASSUMPTIONS ABOUT MAN AND SOCIETY

One of the major assumptions in sociological theories of personality is that personality is an open rather than a closed system. That is, its characteristics are determined by social experiences rather than merely channeled or modified by them. This is now a prevalent position in sociology, although historically there have been various doctrines regarding man.

Before the middle 1850s there were essentially two prevalent notions about the nature of man. The Theological doctrine regarded man as an agent guided by God, and the Philosophical doctrine saw man as a creature with the ability of free choice who conducts himself on the basis of reason. These doctrines persisted unchallenged until Darwin published the *Origin of Species* in 1859 and *The Descent of Man* in 1871. The main contention of these works was that man was an animal and differed from lower animals only in that he had acquired a higher level of physiological development. Since it was believed that animal behavior was determined by instincts, it followed that man was also a creature of instinct and that certain inner determinants guided his behavior. The Instinct thesis, sometimes called Social Darwinism, strongly influenced the development of personality theory in sociology.

Theories of personality and theories of society based on innate needs and biological motivations proliferated. By the early 1920s, the situation had beome confusing. Sociologists were unable to agree on how to define an instinct or how many instincts there were. The instinct doctrine was attacked on the basis of sometimes absurd categorizations (i.e., home construction, curiosity, sugar-licking, righteousness) as well as being unamenable to scientific investigation.[5] Under the criticism of sociologists such as L. L. Bernard [6] and E. Faris,[7] instinct theory in sociology eventually

[5] For a more complete description of the rise and fall of instinct theory, see "Inadequacy of Biological Motivation," in Robert E. L. Faris, *Social Psychology*, Ronald Press, New York, 1952, pp. 11–33. See also "Instinctive Nature," in Kimball Young (Ed.), *Source Book for Social Psychology*, F. S. Crofts and Co., New York, 1935, pp. 146–168.

[6] L. L. Bernard, "The Misuse of Instinct in the Social Sciences," *Psychological Review*, 28: 97–119, 1921.

[7] Ellsworth Faris, "Are Instincts Data or Hypotheses?" *American Journal of Sociology*, 27: 184–196, 1921.

collapsed, although not without a brief resurgence of "substitute" theories wherein the old instinct notion was subsumed under newer terminology.[8] The emergence of Watson's behaviorism, which accounted for behavior by conditioning principles, facilitated the demise of instinct theory.

Even when instinct doctrine was popular in the social sciences, it was not accepted by all. The social psychologies of William James, John Dewey, and James Mark Baldwin represent a transition between instinct doctrine and Social Determinism, the doctrine that the nature of man is socially acquired. James contended that instincts existed, but only for the sake of giving rise to habits; once formed, the instincts lost their functions and consequently "faded away."[9] Dewey, while subscribing to classic instinct doctrine in his early work, shifted his position to intimate that the instincts do not make the institutions, but rather the institutions make the instincts.[10] A more radical departure from animistic presuppositions was evident in the work of the symbolic interactionists Charles H. Cooley and George H. Mead.[11] They saw the nature of man as did the philosopher John Locke, as a blank tablet upon which experiences were written. No assumptions were made about

---

[8] The appearance of "substitute" theories was more prevalent within psychology and related disciplines than sociology. Sociologists usually employed euphemisms from the beginning. Albion Small used the term "interests," *General Sociology*, University of Chicago Press, Chicago, 1905, pp. 425ff. W. I. Thomas posited "four wishes," *The Unadjusted Girl*, Little Brown and Co., Boston, 1923, p. 4, and "irreducible factors" of food and sex, "The Scope and Method of Folk-Psychology," *American Journal of Sociology*, 1: 434–445, 1895–1896. However, the term instinct was used in other work; see his "The Gaming Instinct," *American Journal of Sociology*, 6: 750–763, 1900–1901.

[9] William James, *Principles of Psychology*, Henry Holt and Co., New York, 1890.

[10] John Dewey, *Human Nature and Conduct*, Henry Holt and Co., New York, 1922. See also James Mark Baldwin, *Social and Ethical Interpretations in Mental Development*, Macmillan Company, New York, 1913.

[11] Charles H. Cooley, *op. cit.* Also his *Social Organization*, Charles Scribner's, New York, 1909; *The Social Process*, Charles Scribner's, New York, 1920. George H. Mead, *Mind, Self, and Society*, University of Chicago Press, Chicago, 1934; this summarizes his position, although his periodical publications appeared as early as 1909. See also Charles A. Ellwood, *The Psychology of Human Society*, D. Appleton and Co., New York, 1925.

inner determinants of behavior. Instead they posited that man was a social creature, a part of society, and whatever characteristics and traits he displayed were acquired through social experiences. At the time these views were advocated, they were not taken seriously by many sociologists, since the majority were not yet concerned with man as a legitimate unit of sociological investigation, and those who were social psychologically oriented tended to subscribe to the prevalent instinct notions. However, social determinism was to have strong influence upon the later course of the sociology of personality.

THE "NEW APPROACH" TO PERSONALITY

Empiricism was rather slow in coming to sociology. During the first decades after the turn of the century the majority of sociologists associated with the symbolic interactionist approach tended to speculate about the nature of man, his development, and relationship with society. The tendency was to depend upon personal experiences and informal observations, rather than systematically examining either the individual or society. Persons associated with what was to evolve into the Social Structure approach were also highly speculative. The tendency was to construct rather elaborate schemas to account for society and individuals. When the individual was introduced, data often came from secondary rather than primary sources. In addition, more attention was given to the socializing agents (society, formal organizations, social institutions) than to the individual.

By the middle 1920s, particularly at the University of Chicago, a number of researchers were exploring the relationship between the individual and his social environment from a different perspective and with new techniques. Burgess called this movement the "new approach to the study of personality." [12] It drew from work in

---

[12] The "new approach" is identified and brought together in Ernest W. Burgess (Ed.), *Personality and the Social Group*, University of Chicago Press, Chicago, 1929. This volume is based upon papers presented at the 22nd annual meeting of the American Sociological Society, at which the central topic of discussion was "The Individual in Relation to Society."

SOCIOLOGICAL PERSPECTIVES ON THE PERSON 195

social organization and symbolic interactionism, as well as from European collective behaviorists, social geographers, and social economists.[13] It also focused upon the smaller social units which comprise society, such as the family and complex organizations, rather than entities as vast as society and culture. But most important, it introduced the use of primary data such as personal documents, case histories, and first hand observations of groups and individuals. The approach stressed that individuals and groups could be viewed and objectively investigated as facts by standardized methods of science. Hughes examined the division of labor in relationship to professions and the personality types that evolved in occupational socialization.[14] Hayner focused specifically upon hotel life, the personality types that evolved, and how persons accommodated to this social environment.[15] Burgess explored the relationship between the family and the person, making use of life history materials.[16] Reuter examined the peculiar and complex environment into which an individual of mixed blood was born and the personality adjustments which came about as a consequence of the individual's unique position.[17] Types of political personalities were the topic of Lasswell's work.[18] Thomas stressed the importance of the situation in determining personality and individual behavior.[19]

[13] During these early years considerable effort was directed toward the development of typologies of personality. Typologies were traditional within criminology, and were not uncommon within the area of social organization. Since the 1940s typologies have become less popular. Riesman is one of the few sociological theorists to retain the typological approach. Typologies are more frequently employed by contemporary criminologists.

[14] Everett C. Hughes, "Personality Types and the Division of Labor," in Burgess, *op. cit.*, pp. 78–94.

[15] Norman S. Hayner, "Hotel Life and Personality," in Burgess, *op. cit.*, pp. 108–120.

[16] Ernest W. Burgess, "The Family and the Person," in Burgess, *op. cit.*, pp. 121–133.

[17] E. B. Reuter, "The Personality of Mixed Bloods," in Burgess, *op. cit.*, pp. 55–63.

[18] Harold D. Lasswell, "Types of Political Personalities," in Burgess, *op. cit.*, pp. 151–161.

[19] W. I. Thomas, "The Behavior Pattern and the Situation," in Burgess, *op. cit.*, pp. 1–15. This paper represents a departure from Thomas's earlier work in that instinct notions have disappeared.

PERSONALITY AND INTERACTION

Interactionism has proceeded in several interrelated directions, all having some tie to early symbolic interactionist contentions. Three major distinctions are discernible: symbolic interactionism, neo-symbolic interactionism, and social interactionism. These distinctions are not discrete and there is considerable overlap among them.

Symbolic Interactionism

Initially an oral tradition associated with midwestern sociology, symbolic interactionism was not assimilated into the mainstream of sociological thought until the collapse of instinct theory and until it was given more articulate expression by those advocating the "New Approach" to the study of personality. However, since the mid 1930s many of the ideas of the early symbolic interactionists diffused throughout the discipline of sociology to become a general orientation for the understanding of self and social behavior.[20] The idea that the self is socially formed through man's ability to symbolically interact with others was widely accepted. Through interaction and the manipulation of symbols a "world" of experience made up of self and other evolved.

In the period between the 1930s and the middle 1950s symbolic interactionist theory gained in popularity. This was an important period for the crystallization of the approach and the development of understanding that it had ramifications other than for explaining selfhood and child socialization. Various investigators began to apply symbolic interactionist ideas to adult socialization, attitude change, industrial relationships, and social organization. Some of the inquiries took the form of descriptive analyses of the particular

---

[20] The diffusion of the symbolic interactionist tradition within sociology is discussed in Manford H. Kuhn, "Major Trends in Interaction Theory in the Past Twenty-Five Years," *Sociological Quarterly*, 5: 61–84, 1964; and Arnold M. Rose, "Preface," in Arnold M. Rose (Ed.), *Human Behavior and Social Processes*, Houghton Mifflin Company, Boston, 1962, pp. vii–xii.

phenomena in terms of symbolic interactionist contentions, but other investigators were considerably more empirical.

During the same time, symbolic interactionist theory itself became a topic for scrutiny. Classical symbolic interactionist theory is not stated in a way that facilitates empirical testing. One development was to formalize symbolic interactionist theory by the identification of major assumptions and hypotheses, and to translate hypotheses into testable propositions.[21] Other investigators chose specific hypotheses and tested them by means of the scientific method. Among the most popular propositions are those pertaining to self-appraisal. According to Mead the self-concept is the result of the reactions of others. Aspects of this hypothesis have been explored in several investigations.[22] Self-feelings arise somewhat differently according to Cooley. Cooley's "looking glass self," which results from the imagined appraisals of others, was the topic of investigation by Sherwood.[23] Role taking, another central contention of Mead, has been investigated by Brown[24] and Stryker.[25]

Neo-Symbolic Interactionism

Concomitant with the popularization of a theoretical approach, modifications and extensions quickly appear. Beginning in the 1940s

[21] Examples of these trends can be seen in the following: Herbert Blumer, "Sociological Analysis and the Variable," *American Sociological Review*, 21: 683–690, 1956; Alfred R. Lindesmith and Anselm L. Strauss, *Social Psychology*, Dryden Press, New York, 1956; Maurice Natanson, *The Social Dynamics of George H. Mead*, Public Affairs Press, Washington, D.C., 1956; and more recently, John W. Kinch, "A Formalized Theory of the Self," *American Journal of Sociology*, 68: 481–486, 1963; also, Arnold M. Rose, "A Systematic Summary of Symbolic Interactionist Theory," in Rose, *op. cit.*, pp. 3–19.

[22] See S. Frank Miyamoto and Sanford M. Dornbusch, "A Test of Interactionist Hypotheses of Self Conception," *American Journal of Sociology*, 61: 399–403, 1956; Carl J. Couch, "Self Attitudes and Degree of Adjustment with Immediate Others," *American Journal of Sociology*, 63: 491–496, 1958; Richard Videbeck, "Self Conception and the Reaction of Others, *Sociometry*, 23: 351–359, 1960.

[23] John J. Sherwood, "Self Identity and Referent Others," *Sociometry*, 28: 66–81, 1965.

[24] J. C. Brown, "An Experiment in Role Taking," *American Sociological Review*, 17: 587–597, 1952.

[25] Sheldon Stryker, "Conditions of Accurate Role-Taking: A Test of Mead's Theory," in Rose, *op. cit.*, pp. 41–62.

sociologists sympathetic to the symbolic interactionist approach began to incorporate information from other theoretical approaches with aspects of symbolic interaction. This was partly because symbolic interactionist theory is weak on explaining motivation and unspecific as to how social learning takes place. Among the various sources of influence were psychology, psychoanalysis, and social anthropology.

Kimball Young can be regarded as one of the first persons to attempt to integrate the symbolic interactionist approach with personality theory as developed in psychology, cultural anthropology,[26] and within the psychoanalytic movement.[27] According to Young, the self is the core of personality and includes the more or less organized body of ideas, attitudes, traits, and response habits that characterize a given individual. He focused upon internal mechanisms (learned characteristics, biological influences) and external mechanisms (society, culture) which operate in the formation of personality. The manner in which these mechanisms are organized and expressed is ultimately determined through social interaction, for personality is built into the roles and statuses for dealing with others and with oneself. In this respect, Young has expanded considerably the social act as conceptualized by Mead in

---

[26] Sociologists quickly assimilated the idea of culture into their views of personality. However, the "modal personality" approach which arose within cultural anthropology has not been incorporated, to a large degree, with sociological thought. For an excellent summary of the modal personality approach and its relevance for sociology, see Alex Inkeles and Daniel Levinson, "National Character: The Study of Modal Personality and Sociocultural Systems," in Gardner Lindzey (Ed.), *Handbook of Social Psychology*, vol. II, Addison-Wesley Publishing Co., Reading, Mass., 1959, pp. 977–1020.

[27] Young was also one of the first sociologists to employ Freudian concepts. Various other investigators in the 1920s such as Eliot, Ogburn, Rice, and Groves used psychiatric classification in the analysis of social behavior, particularly collective phenomena and personality deviations. Robert E. Park and Ernest W. Burgess's *Introduction to the Science of Sociology*, University of Chicago Press, Chicago, 1924, was the first sociology textbook to include psychoanalytic concepts and findings. However, sociologists have generally been inclined to reject psychoanalytic formulations because of their lack of scientific derivation, their association with instinct theory, and because of a negative attitude toward reductionism in theory construction. They have tended to be more sympathetic toward neo-Freudians such as Sullivan and Fromm.

that he shows what factors insure that social acts will occur and the forms that they happen to take for particular individuals. The superego and defense mechanisms are also part of Young's theory, but are less closely integrated with symbolic interactionist notions.[28] Symbolic interactionist theory, and aspects of psychoanalytic theory have also been integrated in the writings of Gerth and Mills.[29]

Gestalt psychology emphasizes how the perception of forms and figures is influenced by the context in which they are embedded. Among the first sociologists influenced by Gestalt theory were Walter Coutu and Robert E. L. Faris. Coutu attempted to integrate the contributions of Mead with the general Gestalt orientation and Lewinian field theory. His general point of view is that man always behaves in accordance with what the situation means to him. Specifically he regards aspects of human behavior such as role playing and aspects of individual cognitive organization as influenced and determined by field forces. The forces in the field are the groups to which an individual belongs and with which he identifies. Language is the concept used to link the individual to the field.[30] Faris also drew from Gestalt psychology the contention that the human organism is an energy system and is always in a state of restlessness. Especially evident are Gestalt principles of closure and complexity in order to account for motivation. He also drew from Gardner Murphy's biosocial personality theory the idea of canalization to explain how generalized activity became differentiated into specific needs through association principles.[31] Lewinian field theory is evident in recent work by Yinger who developed a model that takes into account both individual tendencies and "field" influences.[32]

Influences on neo-symbolic interactionists often originated within psychology and psychiatry, although influences from sociological sources are also evident. Among the sociological influences, refer-

[28] Kimball Young, *Personality and Problems of Adjustment*, Appleton-Century-Crofts, New York, 1952.

[29] Hans Gerth and C. Wright Mills, *Character and Social Structure*, Harbinger Books, New York, 1956.

[30] Walter Coutu, *Emergent Human Nature*, Alfred A. Knopf, New York, 1949; see also excerpts reprinted in this volume.

[31] Robert E. L. Faris, *Social Psychology*, Ronald Press, New York, 1952.

[32] J. Milton Yinger, *Toward a Field Theory of Behavior*, McGraw-Hill Book Co., New York, 1965. Also see his article reprinted in this volume.

ence group theory and role theory are among the most important.

Reference group theory attempts to explain how social-cultural norms are channeled through smaller societal segments and learned by individuals and how the groups with which individuals identify determine individual behavior. Drawing upon reference group theory as formulated by Hyman[33] and Merton and Kitt,[34] Shibutani not only has shown how reference group theory and symbolic interactionist theory are complementary but also how they may be integrated to open further avenues of research.[35] Role is also a central concept in Shibutani's formulations.[36]

In addition to reference group theory, Manford Kuhn was also influenced by cultural anthropology, and attempted to incorporate aspects of these approaches with self-theory. Mead regarded the self-concept as developed and maintained in human association and discussed it primarily from the perspective of its changing and shifting nature. Consequently, some followers of Mead focused on the processual nature of the self, but Kuhn directed his attention to its stable characteristics. He concentrated upon the structure of self-attitudes and developed an instrument (the Twenty Statements Test) by which the self could be measured. Kuhn's contentions also differed from classic symbolic interactionism in that he was more explicit about how the self-concept functioned as an organizer of behavior.[37]

Social Interactionism

As early as the turn of the century Simmel suggested that the proper topic for sociological investigation was interaction, and that

[33] Herbert Hyman, *The Psychology of Status*, Archives of Psychology, No. 269, *38*, 1942.

[34] Robert K. Merton and Alice S. Kitt, "Contributions to the Theory of Reference Group Behavior," in Robert K. Merton and Paul F. Lazarsfeld (Eds.), *Continuities in Social Research: Studies in the Scope and Method of "the American Soldier,"* Free Press, Glencoe, Ill., 1950.

[35] Tamotsu Shibutani, see selection reprinted in this volume.

[36] Tamotsu Shibutani, *Society and Personality*, Prentice-Hall, Englewood Cliffs, N.J., 1964.

[37] See Manford H. Kuhn, "Self-Attitudes by Age, Sex, and Professional Training," *Sociological Quarterly*, *1:* 39–55, 1960; also Manford H. Kuhn and Thomas S. McPartland, "An Empirical Investigation of Self-Attitudes," *American Sociological Review*, *19:* 68–76, 1954.

society could be viewed as made up of reciprocally interacting selves.[38] Interaction was also a central topic among the early symbolic interactionists and was given its clearest expression in the writings of Mead. According to Mead the social act is the unit around which all coordinated human behavior revolves.[39] With these influences it is not surprising that personality is now often studied within the context of interaction.

The social interactionist orientation differs from the neo-symbolic interactionist orientation in several subtle although recognizable respects. As a rule the social interactionists pay more attention to the social act than to the organization and dynamics of personality. Moreover, symbols are not a crucial analytical construct in their theoretical formulations. In most instances the neo-symbolic interactionists have retained the classic symbolic interactionist contention that symbols provide the meaning for social objects. While the contention is not denied by the social interactionists, it is tacitly assumed and if introduced is not emphasized. Rather than viewing the symbol for an object as providing the motivation for action, generally the social interactionist approach employs the object itself as a motivator. A jump is made directly from acquired needs, motives, identities, etc., to situational behavior. The social interactionist approach can also be distinguished from other related approaches by examining how the social act is viewed. Here the social act is rarely equated with any act occurring in a social context. Instead, it is a basic unit of observation involving action-reaction segments with a more or less clearly defined time sequence which can be abstracted from an ongoing process. This is not to say that personality is regarded as a mere by-product of interaction in this approach, but the interaction situation is the place where personality emerges and can be studied.

Among those contemporary theorists who have paid particular attention to the social act is Leonard Cottrell, who stresses that personality can only be understood as part of a situation comprised of interacting selves. According to Cottrell the social act is ". . . a series of reciprocally related acts by units called selves, which . . .

---

[38] Simmel, *op. cit.*
[39] George H. Mead, *op. cit.*

forms a dynamic perceptual unit."[40] Personality refers to ". . . the population of self other patterns and their intra-personal organization."[41]

Another theorist for whom the social act is an integral concept is Erving Goffman.[42] The importance given the social act is evident in the titles of several of his books: *Presentation of Self in Everyday Life; Encounters: Two Studies in the Sociology of Interaction; Behavior in Public Places;* and *Interaction Ritual.* One theme in most of Goffman's work is that the proper unit of study is neither the individual nor his audience, but is rather the interaction between individual and audience. Specifically, Goffman endeavors to describe the "syntactical" relation among acts of different persons mutually present to one another.

The social act is also found in the theoretical formulations of a number of other sociologists. Foote posits that identity provides the motivation for adequate role performance.[43] McCall and Simmons have also incorporated the social act with an identity model.[44]

PERSONALITY AND SOCIAL STRUCTURE

An orientation with a major concern for the relationship between society and the individual was expressed in modern terms by the turn of the century. However, systematic work on this topic was slow in developing because of the lack of empiricism as a research tradition and because of the distraction of the instinct doctrine. However, by the middle 1920s the instinct school was in decline and the symbolic interactionist position was gaining recognition. The incorporation of the symbolic interactionist orientation with a social organization orientation had also come about through the

[40] Leonard S. Cottrell, Jr., "The Analysis of Situational Fields in Social Psychology," in A. Paul Hare, Edgar F. Borgotta, and Robert F. Bales (Eds.), *Small Groups*, Alfred A. Knopf, New York, 1955, p. 67.

[41] *Ibid.*, p. 64.

[42] Erving Goffman, see excerpt reprinted in this volume.

[43] Nelson N. Foote, "Identification as the Basis for a Theory of Motivation," *American Sociological Review, 16:* 14–21, 1951.

[44] George J. McCall and J. L. Simmons, *Identities and Interactions*, Free Press, New York, 1966. The second Miyamoto article reprinted in this volume takes up the matter of the social act more explicitly.

efforts of sociologists associated with the "New Approach" to the study of personality. Consequently, the study of personality as a topic of "pure" sociological (not merely social psychological) investigation was legitimized. With the refinement of structural functionalism as a program for theory construction and empirical investigation, personality could be incorporated into a larger system of sociological analysis. Since functionalism stresses the examination of relationships among components, its adherents have frequently been interested in the relationship between personality and social structure.

The social structure approach has developed in several major directions. One direction which may be called the systems approach emphasizes that personality, social structure, and culture taken together constitute a system, with no one entity superordinate to the others. Another avenue of approach takes social structure as an independent variable and personality as a dependent variable. A third approach takes personality as an independent variable and social structure as a dependent variable. A fourth avenue regards personality as a variable that determines responses or adjustments to various aspects of the environment.[45]

The *systems approach* is a relatively recent development. As developed by Sorokin the task of sociology is the study of superorganic phenomena.[46] A superorganic phenomenon is the product of the interaction of culture, social structure, and personality. These components represent an indivisible and indispensable triad, each existing by virtue of the existence of the others and each reflecting the others. Together they constitute a system. Personality is roughly the organization of minds and behaviors of individuals. Society is the totality of interacting personalities with their socio-cultural relationships and processes. Culture is the totality of meanings, values, and norms possessed by the interacting persons and ". . . the totality of the vehicles which objectify, socialize and convey

---

[45] With the exception of the fourth avenue, it is arbitrary whether these represent separate avenues or merely subdivisions within one major approach. In many respects the independent-dependent variable approaches are special cases of the systems approach, with choice of one level over the other as a beginning point for analytic purposes.

[46] Pitirim A. Sorokin, *Society, Culture, and Personality*, Harper and Brothers, New York, 1947.

these meanings."[47] Sorokin conceives of four culture types (ideational, sensate, idealistic, and eclectic) with four corresponding personality types. From Sorokin's perspective the quarrel between partisans of the supremacy of any one component over the others is meaningless.

The systems approach is also exemplified in the work of Talcott Parsons. He suggests the theoretical existence of three systems: a cultural system, a social system, and a personality system. Behavior can be understood only when all three systems are involved. The personality system provides the motivational energy and orientation for action. The cultural system provides the value orientations and meanings which are attached to objects with which the individual interacts. The social system provides the setting and structure in which action can take place. Participation in the social system is organized and structured by sets of expected behaviors and is regulated through the development of appropriate and stable motivations. The sets of expected behaviors or roles are internalized to constitute parts of the personality. Because of interpenetration, the three systems have consequences for one another.[48]

Parsons has shown a strong interest in the personality system, and how the other systems impinge upon it. This is undertaken from the point of view of childhood socialization and the analysis of social role learning.[49] In some of his writings, Parsons draws heavily upon psychoanalytic terminology and conceptions to facilitate the analysis

---

[47] *Ibid.*, p. 63. To illustrate, Sorokin would regard the students and professor in a classroom as the personalities, with each personality mirroring his social and cultural universe. The society of the classroom is the norms of their relationships, and reflects the component individuals and their cultural patterns. The culture of the classroom is the ideas possessed and exchanged by the individuals and the physical facilities in which all are embodied. The culture manifests its human members and their normative organization.

[48] The term system is employed differently by Parsons and Sorokin. Sorokin conceives of three components as constituting a system. However, for Parsons each component is in itself a system; taken together the three systems form an even larger system. Parsons also differs from Sorokin in that the systems are not mutually reflective; the major characteristics of any one cannot be derived from the others. See Talcott Parsons, *The Social System*, Free Press, Glencoe, Ill., 1959.

[49] Parsons, *op. cit.*, see especially Chapter I, "The Action Frame of Reference and the General Theory of Action Systems: Culture, Personality and the Place of Social Systems," pp. 3–23.

of the development, organization, and dynamics of personality.[50]

Analytically, employing *social structure as an independent variable and personality as a dependent variable* has been the most prevalent approach utilized by sociologists of the social structure and personality inclination.[51] Merton's classic work on bureaucratic structure and personality comes to mind when this topic is discussed,[52] although a host of other investigators have also made related contributions. Riesman's analysis of stages of demographic growth of societies and the character types that emerge is one example.[53] Work on childhood socialization, adult socialization, individual consequences of social change within small social units such as the family, or larger units such as society also exemplify this approach.[54]

The third avenue of approach has taken *personality as an independent variable and* some aspect of *social organization as the dependent variable*. Here concern is with how personality contributes to the maintenance and organization of cultural groupings, bureaucracies, and social institutions. Inkeles and Levinson developed an analytical schema for examining the influence of personality on bureaucracies, specifying dimensions along which both personality

---

[50] See Talcott Parsons, *Social Structure and Personality*, Free Press, New York, 1964.

[51] Some of the work done within the systems approach could just as well be included here, particularly when concern is with the interpenetration of the culture or social system on personality. Parson's work on the incest taboo is one example. *Ibid.*, pp. 55–77. Levinson's investigation of personal role definition as a concept linking personality and social structure could also be cross-classified. See Daniel J. Levinson, "Role, Personality, and Social Structure in the Organizational Setting," *Journal of Abnormal and Social Psychology*, 58: 170–180, 1959.

[52] Robert K. Merton, "Bureaucratic Structure and Personality," is, Robert K. Merton, *Social Theory and Social Structure*, Free Presn Glencoe, Ill., 1949, pp. 195–206.

[53] David Riesman, *The Lonely Crowd*, Yale University Press, New Haven, Conn., 1950; and see excerpt reprinted in this volume.

[54] William H. Sewell, "Infant Training and the Personality of the Child," *American Journal of Sociology*, 58: 150–159, 1952; Delbert R. Miller and Guy E. Swanson, *The Changing American Parent*, John Wiley and Sons, Inc., New York, 1958; Norman S. Hayner and Ellis Ash, "Socialization in a Prison Community," *American Sociological Review*, 5: 557–583, 1940; Sanford M. Dornbusch, "Socialization in a Coast Guard Academy," *Social Forces*, 33: 316–321, 1955; Alex Inkeles, "Social Change and Social Character: The Role of Parental Mediation," *Journal of Social Issues*, 11: 12–23, 1955.

and social organization can be viewed.[55] Consequences of personality change in the form of mental illness on family organization have also received inquiry.[56] Another topic that has been examined is the relationship between personality and interaction networks.[57]

The fourth approach endeavors to use personality data to contribute to a more complete understanding of problems of sociological importance. Concern is with how some aspect of *personality is predictive of accommodation within organized social settings*. Research in this area has typically raised questions associated with recruitment into occupations and other status positions, and the quality of role performance. Rosenberg found that occupational choice was closely associated with personality characteristics, with submissive and dominant persons choosing different occupations.[58] Coser reasons that a person's personality predispositions determine his reactions to institutional life. Some patients respond to the hospital as a source for the gratification of primary needs, while others respond to the hospital as an organization instrumental for recovery.[59] Stern, Stein, and Bloom, found that the adjustment of the rigid, dogmatic, unyielding (stereopathic) person to college life was less successful than that of the less rigid person.[60]

With notable exceptions, personality is conceptualized somewhat differently from a Social Structural approach than from an Inter-

[55] Alex Inkeles and Daniel J. Levinson, article reprinted in this volume.

[56] John A. Clausen and Marian R. Yarrow, "The Impact of Mental Illness on the Family," *Journal of Social Issues*, 11: entire issue, 1955; Charlotte G. Schwartz, "Perspectives on Deviance—Wives' Definitions of their Husbands' Mental Illness," *Psychiatry*, 20: 275–291, 1957; Harold Sampson, Sheldon L. Messinger, and Robert D. Towne, *Schizophrenic Women*, Atherton Press, New York, 1964.

[57] Bruce W. Tuckman, "Personality Structure, Group Composition and Group Functioning," *Sociometry*, 27: 469–487, 1964; also Arthur R. Cohen, "Experimental Effects of Ego-Defense Preference on Interpersonal Relations," *Journal of Abnormal and Social Psychology*, 52: 19–27, 1956.

[58] Morris Rosenberg, *Occupations and Values*, Free Press, Glencoe, Ill., 1957.

[59] Rose L. Coser, "A Home Away from Home," *Social Problems*, 4: 3–17, 1956.

[60] George G. Stern, Morris J. Stein, and Benjamin J. Bloom, *Methods in Personality Assessment*, Free Press, Glencoe, Ill., 1956. One of the earliest works related to this avenue is Paul G. Cressey, "The Motion Picture Experience as Modified by Social Background and Personality," *American Sociological Review*, 3: 516–525, 1938.

actionist approach. Although the Social Structure approach is giving increasingly sophisticated attention to the linkage between society and the individual, during recent years interest has been drifting more and more toward social structural variables at the expense of personality variables. Consequently, personality is often thought of as synonymous with any single factor (behavior, trait, attribute, etc.). This presents no particular problem as long as the factor is conceptualized as a portion of a larger domain of factors, but when a particular factor is not thought of in conjunction with any identifiable universe, it can be argued that the term personality has been overgeneralized.

SUGGESTED READINGS

HERBERT BLUMER. Sociological Implications of the Thought of George Herbert Mead, *American Journal of Sociology*, 71: 535–544, 1966 (Comment on Herbert Blumer's paper by Robert F. Bales, pp. 545–547).

EDGAR F. BORGOTTA. Sidesteps Toward a Nonspecial Theory, *Psychological Review*, 61: 343–352, 1954.

ELLSWORTH FARIS. *The Nature of Human Nature*, McGraw-Hill Book Co., New York, 1937.

HERBERT GOLDHAMER. Recent Developments in Personality Studies, *American Sociological Review*, 13: 555–565, 1948.

PATRICKE JOHNS HEINE. The Problem of Personality in Sociological Theory, in Joseph M. Wepman and Ralph W. Heine (Eds.), *Concepts of Personality*, Aldine, Chicago 1963, pp. 385–409.

GEORGE C. HOMANS. Contemporary Theory in Sociology, in Robert E. L. Faris (Ed.), *Handbook of Modern Sociology*, Rand McNally and Co., Chicago, 1964, pp. 951–977.

FAY BERGER KARPF. *American Social Psychology: Its Origins, Development, and European Background*, McGraw-Hill Book Co., New York, 1932.

MANFORD H. KUHN. Major Trends in Symbolic Interaction Theory in the Past Twenty-Five Years, *Sociological Quarterly*, 5: 61–84, 1964.

CHARLES K. WARRINER. Groups are Real: A Reaffirmation, *American Sociological Review*, 21: 549–554, 1956.

DENNIS H. WRONG. The Oversocialized Conception of Man in Modern Sociology, *American Sociological Review*, 26: 183–193, 1961.

*Note

By the Editors of the Series

In the field of psychology we believe that the student ought to get the "feel" of experimentation by reading original source materials. In this way he can acquire a better understanding of the discipline by seeing scientific ideas grow and change. However, one of the main problems in teaching is the limited availability of these sources, which communicate most effectively the personality of the author and the excitement of ongoing research.

For these reasons we have decided to edit several books,* each devoted to a particular problem in psychology. In every case we attempt to select problems that have been and are controversial —that have been and still are alive. We intend to present these problems as a set of selected original articles, arranged in historical order and in order of progress in the field. We believe that it is important for the student to see that theories and researches build on what has gone before; that one study leads to another, that theory leads to research and then to revision of theory. We believe that *telling* the student this does not make the same kind of impression as letting him see it happen in actuality. The idea is for the student to read and build ideas for himself.

Suggestions for Use—These readings books can be used by the student in either of two ways. They are organized so that, with the help of the instructor (or of the students if used in seminars), a topic can be covered at length and in depth. This would necessitate lectures or discussions on articles not covered in the series to fill in the gaps. On the other hand, each book taken alone will give a student a good idea of the problem being covered and its historical background as well as its present state and the direction it seems to be taking.

* (Pub. note: a sub-series within the Insight Book Series.)